HALLE EAVELYN

RED GODDESS RISING

a spiritual travel memoir

INTRODUCTION

Under everything in Egypt runs a current of energy, powerful and implacable. It's as if the Nile is calling to you no matter where you are, singing to you from beneath the land. Egypt changes people. It changed me. This is the story of my first trip down the Nile and the spiritual awakening that I, like so many before me, experienced during that journey. I am literally no longer the person I was before I heeded that call, and it is Egypt herself I have to thank for that.

In telling my story, I have structured this book to follow my first visit to Egypt as an unwitting tourist, although it includes moments from other experiences that have since made their way onto Spirit Quest Tours' itineraries. Every person in this book is real, though I have changed many of the names and made some of them amalgams. Every story in this book is true, but in some places I have changed the chronology to create a cohesive tale. Please indulge me; the experiences themselves were all as I have written them.

A note on the spirituality: I don't think religion and spirituality have much in common, and I am not trying to get you to change your religion as you read my story. From my own experiences, I can now say without reservation that we reincarnate to learn our life lessons. And that believing or not believing in reincarnation, or in any particular religion, has zero effect on the process. In any spiritual descriptions in this narrative, I have tried to give my best impressions and memories of exactly how I felt, vague or specific, and not embellish in any way.

Some people have asked me how my partner Greg and I started Spirit Quest Tours, and why this is not included in the book. All I can say is, that's a different story but Spirit Quest Tours came from a deep desire we had and from the suggestions we received from our Egyptian partners, who you will meet in these pages. It evolved into a company without us really intending for it to do so. The call of Egypt is unmistakable, and this was our way of sharing what happened to us there, in hopes that others might experience their own openings of spirit.

CONTENTS

Prelude: Awakening Hathor 1

Momo and Shakky 5

Where I See the Sphinx 15

The Desert 21

The Galabeya Boys 27

The Man and Secrets of the Night 39

The Khan is… the Khan 49

Religions of the World 57

Where We Learn the Consequences of Ignoring Instincts 67

Hanging With Kojak 75

Alex..85

Where I Get the Yellow Fire 93

Woo-woo Time 99

After a While, Crocodile 111

As the Hawk Flies 117

Broadway Show References 123

In the Valley, in the Valley of the Kings.......................................131

Hot Chicken Soup 139

My Name is Ozymandias...145

Egyptian Prom 153

The Night Market 159

The Dogs of Egypt 173

Getting Sekhmetized 179

Where We See the Flower of Life 183

House of Horus 191

Where We Party Like It's 1999 197

I'm a Soul Sister 203

The Long Cruise 211

The Moon Over Mohamed Nazmy 217

The Little Prince 223

Where I Find Music In the Wilderness 231

Climbing Gebel Musa 241

What If Moses Had A Cell Phone 251

An American Thanksgiving in Cairo 263

The King's Chamber 279

Acknowledgments 289

About The Author 291

PRELUDE: AWAKENING HATHOR

2011

The crowd is getting restless. It's almost 9am and the throng at the entrance to the Cairo Museum is jockeying for position. Our group has made it past security and the tourist police, their machine guns at the ready. Ignoring the sculpture garden with its precious statues commissioned by the pharaohs, we now stand at the head of the line, waiting for the doors to open. Behind us, the cacophony of voices from Italy, Germany, America, and Japan grows louder as the minutes tick down.

An Egyptian woman comes to the top of the stairs, her head modestly covered in a bright scarf but wearing modern slacks. Polyester in this heat? We must have different genes. She nods to the ticket takers below. The surge is on. Though we had been first in line, our group is suddenly swamped by a gaggle of excited Japanese tourists. We're buffeted on all sides but push through as best we can, still trying to be reasonably polite. Like salmon rushing upstream, we burst past the marble steps, submit to another security check and then pass into the cool lobby.

Our group follows orders, sticking like glue to my partner Greg and our Egyptologist guide, Shakky. All except me. I need to get to the rear of the museum, an irresistible urge that hits me every time I'm here. With an acknowledging nod from Greg, I peel off from the group and turn down a corridor into a separate wing. The babble of languages fades behind me as the tour groups scuttle off to see the museum's biggest draws: the King Tut exhibit and the Hall of Mummies. Vaulted ceilings soar above me, and my soft Egyptian slippers glide quietly along the marble floors as I make my way past silent galleries. I've already seen all the museum's big exhibits more than a few times, so I'm not missing anything as I steal this time to explore alone.

I pause at a side room that holds a statue of a pharaoh receiving a benediction from two Egyptian gods. It is an outstanding work of art, beautifully rendered from a single massive block of speckled granite, the three figures nearly life-size. Falcon-headed Horus, god of the Sun and husband of Hathor, stands at the pharaoh's right; the god Set, Horus' sworn enemy and the god of Chaos, is on his left. My heart lifts as I look at the statue: both gods hold their hands to Pharaoh's temples, as if supporting him, but neither actually touches him. They are "activating" the king, sending him the energy of the divine so he can do his work on Earth. Like most Egyptian art, the piece speaks on many levels. It tells of the juxtaposition of light and dark, of good and evil, of man balancing the two and mastering both. I can see this hidden message now—I know what to look for—but I am sure there is more beneath even these layers.

In the main wing, I'm abruptly drawn up short, struck by a statue I've never noticed before. It is a sculpture of the goddess Hathor, six or seven feet tall, carved from a single piece of white granite. The body of the statue is a sculpted pillar called a djed, or the "backbone of Osiris," thus named because it resembles a spine. Representing stability, it's another symbol and tool of activation, like the hands of the gods blessing the pharaoh. A bust of Hathor sits atop the djed. Associated with the image of cows, Hathor is the goddess of love and motherhood, health and prosperity, the goddess of joy. She has become my totem—her cute cow ears, her long thick hair. Shakky, our guide, saw me come down to breakfast one day with my red hair tucked behind my ears, and shouted happily, "Hat-hor! You are Hat-hor!" (Being Egyptian, he pronounces it as a hard "t" instead of a "th" sound.) And ever since, I am "Hat-hor" in Egypt.

Hathor's face is heart-shaped, her head the same outline as the ancient hieroglyph for "heart." That symbol also looks like a jar—Hathor's cow ears could easily be a jar's handles—there is poetry in this image, I think as I walk slowly around the statue. The heart, after all, is a vessel for holding love—another example of the Egyptians' unique genius, their ability to nest symbol, meaning and form together.

I didn't notice these nuances the first time I came to the Cairo Museum. Like most museum-goers, I was overwhelmed by the sheer mass of sculptures, paintings, pottery, jewelry, funerary artifacts, canopic jars, spears, shields and mummies, cheek-by-jowl in a crazy jumbled collection spanning almost all of recorded time. I also didn't know Egypt, about the way it can work on you until it's in your blood, your bones, your canopic jar heart. In those days, I was half-awake, living mostly on autopilot, aware only of the vaguest notions of spirituality, none of which I related to. I am no longer that person.

I am so taken by Hathor's statue that I pull out my journal and sketch her: the only time I have ever added a drawing to my notes. Hathor, goddess of music, of childbirth and all things domestic: if Aphrodite and Demeter had a baby, it would be Hathor—except that Hathor existed centuries before those usurping hussies emerged to refashion the older goddesses. Joy is Hathor's gift, and I have made it my own.

Gazing at my little cow-eared sketch, I recall my first visit to Egypt as a tourist, before I came to lead other visitors on journeys through this amazing country. That was before Hathor's land taught me simply to live, to move past fear into love. My own natural set point for joy had always been quite high. But over the years, that set point was challenged, sometimes terribly. I have now learned to make deliberate choices to be happy no matter what my external circumstances are, and in returning to that natural place of joy, I have felt all my burdens ease; it's become easier for me to meet whatever challenges come up. And it's made me more adventurous, more willing to face my fears.

Down the hall, I hear approaching footsteps and a rising swell of voices. It's time to close my notebook and rejoin my group. I turn away from the Hathor statue, carrying my goddess with me.

MOMO AND SHAKKY

In the fall of 1997, Greg came to me. We were working a hundred hours a week (each) on a project, and we were exhausted. Greg had recently become a Rosicrucian, which these days is a home study program based on the teachings of an ancient mystery school. In it, you learn all kinds of esoteric techniques, like energy healing or reading auras, and perform experiments designed to teach you a rational basis for faith. If you're interested, the program's open to anyone, and you can sign up for the home study course, which is how Greg got involved. But since it is a private mystery school, the secrets of which are only taught to initiates, you'll have to find out the rest for yourself. I was not that interested in the Rosicrucians—the idea of a spiritual system of study was intriguing, but academic approaches had a tendency to make my eyes glaze over, and to be honest, I was lazier in those days and more likely to ignore something I might have to work at.

"There's this trip. To Egypt. I want to go," Greg says.

I blink, confused, overtired. "Egypt? Why?"

"I saw it in a magazine." He comes over, holding a copy of the Rosicrucian magazine open to the last page. I see a drawing of a cruise ship. *Sail the Timeless Nile*, it invites me. "You want to come?"

"What about work?" Running a small company took almost every waking moment, and the only time we left town was on business trips.

Greg shrugs. "They've made do without us before. Don't we need a break? "He pauses. "It's a cruise. Up the Nile. For two weeks."

Two weeks? I thought about it. At the time I couldn't have cared less about Egypt, but the idea sounded much better than eating Mickey D's and sleeping in the office. It was a turning point in our relationship, the fact that he had asked me to go—a real vacation together that wasn't tacked on to a work trip. The following May, we made what was to become an annual pilgrimage.

Egypt is an incredible place, and though many flowery descriptions have been written about it, no one ever exaggerated. It's also an often-confusing dichotomy of the ancient coupled with the not-so-old-but-still-pretty-run-down. Nothing in Egypt seems new; they are about twenty years behind America, just the same as any developing country. This, plus a thick layer of sand, dust and dirt, keeps many things looking much older than they are. We have always found the people there friendly to the point where we call them family when we see them again. During the Bush years, they would tell you to your face: they love Americans; they hate our president. They don't even seem to blame us for voting for him… twice. These days, they greet you with "Obama! Obama" and tell you they love our president. It's early in the Obama legacy, but he's already improved tourist relations.

*   *   *   *   *

The first time I saw Cairo, Greg and I both thought, *Good Lord, what have we done?* The flight was circling to land, and all we could see were these buildings, many looking no better than sand huts, all drowning in the desert. The smog was so thick I was afraid I wouldn't be able to breathe on the ground. Not much of an improvement, since in those days they still allowed smoking in the back of international flights, as if the canned air in the rear of the plane wasn't toxic to those in the front. At least after landing we would be out in the open.

The Cairo airport did nothing to improve my initial impression. Now it's been remodeled, with lots of shopping, vast halls of marble and carved stone and a brand new terminal, but at that time it looked dilapidated, like a crumbing, leftover relic from the Soviet Bloc.

I'm shell-shocked, underwater from having slept badly on the plane. We stand in a sprawling group, waiting for everyone's luggage to arrive and be identified. Greg has his arm around me, and I doze on and off, resting on his shoulder.

I never traveled in a group before, despite extensive trips all over Europe since I was very small. No one had really introduced themselves on the flight and now, after sixteen hours of travel, everyone is too tired to socialize. But we notice a blond woman, her hair down to her waist, traveling alone. Greg nudges me and points to her with his eyes. I look at her friendly features, her stick-straight mane the color of sunshine, her slender, almost coltish arms and legs. Despite our exhaustion, we are both drawn to her. I could make friends with an inanimate object if I thought it would let me. I go over, and she gives me a warm look.

"I'm Halle. Hi. You're by yourself? "She nods, reaching out a delicate hand with a surprisingly firm handshake.

"I'm Lyra. Yes, I'm by myself. You? "

"I'm with my—Greg." I never know what to call Greg. Business partner, lover, soul mate, plus-one... he is all these things, just not my husband according to law. And though we are married in our hearts, that's not easy to describe in a single word. I once met a Meg Ryan-esque woman at a party. She shook her curly blonde mop at me and said, "Call him your LOVAH!!!" the last word at extra loud decibels. It was cute, if you like being embarrassed by such things, but I desire a single defining word. Like when my friend Laurel calls her ex her "wusband." Just like that, only for the one who means everything in the world to you.

I introduce Greg to Lyra, who stands next to us, comfortable. I feel like we've known her a long time. Honestly, how can groups help but grow close quickly? Everyone's exhausted, wearing the same rumpled clothes for over two days, all smelling of unwashed teeth and armpits. The choice is, bond or hate each other. Perhaps this is how early humans survived. But Lyra smells fine and still has a sense of humor despite all the travel. I am glad to have already made a friend.

Eventually, after passport control and a forty-five minute ride to the hotel, we get a glimpse of the famous Mena House Hotel. The lobby is surprisingly ornate, all glass chandeliers and gilt mirrors, featuring a low gold ceiling. In the middle of the night, on the way to our rooms, I have a muddled view of a sprawling set of buildings with gardens, then we collapse. They tell us the Pyramids are right outside our windows, but by this time, it is too dark to see. They will have to wait until morning.

The next day, I awaken in cool, smooth Egyptian cotton sheets, the thread count so high I want to drape them around me and wear them to breakfast. Heavy damask curtains cover the windows—I'm not even sure it is morning, but the balcony of our room beckons, and I pop out of bed to see our view. The green rolling lawns are a surprise, as is the blue water of the pool; I naively thought they wouldn't have swimming pools in the desert. As my pleased eye sweeps up, I finally see what all the fuss is about—the Pyramids and the famed Giza Plateau seem as if they are only across the street.

These triangles of stone are inexplicable. From the outside, even from a distance, they seem infinitely more romantic than their simple shapes would warrant. The view from our window, like much of the Mena House Hotel, features the Great Pyramid itself, the largest of the three structures that make up the pyramid complex. It's like a mountain range, if the mountains were shaped exactly like triangles and there were only three of them. They draw my eye constantly as I walk around the area.

The Mena House is legendary, the most historically important hotel in Cairo. A former hunting palace, the Big Three confab was held here during World War II, so Roosevelt, Churchill, and Chang-Kai-Chek all have been guests, along with everyone from Princess Grace to Princess Di. It has a vaguely Moroccan theme, which suits the over-the-top décor in the main lobby. I love the late nineteenth and early twentieth century pictures adorning the walls, which feature the couple who owned the hotel, their guests, and the many servants, horses and camels who made up the bulk of any establishment's staff. My favorite is the lady of the house, setting off on her afternoon ride, sidesaddle, with a full skirt and a Gibson Girl hairdo. A little black boy waits beside her in a resplendent uniform. It might have been a hundred degrees that day, but there she goes, off into what can only be described as an uncivilized heat. Between the Egyptian and Indian climates, they seem to have built the English hardier in those days. As I go down to breakfast that morning, I imagine what it would have been like to be the owner of all this, when it was still a private palace. My steps become mincing and my bearing more regal as I pick my way daintily down the flights of stairs to the dining room.

The central restaurant also overlooks the Great Pyramid— well, not so much overlooks as "sits right next to"—the first day we are all overwhelmed by this iconic image, sort of looming about the table like the proverbial elephant in the room. The Pyramid is so tall, and we so close, that when you stand up you can't see the top, which becomes a distant, grayish wall. But then you sit down, and there is the Pyramid again, practically having breakfast with you at your table. I am dining with Greg, Lyra, and her roommate Rose, a friendly, elderly blonde whose accent is foreign.

My mother, Judith, has just joined us. She flew in from her home in London early this morning, and we have had a joyful reunion. Judith is a quick and charming redhead who prides herself on looking much younger than she is. You might not want to travel with your mom, but I sure do. She is more friend than mother to me as an adult; the sort of woman about whom people regularly say, "That's your mother? You are so lucky." Indeed.

Many of the Egyptian hotel and restaurant staff people are trained in the way of French cuisine and service. They do a wonderful job with food in Egypt, while there is none of the reputed French attitude (in France, a waiter almost kicked Greg out of a restaurant for ordering coffee, bread, cheese and fruit— at the same time, quelle horreur!) The breakfast is sumptuous at the Mena House, and you can pick from made-to-order or a full buffet. I want to try the local yoghurt and black honey—dark and treacly, it looks the same as molasses, which is exactly what it turns out to be, despite its exotic name. They do the whole silver tea and coffee service, and the waiters and kitchen staff fawn on you. One day I asked the waiter to exchange my scrambled eggs for fried, and the chef himself brought out my plate to make sure I was satisfied.

My first Arabic words are, Chai, bi laban (shay, bee lahbahn). This means "tea with milk." The waiter teaches me, smiling at my attempts at pronunciation as he pours my tea. With milk.

"Min fud'lak," he tells me.

"What does that mean?"

"Please," he translates.

"Oh, min fud'lak."

"Yes. To a man," he says.

"Excuse me?"

"'Min fud'lik' if it's to a woman, and 'min fad'lak' to a man." Greg and I try to sort that out.

"Okay," I say, "it's 'lick' if it's a woman, and 'luck' if it's a man."

Greg nods eagerly. "I thought of a phrase that can help you remember. 'Lucky men lick women.'"

I narrow my eyes at him. "I think that's enough Arabic for a bit." The waiter turns away, but not before I see his smirk. Lyra and Rose laugh, as does Greg, pleased to be our entertainment. Judith laughs loudest of all; she and Greg have always gotten on famously.

Food helps to ground me, but for two days, I founder as we travel from site to site visiting Cairo. Jet lag, the newness of the Middle East, the strangeness of the "getting to know you" period and my general work exhaustion, all seem to overwhelm me until I feel I am swimming through sand. We meet our guides for the trip, Mohamed and Shakky. They are the reason we return to Egypt year after year, and it was at their suggestion that we eventually began to lead trips.

Mohamed Nazmy, the President of Quest Travel, has always been a bit of an enigma to me. My primary impression is that a bear and a beagle had an Egyptian baby. He is formidable, a big man with a full face, smooth olive skin, heavy-lidded eyes, and jet black hair with a white Bride of Frankenstein streak at the front. These days, Mohamed wears Armani suits, and his every gesture is elegant. His staff is obviously both afraid of him and worshipful of this father figure, who acts as sort of a benevolent dictator. Everyone in the hospitality business knows Mohamed; I once scared off a taxi driver on the street who was trying to hustle me, just by telling him, "I know Mohamed Nazmy." I believe Mohamed has done more for spiritual travel in Egypt than possibly any other person, and he counts Marianne Williamson, Gregg Braden, John Anthony West and Graham Hancock among his many luminary friends.

To Greg and me, Mohamed is a teasing boy, who giggles and loves practical jokes and surprising people with gifts, unexpected opportunities, or little extras that he knows will make his guests happy. On this first trip, he looked in Greg's and my eyes and called us his brother and his sister. He obviously saw something there we did not, since at the time we had no way of knowing we would start Spirit Quest Tours.

Eventually, I nicknamed him Momo; to my surprise, the name stuck, and now Mohamed has taken to signing his e-mails Momo. In typical Momo fashion, woe to the staff member who calls him by his nickname! They all still refer respectfully to "Mr. Mohamed," at least to his face.

Momo is the most ingenious marketer I have ever met, and has shared many of his secrets with me over the years. But beyond any trick of the trade, he has a genius for understanding the myriad dynamics of his guests, and always knowing precisely how to give them nothing less than the trip of a lifetime. For each of his visitors this is his personal goal; that he typically succeeds, and in Egypt, can sometimes be nothing short of a miracle.

Shakky and Momo have been friends for over twenty years. Shakky is not his real name, but a play on "El walid el shakky," Arabic for "the naughty boy"—which describes him perfectly. He was born in Luxor, not merely in the city, but on the actual grounds of Luxor Temple, which in those days was still full of crude mud houses. Standing at the front entrance to the temple, Shakky points at a section of wall directly behind the towering Colossus of Ramses. "I was borned—right there!" He stabs fiercely towards the wall of the temple itself with his finger. "Our home was mud brick, attached to the wall—it was our wall!" Egypt is truly in his blood.

When Shakky was a child, the authorities came into Luxor Temple, anticipating the growing tourist trade that would be created by the advent of cheap plane travel. They kicked everyone out of the temple and demolished all the homes, making way for badly needed refurbishment and ushering in the era of modern tourism. Now, over fifty years later, they are doing that to much of Luxor as they transform it into the "Paris of the Nile." I hope they don't ruin it with casinos and high-end hotels, but of course they will.

Shakky was, by his own gleeful admission, a bad boy, so it is the perfect pseudonym for him. He will tell you as many stories as you like to prove this to you. This is a typical Shakky story: "I was a kid, six, seven maybe. An old man lived near my house. He married a beautiful girl. Zero mileage, you know?" The group, listening raptly, looks a little confused. "Zero mileage! She had never been —" He makes a rude hand gesture. Everyone nods, the light bulb now on. "He was having sex with her—every night! Their bedroom was on the second floor, you know, up?" He points a little ways above his head. Then he cackles gleefully, covering his mouth—the teeth cracked and yellowed from years of smoking. His round face looks like a little kid's. "I would go up the gutter and put my head next to the window so I could watch, you know? But somehow, someone told the old man. He wired the pipe—with 'lectricity." (I wince in anticipation of the outcome.) "The next time I go up, I grab the pipe—woo! The 'lectricity knocked me straight across the alley!" Shakky laughs uproariously and slaps his leg.

At fifteen, Shakky got into enough trouble that his mother decided he had to leave Luxor. She sent him away to school in Cairo. Eventually, he went to Cairo University and became an Egyptologist, and it was in this capacity that he met and began working with Mohamed. Shakky's a few teeth shy of a full set, and has very little hair, but women for some reason find him devastatingly attractive. On every trip, they fight over Shakky. "He'll visit me in Vancouver next year!" "No, he's visiting me in Albuquerque!" I've seen a seventy-year-old and a thirty-year-old go nuts over the guy. Shakky gets the last laugh, flirting with everyone, making all kinds of promises, but when I ask him if he ever follows through, he says, "No! I am a good boy," gesturing dismissively. I almost believe him, though the seventy year-old seemed especially determined.

In the last couple of years, both Momo and Shakky have faced enormous health challenges. Shakky has had two heart attacks and now sports several stents. Momo had a debilitating stroke, and has relearned to walk and write. Though both are recovering well, it's been strange to see these two strong men brought down by their own hearts, despite being full of love for the guests they help each week. However, Egyptian men are also quick to anger, and hold full sway over their respective dominions, which requires huge outlays of energy. I cringe every time I hear either of them raise his voice, worrying that it will have some lasting detrimental effect.

The thought of losing either of these two larger-than-life personalities is unthinkable. They are both so vital, and their work touches so many. But everything is a choice, and whether they choose to stay with us or continue down the paths that led to their physical deterioration is their decision alone. It is like this for each of us, and they serve as lessons, cautionary tales for their families and loved ones, and of course for themselves.

WHERE I SEE THE SPHINX

Too early in the morning, we stumble out of bed, eating nothing and drinking only water, and board the coach for the Giza Plateau. I cannot quell the butterflies in my stomach.

We initially drive in the opposite direction from the Pyramids, as Shakky says we have to pick up the key to the Giza Plateau—I imagine some great ornate gold thing. Ten minutes later, we stop at the side of the road, and the bus idles there. Most of us have been lulled to sleep by the throbbing motor, and now we wake at the sound of Shakky's voice over the microphone. "I want to introduce... the Key." The doors *psssht!* open and a little man hops on. I expect him to hand Shakky the key, but he *is* the key; without him accompanying us, we cannot get into the Giza complex. He is Mohammed, another Mohammed; the name is as common here as John is in the States.

Just after 5am, in the early morning gray right before dawn, we clear the guard's gate with the Key, pass the outlines of the three pyramids and drive down to the Sphinx. The bus must approach the Sphinx from the rear, and can park on the side just long enough to drop us at the gate, so we don't really notice the Sphinx in our hurry to grab our things and get out.

It's difficult to properly perceive the great statue of the pharaoh-headed lion who guards the Pyramid complex; the Sphinx is truly so big that you don't notice it right away. I have heard stories of native tribespeople who cannot see something in front of them we would take for granted, like a doorknob, because they don't understand it and have no way to comprehend it. Deep down, we are surely all that way, but it requires a lot to take a TV-savvy modern American completely by surprise.

In the half-light of dawn, I am caught up trying to navigate my way down the wooden steps and walkways and don't realize I am at the Sphinx until I have stopped. I look up and suddenly see: I am standing at the great lion's paw, which is about a story-and-a-half high. The creature is almost too big to be allowed; no matter how many movies you see with live dinosaurs and carvings from history coming to life, to stand next to this magnificent work of art is a marvel that makes you believe it might inexplicably begin to move. It's enough to actually make me catch my breath, and I look over at Lyra's roommate, Rose; she is staring up at the face, tears running swiftly and silently down her cheeks. I grin over at Greg and Lyra, who look as pleased as I feel. As my eye passes across the enormous beast, I see the placid face of the pharaoh carved out high above me, his cat body resting across nearly seventy yards.

The Sphinx enclosure is walled to twenty feet, and there is enough room on either side of the statue for six or seven men to walk abreast around its circumference. Most of the tourists who come to visit must content themselves to stand in the viewing gallery high above, but like everything in Egypt, you can pay for a private visit, which is incredibly worthwhile. It seems as if there is nothing here except the Sphinx, though that's not accurate; there are little cave-like openings in the rock, a large set of colored lights (right in front of everything) for the "Sound and Light Show" they put on at night, and even a small temple next to the walkway. But inside the enclosure, it feels as if it's just you and the Sphinx, and that's plenty. The sandstone sculpture faces away from the Pyramids, leading some to say he is guarding them like a faithful watchdog, his chest lifted and his paws stretched out; between them sits a small sandstone altar, and behind that, a recessed stele (pronounced "stella").

The stele was created around 1400 BCE, which stands for Before Common Era—I was surprised to discover that since I left high school, the terms Before Common Era and Common Era have replaced BC and AD. Since the notation is a little more historic and a little less religious, I have adopted the modern abbreviations throughout this book. Not realizing he was before or during any era but his own, King Thutmose IV had this oversized tombstone of a stele made. It tells the hieroglyphic story of when Thutmose the prince went hunting and fell asleep in the shade of the Sphinx's chin. He dreamt the Sphinx spoke to him and asked him to clear away the sand, which at that time was all the way up to the neck of the lion. The Sphinx told him that if he did this, he would become Pharaoh. Thutmose complied with the request, and indeed became Pharaoh, and the "dreaming stele" was put there to commemorate his experiences. Even by accepted Egyptian standards the Sphinx is at least 5000 years old, and civilization itself is only about 6000 years old, which means that as the Neolithic period was ending, man was also capable of carving the Sphinx.

The Sphinx has had several books written about it in recent years, and authors such as Robert Schoch, John Anthony West, Graham Hancock and Robert Bouval have a lot to say about the actual age of the Sphinx. What I know to be true now is that the Sphinx is older, much older than we have been told. While this offends the current administration, in my opinion, all you really have to do is look. Hancock's work (especially *Fingerprints of the Gods*), that of a journalist who set out to disprove the rumors and then ended up by furthering these alternate theories, makes a compelling case all its own. Schoch's writing came about the same way, as he was flown to Egypt to disprove some of the "heresies" and instead became an ardent supporter of them. Here are the most pertinent facts, according to Halle (you can read the original authors' work for more details and specifics):

The Sphinx shows signs of heavy erosion, supposedly from the wind whipping it for centuries. Wind erosion runs horizontally, but rain erosion leaves vertical tracks. Look at the Grand Canyon for examples. There has been no rain on the Giza Plateau for ten thousand years, yet geologists have proven that there is erosion on the Sphinx from water, not just wind.

The Sphinx has been buried in sand for all of recorded history—the dreaming stele talks about the Sphinx being found, buried up to its neck, in the fourteenth century BCE—and none of the other temples exposed to the same wind have any of the erosion of the Sphinx.

The head of the Sphinx is quite small compared to the body. Pharaohs were known to re-carve statues in their own likeness when they ascended the throne, so it is possible the head was originally a lion. Hancock performed a computer simulation of the precession of the equinoxes and discovered that in 10,970 BCE, we were in the zodiac sign of Leo, that the stars in Orion aligned perfectly with the Pyramids, and the Sphinx would have also been in alignment with the constellation Leo.

Guess what else there was during this era? A fertile Nile Valley, with a tropical, non-desert climate, and frequent rainfall.

There is much more, but this is compelling evidence. However, it's scary to many people because it means that civilization is more than 6000 years old, and that would mean… well, that a lot of things we think accurate are off by millennia. For the Egyptians, it would mean their people probably didn't build the Pyramids or the Sphinx. Isn't that cool? Wouldn't even more tourists go if it were proven that it was alien technology, or an advanced civilization no one ever believed existed, such as displaced Atlanteans? (The ones from Atlantis, not Georgia.) But people, especially powerful people, are threatened by change, by information—they might lose their power if access to that information isn't tightly controlled and disseminated. So the Sphinx continues to stare out across the Nile, its face lit at night by the colored lights of a meaningless show, instead of helping us solve the biggest riddle of humanity: when we got here, and why.

Once our brief welcome ceremony between the paws is complete, everyone cozies up for a group picture. Then a Quest photographer treats us to individual pictures. He can pose you so that you seem to be kissing the Sphinx's cheek or holding a model of the Great Pyramid in your hand. At dinner in a few hours, we will receive the color glossies, each tucked into a bright folder frame with pictures of the Giza Plateau all over it.

As we walk up the wooden platform, I hear little yips, and look down to spot a litter of fierce puppies determined to protect their home under the walkway. Momma is nowhere in sight. I drop down to the side of the walkway to try to entice them, but they withdraw until I can no longer see them. Who are these creatures of the desert? How do they survive and breed out here in the heat and the sand? I worry about the puppies, but we are out of time and Shakky is calling us onto the bus. As we board and head up the hill to begin the rest of our pilgrimage, I see the mother dog, the same shade as the sand, slinking into her den. I breathe in relief and relax back into the seat.

THE DESERT

Most everyone who visits Egypt wants their picture taken on a camel, which makes our groups vulnerable. There's no shortage of enterprising young men, hovering as close as the Pyramid police will allow, offering to put you on their camel—I call them camel jockeys, because they are always jockeying for position. It used to be that you would get in the saddle and have a picture taken, for free. Of course, it costs a dollar or two if you want to get down! These days, the camel jockeys also all carry stock packages of "Lawrence of Arabia" head wraps; as you are trying to maneuver your way up onto said camel, they will thrust them on your head (whether you are male or female) and ask you to pay for that, too. Five bucks will cover it, less if you try to give it back.

I do not care a bit for sitting on or riding camels, though I have done my fair share. The first time I rode one, he complained about having to kneel down so I could climb into the saddle, about getting up again with me on his back, about being led around, and the way I sat—probably no more comfortable for him than it was for me. Camels are the boniest creatures—but how would you enjoy someone sitting on your spine? A complaining camel sounds just like Chewbacca, the giant brown Wookie from *Star Wars*. As deep, as resonant, and come to think of it, exactly the same pitch. This realization caused me to look up Chewbacca's voice on the Internet. Wikipedia confirms that indeed, camels were among the sounds used to create Chewie's freakish growl (and bears, and a walrus).

"Come get on my camel! Free! You come now!" This from a young guy in Western clothes; his own head covered in a black-and-white cotton head scarf and bound with a plaited black rope. He approaches our group like a carnival barker.

Carter, a tall, balding man from East Texas, declines in his distinctive twang, "No, thank yew."

The camel jockey, not much bigger than I am, suddenly comes around behind Carter and hoists him around the waist. Carter is surprised and slightly entertained. "No, Ah do not want a ride, thank yew very much, cowboy!"

Still protesting, he somehow ends up on that camel. Based on the five minutes and average two dollars someone spends on a camel, these entrepreneurs are clearing a hundred bucks a day easy. Which is rather incredible in a country where the average salary is $400 a month.

*   *   *   *   *

After the Sphinx, we go to Lake Moeris, a site sacred to Rosicrucians. They will have a ceremony there, which Greg can participate in but I cannot, as I am not a member of the order.

As I look out the bus window, trying to gain a foothold on the cascade of information flowing from Shakky's lips, he talks about building cities in the desert, his accent so thick you have to strain to make out the words. Shakky says "hunjry" instead of "hungry" because he is from the South, where they say a J for a G; as a joke, he calls Greg "Jrej," which comes out sounding like Dredj—everyone on the trip picks it up, and soon Greg has a new nickname. Shakky supplies us with never-ending outrageous stories and is truly one of the best guides in Egypt.

Shakky tells of giving free homesteads to young men, tractors to clear the land, and long-term loans to build. In ten years, he says, they will reclaim the desert, rerouting the Nile to create fertile land, and Egypt can again feed Europe as it once fed Rome. It's a nice ideal, and by now, a dozen years later, gated communities have started to spring up in the desert—Western-style suburbs literally in the middle of nowhere. A New Cairo is going up outside Cairo, and a New Thebes rises on the outskirts of Luxor.

Unfortunately, there is a remarkable contrast to the splendor of the villas and the voracious construction: people living in squalor, people littering everywhere. Piles of trash, sometimes enormous, are scattered about as if everyone who ever walked through the desert left something behind. On the way to Lake Moeris we pass many buildings under construction, almost all half-finished, but with people obviously living in most of them. I learn later that the Egyptian government does not tax you until your building is complete. So many people simply never finish the exterior. While this means no windows, no stucco, no paint, and everything simply open to the air, it's no different from how Egyptians have been living for thousands of years, so it only seems a lousy trade-off if you're a Westerner on an air-conditioned bus. But the whole thing adds to the atmosphere of decrepitude and, to my eye, of an unbalanced culture only inching towards its modern goals. This lack of balance was surely part of what eventually led the Egyptian people to take to the streets in the recent revolution.

Even in Cairo, which is far more populous than the desert, and, for the most part, lacking in larger garbage piles, the standard of living is simply different from what the Western mind expects. On the way into the main part of the city, there is an enormous cemetery. After the brief, disastrous Six Days' War with Israel, hundreds of thousands of refugees from the Sinai flooded into Cairo. The Egyptian government allowed them to move into the city's largest cemeteries temporarily. That was over fifty years ago, and now the City of the Dead is a permanent home for up to a million residents.

The typical American might find this lifestyle abhorrent. But according to Jeffrey Nedoroscik's excellent book, *City of the Dead*, the culture of Egyptian death and burial is what has enabled this environment. Even before cemeteries belonged wholesale to the living, mosques and schools would spring up inside of them. It was common to build tombs inside of small buildings, to house those who would visit the dead, staying for a full forty days of mourning or making a lengthy pilgrimage to visit their deceased loved ones. Over time, and due to the housing crisis caused by a current Cairene population estimated at eight million at night but swelling to eighteen million by day, more people moved into the cemeteries as permanent squatters.

The City of the Dead has no running water, electricity, or sewage, and you can imagine the inconvenience of living in a ghetto without basic services. Many people are housed in single-room tombs with gravestones, now converted to bases for shelves or tables. Often, people are buried under the floors, so the surfaces are flat with no tombstones and the rooms can be quite spacious. As long as you don't mind walking on the dead, it is a decent home. Every tomb is now occupied, with entire families living inside. While one-room living is not uncommon in Egypt, it makes for extremely close living quarters. However, this occurs even out in the farmlands where you can make your own mud bricks and build out as much as you choose. I cannot imagine Americans living in a cemetery, let alone inside the tombs themselves. It is a glimpse into the cultural differences between us, and into the remarkable canon that is Egypt's symbiotic relationship with death.

When my elderly uncle died unexpectedly last year, my aunt moved into a retirement home within two months, unable to face her growing dementia and the big empty house she had raised her family in and shared with my uncle for so many years. She refuses to call her new apartment "home;" instead she refers to it as a "stopping-off place," which it is, at best. Now we call her less, see her less—she has effectively retired from her life. It's the big bugaboo none of us wants to face, because we don't really know what will happen to us when we get old. We don't want to burden our families, or ourselves, and we ignore death because we are terrified of the unknown. But in Egyptian culture, your family takes you in when you get old, even if it's inconvenient, even if they have only a single room in the middle of a cemetery. And what happens after you die is richly developed, often so much more important to them than the time you lived (though you must live morally while you are on earth, of course) that it shifts death to the fore, not merely an accepted part of life, but a celebrated one. This is not a judgment against my own culture; it's just recognition of a different—vastly different—view from what I've known. In the West, we sanitize everything and sweep it under the rug—sickness, old age, and especially death. Egyptians celebrate death and revere the ancient.

We haven't gotten into the rhythm of anything yet. By the time we get to the lake, all the ladies have to potty. Unfortunately, this is a lake surrounded by not much of anything other than desert, but there is something called an "Emergency Beach Unit," which seems to translate from Arabic into what is commonly known as a "Turkish Toilet," or "tiled hole in the ground." There is only a single stall in a small squat house—the floors are wet and muddy, and next to the concrete hole in the floor is a bucket you can fill with water and use to "flush." It smells like a zoo, and between the smell and holding my trousers so they won't get anywhere near the floor, and also so I won't pee on them, I can barely manage; I feel quite sorry for several corpulent women in our group.

Back on the road, Shakky looks sheepish as he grabs the microphone. "There is—a, uh, a bathroom on the bus."

Groans filled the air. "Why didn't you tell us?!"

Shakky shrugs. "I forgot," he apologizes. That was the last Turkish Toilet I saw on that trip.

Greg gets us water at the front of the bus, paying five Egyptian pounds—about a dollar—for two bottles. Ten years later, it's still the same price. We buy bottled water from the driver, so no one ever has to stop for more. Nestle is a popular brand, as is Baraka—neither of which they sell in the States. I am grateful as he slides into the seat and hands me a bottle of icy liquid. He remembers to check the top to make sure it's factory sealed before he cracks the cap, as we've been warned against refilled bottles with the caps melted into place. Greg is alert, engaged fully in this culture shock, and has skipped right over the parts that bother me. I am still sipping when we arrive at our destination.

At Lake Moeris, I sit observing the brief ceremony with the other ineligibles—spouses and partners of Rosicrucians, including my mother. There are different schools of thought about who participates in initiations, the sacred ceremonies so many people come to Egypt for. The Rosicrucians make a distinction based solely on whether you are a member of their order, which seems sensible. Sometimes I hear about people being denied if they are not considered "worthy." Our attitude for our groups now is, if you come here and you want to participate, you are welcome. It's being here that is the real initiation, but I didn't know that my first time. I watch the ceremony; from a distance, a singularly uninteresting conversation.

On the ride to the hotel, I turn to Greg. "So, how was it, Dredj?" He looks a little puzzled.

"Pretty great. Did you, uh, notice anything funny from where you were sitting?"

I shake my head." No, not that I could tell."

"Well, I could see Dennis' aura." Dennis was the man leading the ceremony.

"What did it look like?"

"Sort of blue and purple. But vibrant. Like a big halo all the way around his head and body. It was cool!"

Greg has never seen something like this before, and it's a harbinger, though ultimately trivial compared to what is to come. I'm happy for him, but still floating around, not quite in my body, and more than ready to return to the hotel for some sleep.

THE GALABEYA BOYS

The second day, we visit Sakkhara, home of the step pyramid of King Zoser. The Sakkhara temple complex is in the desert, but the way to and from the site is surprisingly green and lush, full of farmland that literally hasn't changed in thousands of years. We rode across the Nile on the way in from the airport, but between the late hour and jet lag, it almost went unnoticed. Today we cheer, as seeing the famed river is a point of celebration during this early part of the journey. It's narrower than I thought the great river would be (in some areas we will see later, it's nearly five miles across) and in ten seconds we are past it, then we follow a Nile tributary as it winds alongside the road. Great white Egrets fly low across the water, and in several spots we are treated to the abundant life the Nile brings. Forests of date palm trees and native plants are visible through the large windows of the bus, along with acres of open farmland where locals are harvesting or tending crops. Donkeys, their backs laden with great mounds of hay, wait quietly for more to be piled on. Occasionally we even see a man out in a field, yoked to his own plow, dragging his livelihood behind him row after row.

There are no sidewalks, and people walking or riding donkeys line the roadways in the busier sections of the tiny towns and villages; you almost never see an Egyptian on a horse unless it's a member of the police or they're locals joyriding on the Giza Plateau. At each crossroads, we slow, and again at checkpoints in each village. Like a movie on native culture, I can sometimes see men on bicycles or women walking, balancing huge loads of green "hashish" on their heads. We all giggle like high schoolers until Shakky explains that hashish simply means "harvest"; it is what they call the grass that the animals eat. None of these players in my personal Egypt movie looks comfortable, but neither do they look rushed. It is just their lives, simply lived. I wonder how they function without a cell phone, a landline, a computer, a flat screen TV. I feel a touch of envy. Not a life I would choose to live, but they seem, if not happy, at least accepting of this land, this fate. It feels peaceful, and I much prefer it to the empty desert.

On our daily excursions, our Egyptologist, the tour coordinator, and an armed security officer always accompany us. Our bus—or, as they are known in the biz, "coach"—is a modern and comparatively huge vehicle that travels easily across paved roads bumpy with gravel and sand, but occasionally must pause for donkeys, cows, sheep or people who wander too close to its path. Once the bus stops at an intersection and cannot continue. After a while, Shakky, ever impatient, jumped off to see what was causing the traffic jam. He came back shaking his head. "Goats!" he grumbled. Indeed, a herd of goats had gotten mixed up in the traffic and their herder was trying desperately to round them up. Fifteen minutes later, the goats presumably under control, the traffic resumed its regular pace and the bus was able to move forward.

Sakkhara, or Saqqara (potato, potahto—most Arabic transliterated into English has multiple possible spellings) is not my favorite locale, although it has some interesting columns in one hall, and a lot of friendly local dogs. The Sakkhara step pyramid is crumbling, and you can't go inside because it is structurally unsound. Sakkhara is supposedly a precursor to the Giza pyramids, but to me it seems a much lesser site, as if a kid built a sandcastle pyramid and it somehow stuck around for a couple thousand years.

Here at the temple I have my introduction to the Galabeya Boys, as Greg immediately christens them. Each temple has two kinds of guards: the Tourist Police and the Temple Guards. The policemen wear uniforms with guns and holsters, boots and berets, and the other guards wear white scarves wound around their heads like turbans, and (usually blue) plain cotton galabeyas. A galabeya is the ubiquitous word for the Egyptian robe. Worn by women, it can be ornate and embroidered; in the "man-dress" form it is usually plain sheeting, but in both cases it reaches to the ground, has long sleeves, and is open at the neck.

Egyptians are weird about their underwear; believe it or not, one of the worst things one Egyptian boy in Luxor can say to another boy is that he knows the color of his mother's knickers. So it's not as if I have asked what the Galabeya Boys wear under these floor-length nightshirts that pass for clothes. I have hinted around a bit, I have had the whole "boxers or briefs" discussion with several Egyptian male friends, but as with Scots and their kilts, they'll never tell. In conversation, Shakky let slip something about shorts. So I speculate that Egyptian men wear boxers under their galabeyas, but I am told that whatever kind of underwear they have under there, they also have machine guns. Uzis. If you ever want to do something criminal at a temple, rethink it, because these men will shoot through their clothes to stop you. When we started going to Egypt, they wore their guns over their galabeyas, but some time after that, they started wearing them underneath. Of course, it could just be a rumor.

All the Galabeya Boys seem to do is smoke and wear turbans and stand around talking. They show up, often unexpectedly, when we are given time to wander on our own. If they can get you alone for a second, they will try to show you something you might have missed, and then ask you for "baksheesh." This is the Egyptian word for tip money; it is heard everywhere, and supplements their meager incomes. In the street, when an Egyptian pulling a donkey gives you directions, you proffer baksheesh. In the hotels, when a staff member does a service for you, baksheesh. Lots of baksheesh when the Galabeya Boys, sensing your woo-woo inclinations, show you some really powerful spot to meditate. Right on that extra-spiritual bird shit. Overall, my experiences have been that the Galabeya Boys are harmless, and occasionally truly moved by our initiations at the temples.

Greg immediately adopts the galabeyas and turbans of these men, so they chat him up right away when they see our group.

Shakky slaps Greg on the back, cackling at everything he says, further endearing him to the Galabeya Boys Club.

*   *   *   *   *

At Sakkhara, Shakky shows us the tombs of the nobles, beautifully decorated specimens built for Egyptians who were high-level workers for Pharaoh—his scribes or his priests—and could afford to be buried in the way of the king, with scenes from their lives intricately carved and painted on the walls. These men worked during their lifetime to plan their own burials and the art, furniture, and decorations that would accompany them into the afterlife. All during their lives, the elements of death were woven into the fabric of their existence. I try to get my head around that concept, try to imagine my life with that added component, but I quickly give up. I don't dare think of death for too long anyway, unless I want to bring on a panic attack in the middle of the tour, in broad daylight.

These panic attacks of mine had been happening ever since I was an impressionable ten-year-old and asked my dad every child's question, "Daddy, where do we go when we die?"

Unfortunately, my dad, the ultimate atheist, responded with his very own rational truth. "Well, you go into the ground and the worms eat you."

Ah.

Parents, in case you were wondering, this is not a good thing to tell a child who practically still thinks you are God. Wait until they are older—teens in full-on rebellion—before telling them your theories of the afterlife. Don't believe in God? Make something up, preferably something with sunny meadows and flowers. For months, all I could think of was lying in a coffin being eaten by worms. Never mind that my father also believes in cremation. I would lie in bed at night, imagining I was dead, wondering what would happen, trying to sense what I would be while my body was being turned into worm food. But nothing was there. Nothing but my growing fear.

This revelation grew into sweaty night terrors and as I got older, panic attacks. I would wake up in the heart of night, looking around the pitch black of the room, unable to see anything. This nothingness seemed like a foretaste of death, and glimpsing nothing but the thick black blanket a dark—senses deadened by lack of input—I could feel the dread of no longer being "me" someday. I wasn't going to be Halle any more, after I was dead. I would try to feel my way into this nothingness that was the only thing before my eyes. I would try to sense "myself" somehow, in that context, but I couldn't and it would terrify me. My ego was all I had, it was all I knew. My sense of self was woven into the bodily senses I could access readily, but there it ended.

I would become claustrophobic and violently afraid, until I couldn't take it any more. I would turn on a light, leap out of bed, and pace around the room, utterly panicked, my mind grasping random thoughts that would allow me to focus on *something* until my breathing had slowed and the panic started to subside. Maybe an attack wouldn't happen again for a week, a month if I was lucky, but it always came down to this one awful truth: I wouldn't be me, ever again.

I carried this swirling secret inside of me, a deep blackness inside of an otherwise sunny space. I really couldn't tell anybody. I tried, but how do you describe the earthquake and the avalanche as they both hit you at once? How do you convey your deepest fears to someone who has never felt this, or worse, has the faith of their own belief to buoy them up when you have none?

To stave off a panic attack in the tomb of a lesser noble, I refocus on Shakky, now showing us a marvelous example of the Egyptians' workmanship: a door surrounded by hieroglyphs that look stamped into the stone. When you get close, you see that the door is false, and all the hieroglyphs have been meticulously hand-carved, so finely that they look like a repeated imprint instead of individual work. It's absolutely exquisite, but I notice that some portion of the reliefs is missing. Shakky explains that they are cut out, restored, and then returned to their original position. Over time, though, I've come to understand that museums all over the world often obtained their pieces this way, and though the latest cuts might be restoration, at least occasionally we are viewing reproductions or pieces that will never be reinstated.

Howard Carter was the man who discovered the tomb of Tut Ankh Amun, whose name means "living image of the sun," or, as Americans call him in our constant desire to level the playing field, "King Tut." Once, Howard Carter was the director of all Egyptian Antiquities, the title Zahi Hawass now holds (with the prefix "Supreme" added, since Zahi's much more of a showman. You know Zahi even if you don't know the name—he's the man in the Indiana Jones hat on Fox News, opening the newly found tombs.) During Carter and his colleagues' period of history, excavations followed "I scratch your back, you scratch mine" methods, where the wealthy (usually British) patrons would fund a dig, provided that some of the choicest bits went to them. No one thought anything about gouging out part of a wall to send to their patron, and it follows a certain logic; after all, no money, no excavation.

There was a recklessness and a rampant, happy-go-lucky approach to archaeology then. The most blatant story I ever heard came from Kent Weeks, a marvelous lecturer who runs the Theban Mapping Project in the Valley of the Kings. Much of the history of the Valley is preserved (or not) by the efforts of the archeologists of the nineteenth century. Kent Weeks told of an Englishman who, while on a dig, found eight large alabaster canopic jars of stunning quality and workmanship. When a pharaoh or other high-born Egyptian was mummified, they took the brain out through the nose and discarded it (as the heart was the center of all feeling to them), opened the abdomen and removed all the internal organs, placing them in canopic jars with the heads of deities on them. Over time, the jars' contents turned to dust, but they were still an important part of the funerary findings. These particular canopic jars were not only alabaster, each was inscribed on the outside. In gold. So this logical fellow writes to Howard Carter—very proudly, mind you —that he has saved both shipping costs and trouble. Alabaster is extremely delicate, hand-carved out of solid quartz until it is so thin it is somewhat translucent. This jackass has scraped all the gold off seven of the eight jars, and mushed it all together, to be melted down. Then he has thrown seven of the jars in the Nile. The eighth has been kept for his benefactor, now made much more valuable by its singularity. Mr. Brilliant has kept the gold, which would have been his right, as the finds were apportioned off to whoever paid for and did the digs, as well as to the government. He explains to Carter that he has made a copy of the drawings off a single jar, which should be sufficient for the archaeological needs of posterity. It's a wonder any of these tombs stayed intact, and not a surprise that most didn't.

We have never been inside King Zoser's step pyramid at Sakkhara, as it's off-limits due to safety concerns (true confession —I recently was snuck in, and saw only a long tunnel, fully under construction as they dig it out and shore it up). However, we usually perform initiations in what must once have been a large temple. Now the walls have almost all fallen to rubble. There is only the ghost of the building—a half-wall to shield you from the unceasing desert wind and some low stones that make up the rectangular perimeter. On our way out, we take turns crouching down to peer into the eye holes of a stone box. Inside, you see the statue of King Zoser himself staring back at you. Using techniques now lost to us, his eyes seem alive, surprising you with their gentle stare. The purpose of the eye holes was not for you to see in, but for Zoser to see out, gazing on the stars for all eternity. This is such a tender gesture, and much forethought must have gone into it. Why the box? Why not just the statue? Since it has been much better preserved this way, I'm grateful they chose this method.

After the brief initiation ceremony, Greg, Lyra and I go wandering off on our own. We do this so often on this trip we become known as the "bad kids." Later, when Greg and I start leading groups, our smaller trips are subtitled the "Bad Kids Tour" since we are usually off the beaten path, doing things Shakky calls "illegal," which is the stuff the tourists don't normally know about, let alone get to do. Shakky, his accent and vocabulary peculiarly Egyptian by way of America, pronounces the word "touristses." Over the years, I've come to think of touristses as the inconsiderate vacationers—the "ugly American" who thinks it's rude when foreigners don't speak English, or the European who wants to wear a low-cut tank top into a town where the locals keep even their ankles covered. Our Spirit Questers embrace the idea that we're not even tourists, we are "ambassadors of peace," building bridges between foreigners by exposing us all to cultures of the world.

The sand is blowing in my face—for some reason, it's always the worst for me at Sakkhara—so Greg buys me a white scarf from a vendor. Wrapping it around my head and face, I can block out most of the wind and sand granules. An Egyptian man offers us horses and camels, and though I protest I can't ride, hikes me up, throws my leg over a horse, and thwacks the horse's side. The horse takes off and, after a moment, I have to concede that as much as my fear would have kept me on the ground, I am thrilled. Trotting through the desert sand, neither guided nor steered, allowing the horse to go where it wants without worrying about stops or other traffic, is both exhilarating and freeing. The horse leans back, sort of tumbling down a hill of sand, and then leans forward, climbing the next soft ridge. All I have to do is mirror the horse's motions, and I am an instant expert. After about half an hour, we return our horses, spending five bucks each for a ride I will always remember.

In the afternoon, after Sakkhara, we stop at a desert oasis for lunch. On our way down the steps to the open-air restaurant, a tiny crew of musicians and dancers serenades us with drums and homemade instruments. On the left, in a covered area about twenty feet square, two women sit on their haunches, busily working fist-sized balls of dough into flat circles. One by one, they slide the rounds of dough into a mud brick oven, and pull it out less than a minute later. The layers of dough have parted, and a huge pita puff emerges. They smile and pass it to those of us watching, and we greedily tear it to bits to share amongst ourselves. The fresh, hot bread is immensely satisfying, and the women laugh, pleased by our expressions. They shyly hold their hands out for baksheesh, which we gladly give, then Shakky bustles us over to the main restaurant.

It is huge, and can easily hold a hundred or more people at the long tables. A soda machine leans against a tent pole, a group of hookahs clumped next to it. The whole establishment is under a big group of tents, and in the many times I have been there, we've never seen the kitchen. Our tables, as is often the case when we eat as a group, are covered in an assortment of Egyptian mezzes, appetizers so plentiful you can make a meal of them alone. Little dishes hold hummus (chick pea & tahini dip), baba ghanoush (a dip made of grilled eggplant), tabouli (granules of cracked wheat with garlic, lemon, parsley and mint), assorted spiced olives, cubed boiled potatoes dressed in oil, a dark green fava bean dip that is a staple of the Egyptian table, and my favorite—fresh white beans cooked al dente, drizzled in olive oil, and topped with chopped onion and parley.

Everything in Egypt is fresh, and for the most part, macrobiotic. On the ships, you can see food being brought in that morning that is picked the day before and will be on your table within hours. The Egyptians eat at least two courses, presuming they can afford it: a salad course consisting of these appetizers, and then a meat course, possibly followed or replaced by a fish course, and fresh fruit for dessert. Pork is unheard of, as it's a Muslim country, and beef is not particularly plentiful or popular, but chicken and lamb are served everywhere. After our appetizers are mopped up with plenty of the fresh bread puffs, plates of grilled chicken and lamb take their place; each has a side of local rice, threads of saffron streaking the soft white grains orange.

The lamb seems unspiced, the taste delicate and rich at the same time. The chicken is tender and perfectly grilled, full of flavor in my mouth. Through a faceful of chicken, Shakky launches into another of his stories.

"They eat so many chickens in Egypt, you know?" We all look up, interested to hear the tale and concentrating because Shakky's accent is entertainingly thick. "A couple years ago they started bringing in chickens from Denmark. The Danish chickens, they are larger and fatter, and our local birds are scrawny!" He gestures with a piece of chicken. "But Danish chicken tastes like nothing! So no one will eat it! Then my friend comes from America to my house in Luxor—I will take you there. He brings his boy over to play. He and my youngest boy are the same age, eight, maybe nine, but the American boy is *huge* standing next to my son. But my boy can run faster, play harder. My boy could even beat up the American boy if he wanted." He cackles, then gestures with more of the meat. "The big boy is Danish chicken!" Shakky laughs, finishing his story by popping a last bite into his mouth.

I am enjoying the food and the atmosphere, and I start to get comfortable in the company of these kind Egyptians, and this interesting group of people. We come from all over the States and from Canada. Eleanor is elegant-looking and tailored, with a bit of a Texas twang. She and Carter, who are not together, are from different parts of Texas; he is a working man from a cattle ranch, she owns cattle and oil investments. Vivian, an older woman who was widowed last year, has big, sad eyes and a gentle disposition. Rusty is wiry-haired, in his late twenties, and quite normal-looking, except for the prosthetic plastic and metal leg he wears below his right thigh. Though Lyra is a new friend, we already feel like we have known each other forever. I glance over at her long blonde hair and feline face, glad she is sitting next to Greg and me. Lyra's roommate on the trip, Rose, is a dear, sweet older woman originally from Poland. I suspect she was there during the Holocaust, but it's not the sort of thing you can inquire about over hummus. We are forty in total, ranging from our twenties to our seventies.

After lunch, I want to smoke a hookah. My mother, Judith, claps her hands like a child. She sports an English accent, having lived in London since I was seven. "Oh, goody. It looks like fun!"

Mohamed laughs. "You mean a shisha, my sister. What kind of flavor do you want?"

Shisha (called a hookah in places such as Turkey) is tobacco cured in molasses. Often, the molasses is flavored, so it's like a little dessert when you smoke it after dinner. It turns out there are many shisha flavors. Apple, mint, and coffee are the most popular in Egypt, but I have also tried honey, cantaloupe, mango, raspberry, strawberry... and new car smell. Not really, but on a recent trip we did get chocolate and cola flavors. It's also fun to mix two or more tobaccos to create a new taste sensation, but that's more likely to happen at the hookah lounges in Las Vegas than in a little outpost of shisha heaven in Cairo.

When the group hears about the shisha, several others want to join us. Carter and Eleanor are both in, since Texas is Marlboro country. Rose smiles but shakes her head. Rusty comes over, walking so smoothly you would hardly know about the metal leg if he weren't wearing shorts. For about a dollar a person, the waiter brings a huge, standing water pipe, the flavored tobacco of our choice on the top of the stand, and a hot charcoal disk on top of that. Most restaurant shishas have at least two pipes, long snaked hoses that end in metal mouthpieces. To share in the States, you get a plastic tip that you can put on as the pipe is passed to you, but in Egypt they simply cover the mouthpiece with a bit of foil. This means you are fairly protected from the last group of people who smoked this pipe before you, but you'd better know the hygiene of the ones you are with.

The important thing to remember is that, while you can inhale the smoke, cooled by the water that is the whole point of this device, an unaccustomed smoker can still get what those in the know refer to as a "harsh toke." In other words, you can really embarrass yourself with a coughing fit. There is nothing more disconcerting than seeing your mother, a shisha ingénue, trying to French inhale when she hasn't smoked in about forty years, causing her to hork up a lung instead. I, on the other hand, occasionally puff a ciggy butt when the mood hits, so I am capable of holding my own on the shisha front.

This mightily impresses Mohamed and Shakky, who, besides blowing smoke rings on a shisha, also indulged in a pack-a-day habit. Eventually, this caught up with Shakky, who had a heart attack and nearly died. Both he and Momo quit smoking then, but only Shakky, touched by death, stayed the course. After Momo had his stroke, he finally gave up the white death sticks as well, but both still enjoy a few puffs on a shisha occasionally.

Sitting near Momo and Shakky, Judith, and a few others in the group, Greg and I grin at each other as we pass the shisha back and forth. We haven't smoked in almost ten years. As we blow smoke at each other and enjoy the ambiance, the camaraderie, the minty flavor of the water-cooled tobacco, and the lovely sun-dappled atmosphere, we start to forget about work, relaxing for the first time in, literally, years.

After lunch, more music and dancing accompany our exit. At the bread ovens, a local woman comes up and points at me.

"Gemila," she says, which is Arabic for beautiful. I look at her shining face, her snapping brown eyes. I point back.

"Gemila." I echo. She laughs and asks for us to have a picture taken together, and we pose, smiling.

As I go out, the music builds, the drumming tempo increases and the zithers manifest a kicky little tune. Unexpectedly, those who have had a glass of wine or beer at lunch are dancing with the musicians, feeling less intimidated than the rest of us, or else more in tune with the music. We all clap and take pictures and leave the restaurant very satisfied.

TUE MAN AND SECRETS
OF TUE NIGUT

The next stop is a carpet school near Sakkhara. The schools take Egyptian kids who would otherwise be roaming the streets, and train them to weave carpets of wool or silk so they can grow up to know a trade. The carpets are sold in the factory next door, to the touristses who come by the busload as we do. The guides get a cut, for bringing their groups here instead of to the carpet factory (or perfumery or jewelry store) across the street, and the tourists get a rug that costs them a lot less than what they would have paid at home.

We are ushered into a large, well-lit space with several carpet looms set up along the walls. The looms are mostly vertical wooden contraptions, strung by hand with hundreds of guide threads. At the base of each one is a narrow wooden bench, almost at ground level. We receive a short guided tour from an Egyptian salesmen, whose English is excellent. The children range from seven or eight to about fifteen, relatively clean and rangy-looking. The kids sit two or three to a bench, weaving all afternoon on the same rug. We are told they study, too, and are taught school subjects.

"The carpets are made the same way they have been for centuries." The salesman points to the lengths of hand-cut and colored wool hanging next to each loom. "They are wrapped around the guide thread and knotted." The child he points to demonstrates, whipping the wool thread around the guide and snapping it into a knot before cutting the thread swiftly with a little knife.

"The rug is made by stacking knot after knot against each other. The colors and pattern become clear as more knots are stacked, until there are hundreds of thousands, sometimes millions of knots! These rugs can take up to a year to weave. Then the carpet is cut down to lie on the floor or a wall." As he talks, I realize that the fringe usually left on a silk rug is all that remains visible of the guide threads used to build that rug. The guide points to a connect-the-dots picture of the pattern on the rug. "A picture is the template now, but as the artist become more experienced, they create their own rug paintings, then each rug is truly a work of art." Some of the designs are done now using software, and it is certainly possible to buy a rug made by machine, but here at some of the carpet schools, it's still done the old-fashioned way.

As the salesman explains the methods used for the weaving, the kids work industriously, smiling at this new group of hourly imports. But as he turns away, the children make the universal sign for money at us, the whispered word "baksheesh." I laugh, thinking it might be a joke, going along with them, but they are serious, insistent. Their eyes are hard, unconnected, their little minds focused only on the money we can provide them. I can almost see the light going out as their childish innocence is turned in, one Egyptian pound at a time. I hate that these kids sound like beggars, when they are here to learn a trade that can support them. I suppose I might as well hate us for having money, for giving it to them. We have taught them by our actions; it's not their fault they already know the ways of the world. I am not sorry when the guide conducts us on to the main point of the tour: the shopping.

Inside, the enormous room is full of wool rugs, some coarse, some fine. It seems there is enough inventory to last forever, these stacks upon stacks of colored squares, as we are waited on by some of the very men who made them. But any halfway-legit buyer is brought into the silk rug room, where you can spend some serious coin. Though both wool and silk rugs can be truly masterful pieces of art, I much prefer the silk, both for the feel and the fine nuances in the designs. As I enter, a man is showing a couple from our group how silk rugs change color. He flips a smallish rug up in the air, giving it a half-turn on the way as if he's making pizza dough. The rug responds by shimmering in mid-air, and indeed, as it lands, the blue is now another shade. The silk gives off differing hues depending on which way the threads are angled, appearing to change color as you walk around the piece. This chameleon factor, I'm told, is what created the legends of flying carpets, as the rugs seem to glow, shift and move when they are airborne. Even without the delightful back-story, they are exquisite. The larger rugs go for ten or twenty thousand dollars, but when you blanch, they are quick to point out that you could easily pay ten times that in the States. Some of my group is converted, and stay to choose their rugs as I sidle out to see what Shakky is up to.

Typically, he is embroiled in a heated battle over prices. Shakky's modus operandi is to look at an item that has been brought to him, give it the once-over, and then say, with a dismissive flick of his wrist, "Give him fifty pounds or let him keep it!" Fifty Egyptian pounds is ten dollars, which would be fine, except the vendor who is selling the item wants fifty U.S. dollars, and up until now you thought that was a fair price. It's weird since all guides get a cut of almost anything you buy, but that's Shakky for you, bucking the system wherever he can—and they all seem to love him. He is loyal, certainly, and if he knows the guy has a good product, Shakky will bring him a group a month for years.

Shakky grabs the large roll of woven silk from Rusty, whose wiry red hair sticks out from under his safari hat, and ushers him over to "The Man." The Man (and there is a similar man at each major shop we visit) is sitting at a desk at the head of the main room, surrounded by chairs and sycophants. He is late middle-aged, and sports gray, close-cropped hair and a formal-looking black Saudi-style galabeya, made of smooth polyester with a flat Oriental collar.

A snap of his fingers and glasses of hot mint tea magically appear. In any of these shops, mint tea or a cold bottle of soda pop means you are bargaining. Woe to any tourist foolish enough to turn down a drink offered by a shop owner. It is the custom, but also signals a relationship, which means you can get a better price later, after you have gotten to know each other over tea. Tea is the currency of the social hour, and if you refuse it, even if it's because you think you are being polite or honestly don't have enough time, you're guaranteed not to get the cheapest price; you're also missing out on a cultural exchange as important than anything that goes on at Camp David.

Rusty intrigues me; he won't talk about his leg, except to say he got a lot of money losing it. He is now spending some of that hard-won cash on a silk rug in Egypt. And Shakky is making sure he gets the best price, possibly even pointing out Rusty's disability to the Man in the process—for leverage.

I move closer and sit unobtrusively in one of the half-dozen chairs set in two neat rows facing each other, The Man's Lounge. Shakky cannot just snap his fingers at this man, and he knows it. He speaks rapidly in Arabic, gesturing like an Italian whose beloved mama has been insulted. He sighs, he rolls his eyes. The Man listens quietly as Shakky gets louder and more intense. He gestures placidly, the movement going only as far up his arm as his wrist. Suddenly, The Man nods his head—once. Shakky stops talking. He takes the rolled-up rug and gives it to Rusty. In English, he announces the price. Looking pleased, Rusty sets an edge of the rug roll on the ground, balancing against it so he can reach for his wallet. Then the next tourist comes forward, hovering in the background until he can have his turn, and Shakky heads into the silk room so he can repeat the process.

In 2006, Greg convinced The Man to design a small rug based on the Flower of Life, a sacred geometry pattern we didn't even know existed on our initial visit to the carpet school. He sent a full-color picture by e-mail, and they downloaded it, printed it, and transferred it to a pattern for a silk rug. The original one cost over $1,500 to make—the time and effort must all go into planning the pattern, choosing the colors, calculating the needed threads, and setting up the loom's parameters. After that, each time they make the rug, it's cheaper and cheaper until it becomes profitable. We have that rug now on our wall at home and each time we go to the school, someone in our group buys a copy of the rug based on that prototype.

Our purchased rugs wrapped into squares and tied with brown paper and white string, we look as if we have spent our time at a bakery, not a carpet factory. The packages are small, but heavy. They will fit neatly at the bottom of our suitcases until we can unwrap them at home and spread them out on our floors, smoothing the fringe at the edges of the rug, and walking over the wrinkles until they are gone. Then we can glide barefoot on the wool or silk for years, thinking of Egypt each time.

*   *   *   *   *

In the evening, we have time off and everyone collapses gratefully in their rooms. We are staying in the Pyramid rooms, a separate wing built across from the palace, facing the Giza plateau. The key they give you for your room (one key, even for two roommates) is a standard-style house key attached to a heavy brass oblong, about an eighth-inch thick, with Arabic writing standing out in high relief against the textured matte gold. The key is too unwieldy to carry on your person and would weigh down any handbag, which is the whole idea. There is a man in the lobby whose only job, it seems, is to check your key when you go out and give it to you when you return. This is the way it was done at hotels for centuries, before plastic key cards and doors with blinking red and green lights. These unfeeling signals inform you whether you can enter your room or have to sit in the hall awaiting security because you put your key card too close to your cell phone and it rang, wiping out the passcode. Much more civilized, instead, to walk your key from the front desk to your room, and to know precisely where it is while you are out gallivanting all over Cairo and its environs.

There is nothing more delicious than coming into a truly fine hotel room in a foreign land; I feel part pampered Westerner, part Mata Hari, the unknown lurking around every corner. The door to the room is a massive wooden sentry that hints at the heavy Middle East furnishings within. The dressers are the same dark wood, the bed a California King on steroids. The floor is covered in a Persian rug, and the hangings and bedspread look Moroccan. Two low, plump slingback chairs hover around a small center table and every afternoon a hotel angel leaves us local fruit, whole on the plate, a knife tucked into a linen napkin next to it. My favorite is the guava, which makes the whole room smell like Hawaii.

Our bathroom is large, the bathtub marble, the ever-present mini-shower sprayer hung next to the loo. Culturally I cannot get used to the idea that I am supposed to wash instead of wipe, because spraying water up into my parts does not seem to take gravity into account. There is never any towel close to hand—indeed, unless you are in a hotel room, none at all—and I do not care to feel like a leaky faucet for hours afterwards. At the occasional bathroom this is the only option, but here at the hotel they are kind enough to provide us Westerners with toilet paper as well, and I admit I have never tried the "potty shower." I am too scared, as I picture myself, Inspector Clouseau-like, unexpectedly fending off an angry water snake with a mind of its own.

But I am fascinated by Egyptian toilet hygiene. Egyptians, for example, do not wash their hands after they use the bathroom, which explains the lack of paper towels in many of them. I believe this is because they did not touch themselves at all, at least not until they had been sprayed clean. Every public toilet in Egypt costs a pound to get in, about 20¢. This seems fair—you pay a quarter in the U.S. or 10p in London. Before you go in, the attendant hands you between two and five squares of toilet paper, which is hardly enough to wipe a trickle, let alone address your needs when you haven't seen a toilet in the last four hours and you're not likely to again for another four. Once, at Philae Temple in Aswan, I watched as the hapless bathroom attendant tried to hand the requisite squares to a burly, mustachioed European man, who immediately began berating her. She handed him another round of paper, and still yelling, he set off towards the bathroom, only to turn on his heel at the door, march over to her, and grab the whole roll out of her hand. As Greg's dad says, "He clearly had important government work to do."

Another time I was at a McDonald's restaurant in Aswan, which has a bathroom to rival the Cairo Four Seasons hotel, very Asian and full of modern stone. My now-favorite Texan,

Eleanor, who has traveled in the company of Spirit Quest Tours several times, came out of the toilet stall, scowling.

"This is the nicest bathroom in Egypt!" she drawled. "I can't believe someone peed all over the seat! And the floor! What is wrong with some people?" I explained about the sprayer, but she shook her head.

"I checked. There isn't one." We were both shocked. But later, I found out that new models of toilet put the sprayer in the bowl itself, so that all you have is a tiny hole at the top in back. I could only imagine some poor tourist trying to use the spray and dousing the seat and floor with jets of water from the in-bowl bidet. However, this new information did help me to understand why the ubiquitous attendant in public bathrooms always wants only to give you four squares of TP. It isn't to wipe yourself, it's to dry off after your potty shower.

Late in the evening, we venture out with a few members of our group. Mother, Lyra, Rose, Carter, Rusty, Eleanor and Vivian have already developed into our regular companions. It's perfectly safe to walk here, at least as far as any crime might go. Despite what you've heard in the media, Egypt has a remarkably low incidence of violence, and against tourists it's almost unheard of. Where your safety might be at issue is the actual walking, as streetlights are rare and sidewalks tend to run in fits and starts, beginning and ending randomly. The street that fronts Momo's office has these haphazard sidewalks, plus enough room for two lanes of cars. But because it runs parallel to a busy main street, cars take it as a shortcut. During rush hour, you can have as many as three lanes of cars going in a single direction, plus two lanes of pedestrians—one walking against traffic, the other walking with it. There is a constant buzzing from all the horns advising you to get out of their way. I've actually been clipped by a car's side view mirror before—that's how close they get—but thankfully it didn't do any damage, as the car was going all of two miles an hour.

This particular evening we don't get too far, as the minute we leave the protection of the hotel's perimeter, we are pounced upon by that venerable old cliché, the Con Man, in this case in the form of "Memo, the local souvenir seller." Memo's shop is barely big enough to turn around in, but he manages to stock about 500 statues, six glass cases stuffed with rows and rows of jewelry, all sorts of Egyptian artifacts, even some Egyptian costumes.

By now, I've known Memo over ten years. I'm convinced he has a mole working for him inside the Mena House who tells him when I am scheduled to arrive and how many in my party. So Memo is always waiting to ambush my people as soon as they venture beyond the Mena House's main gate. "Halle Group? Halle Group! Over this way!" Of course they go. He'll get them even before I have arrived, so they often think I have some business arrangement with this man. The only agreement we have ever had is to make sure he gives a good price to our guests ("No, Memo, twenty-five dollars per silver cartouche is not acceptable. Yes, Memo, ten dollars is much more reasonable," etc.) but that first night, on that first trip, we must have been lambs to the slaughter.

The conversations with Memo have been interesting over the years. He will point to a statue you are interested in and describe it as lapis lazuli. Lapis is one of the semi-precious stones the Egyptians ground up and used in their paints, the cobalt blue which often depicts the skin tones of the god Amon or Pharaoh's hair. Some of the charming ushaptis, the tiny statues that accompany the dead to the underworld, were made from lapis. But almost nothing in Memo's store is older than last week, and these days, much of it is made in China.

"You mean, it's lapis-colored, Memo."

"Yes, of course," he will reply, his hand waving airily.

But my gut tells me that had I not corrected him, the price I was quoted would have been much higher, as it so often was with his less discerning clients. I tell our guests that if I'm not accompanying them they should threaten Memo with: "Is this the Halle price?" If it is not, he knows I will be coming to strong-arm him into a fair deal.

A few years ago, we bought a cool statue that looked stone, but broke in the suitcase when we brought it home. When Greg glued it, I was surprised to see that it was plastic. That statue has broken three times, in nearly the same place, and though Greg knew it wasn't real stone, I don't think he has ever forgiven Memo for selling him the cheapie tourist junk. I thought it was actual rock, but I am a tad bit gullible, even something of a Pollyanna. While this has served me well in some areas of my life, it means that Memo could still pull a fast one on me if he wanted to.

For me, all this pales when I see the back room. Benches span three walls, covered in decorative blankets and cushions. Above the benches, reaching to the ceiling, mirrored shelves line the walls, covered with confections of hand-blown bottles. Between two and ten inches tall, they range from the simple to the sublime: palm trees, teapots, garden sculptures, pineapples and birds, all creating a collection of delicacies in Pyrex and glass. Of course the bottles are really an elaborate army of Trojan horses, designed to better sell Memo's vast selection of essential oils. This is where the Pollyanna part of me kicks in. I am just grateful to be here.

You go in to this mirrored wonderland, sit, and are offered tea, which of course you now know to accept. For about ten minutes, your wrists, hands and forearms (and even biceps, should you run out of other real estate) are liberally doused and smoothed in oils with names such as Queen of the Night, Nefertiti, Royal Lotus Oil, and Priscilla, Queen of the Desert. Sweet tea, with fresh mint sprigs, is endlessly poured for you in little gold-filigreed glasses, despite it being nearly 10pm. Then you have to decide which of the oils smells best, which can be a challenge if you have, say, eight competing scents on each arm.

"Good night, Dredj," Lyra calls, as Greg kisses me good night and heads to the hotel. He escorts Judith, who got in a day later than the rest of us and is still exhausted. All the men from our group have drifted off by now, retreating from this onslaught of senses and shopping, and the women are finally starting to feel like your girlfriends. Once you and the others have chosen your oils, giggling, and chosen your bottles—with much discussion amongst you and maybe even some swapping—you drink even more tea, and then the negotiations begin.

Don't bother asking the price before this point. Memo will merely shrug and tell you, "Wait. See what you want." Try a second time and he will say, "It will depend on how much you and your friends buy." Here's my favorite: "I promise it will be a good price."

Some of the oils are supposed to act as pheromone clouds. Memo tries to get me to buy something called "Secrets of the Night"—guaranteed, he says, to "make your husband feel different." Though Greg had liked the scent a lot, Lyra and I are both too turned off to buy it. To us, it smells like a cross between strawberry urinal cake and cherry rat.

Lyra buys a huge bottle of rose oil, since the Rosicrucians often use it in their initiations. I buy a lovely scented oil, Queen of the Something-or-Other, and a beautiful long-necked orange glass genie bottle, its stopper like a twist of smoke, which still sits on my dresser at home. Several in the group spend hundreds of dollars on their purchases. And why not? Compared to the cost of comparable amounts of these oils in the States, Memo is a bargain. Then there is the added pleasure of being able to say to your neighbors and friends (for at least several years, judging from the size of the bottles), "Oh, yes, my lotus oil was hand-carried from Egypt." I'm sure the most polite among us even manage to avoid smiling gleefully as we say it.

Since we will go home from Cairo, everyone arranges to leave the largest purchases to pick up at the end of the trip. This is the smartest sales technique Memo has. When they return to get their things, he sells them more. And in case they forget and never come back, he can always resell it to the next customer.

THE KHAN IS... THE KHAN

Valentine's Day is extremely popular in Egypt, with street vendors hawking huge baskets filled with giant pink teddy bears and pounds of chocolate, flower bouquets in garish colors and red mylar "I love you" balloons. When we visit a couple years ago, everyone at the Quest Travel office has something for Valentine's Day, and Mohamed offers us three different kinds of chocolates (Egyptians like nougat in their chocolate, but otherwise it could be Belgian it's so smooth and dreamy). The candy is all from important hotel clients and cruise lines, which gives you an idea of the cultural difference—I can't see the Hyatt delivering Valentine's Day chocolates to Donald Trump, here many of the men have boxes of candy or flower arrangements, sent to them by the other men they do business with. Momo tells us that Valentine's Day has become huge in Egypt in recent years, and indeed, it seems to outdo even the States in its hues of pink shinyness everywhere we looked.

This Valentine's Day we've just arrived, and a group of us head to the main restaurant at the Mena House for our opening night's dinner. Everywhere people are celebrating, with romantic tables for two occupied by starry-eyed Egyptian couples or honeymooning travelers. Greg and I are the only couple with our group that night.

"Champagne?" I ask brightly. He knows it's my favorite. He shrugs. It's not his.

"If you like."

I glance down at the menu. "Let's see. Fifteen hundred pounds, at five and a half pounds per dollar. That's...two hundred and fifty dollars?? You've gotta be kidding!"

"Two hundred and seventy-two," Greg smiles, having totted it up on his ubiquitous iPhone. "Still want it?"

I shake my head, laughing. "Let's get some white wine." We do, but though it's also extremely expensive, the Egyptians are much better architects than they are vintners.

Dinner is excellent that night—lamb and couscous served in a pointy, hat-like Moroccan tagine that allows the food to slow-cook, the steam escaping from the hole in the pot's chimney. Over dinner, Greg explains to everyone about Shakky, who they will meet the following morning. I go to the Ladies Room, and when I come back, Greg is talking to Patricia, an irreverent and sweet woman who reminds me of Ethel Merman (had the great lady been born in Boston). Greg is depravedly trying to teach her an Arabic phrase for when she meets Shakky:

He says it several times for her. "Kiss imak." Slower. "Kiss ih-mahk."

Patricia nods, repeating it carefully. "Kiss imak," she warbles, trying to be heard over the crowded restaurant.

Greg shushes her a little, his hands in the air as he indicates that she should keep her voice down. Patricia's eyes narrow. "What's it mean?"

Greg looks around, making sure no Arabs are in earshot. He speaks out of one side of his mouth, in a stage whisper. "Your mother's vagina."

Patricia squints, leans in, and not really hearing Greg, yells, "Your mother's from China?"

When Shakky meets Patricia the next morning, he doubles over in glee when she greets him with her carefully learned phrase. After we tell Momo, he begins to use it against us whenever we say something he doesn't like. It starts off, "Is your mother from China?" But now he looks you up and down, then grins. "Are you from China?"

*   *   *   *   *

The Mena House's big main restaurant, the Khan El Khalili, was named after one of the oldest and most famous markets in the world. I was surprised at the name. Like the market, the restaurant is a melting pot of people from all over, but the Khan is... the Khan.

Row upon row of shops, many not just stalls but permanent stores, line the long narrow streets of the Khan el Khalili, with myriad wares displayed on low tables out front. Goods hang overhead, tantalizing in their beauty and sheer variety. Tourist crapola butts up against expensive jewelry and authentic antiques. Handmade shoes hang on wire racks. Shisha tobacco, T-shirts, inlaid wood boxes, galabeyas, scarves, earrings, paintings, sheets, garish necklaces, and children's toys all vie for space. At the far end of the market, the streets widen into the real jewelry section, and you can purchase expensive heirlooms as well. Everything in the world seems for sale at the Khan.

The center square, which has a lovely large cream stone mosque, is bordered by a whole row of ahwas, the tiny coffee shops whose menus range from coffee to full meals. Each features an outdoor seating area that reminds me of the cafes in Italy, except that instead of individual metal chairs, you sit mostly on carved Moroccan benches and the occasional green plastic lawn chair. You can buy shisha here and smoke for an hour, or enjoy a Turkish coffee with its sluggish fine grounds and rich, chocolatey scent. There are touristses here, of course, but at least as many locals, out for an afternoon in what is possibly the busiest square in all of Cairo.

Here in the market, I feel as if I am on display, much like the wares. I am dressed as a Western woman, in slacks and a long top, but in a nod to the Egyptian style and to keep the sun off my face, I wear a cotton scarf slung about my head. So to my own mind, I'm well covered. Yet the hootin' and hollerin' begins as soon as I step onto the crowded cobblestone path.

"My queen, my queen! Where is your husband? He is a lucky man!" The young shopkeeper laughs as I pass.

"Pashmina, here is Pashmina for you—only ten pounds!"

"Beautiful lady, come look at my junk—no hassle!" This from a portly, middle-aged man with a long beard, wearing a sweater in the blistering June heat. A group of young men gathered around a stall simply stare as we go by.

"Nefertiti, please! Come look—it's free to look!"

It all reverberates, the din of shopkeepers calling to me and the other women, until we are traversing the market wrapped in our own soundscape.

Judith giggles. She looks at me at arm's length, almost as if I weren't her daughter but some strange woman she sees in the market. I roll my eyes at her and tuck her arm into mine so it's clear she's stuck with me. Behind us, Lyra and Greg are deep in conversation. Lyra's Rosicrucian, too, as are many in the group, so they have a lot to discuss that I cheerfully ignore, since it covers topics like astral projection, spiritual scientific experiments and other things I know nothing about. We blend into the swollen crowd of tourists winding its way through the ribbons of streets, nearly overwhelmed by the noises and the colors.

Eventually, we arrive at the back of the market, where fewer people go and the streets are wider. This is the jewelry and antiques area. Down a side street, somewhere in the market, a thin alley leads to a dirty square bordered by tall, boxy apartments. At the center of the square are usually twenty or so of the thousands of cats that live in the Khan, perhaps even outnumbering the tourists. The square is lined edge-to-edge with giant old jewelry safes, rusty now from disuse and time, each relic too big to move or carry off except by someone very determined.

Shakky brings Greg and me here while he negotiates with a merchant for a piece he likes; the rest of the group goes on to lunch. The shop is almost too confined to turn around in— about eight feet wide. Glass cases fill the left and right sides, stuffed with old silver and other metal pieces. The proprietor, a puffy, florid man who I doubt is yet fifty, shakes our hands with stubby fingers. He wears only a single ring, but it's a good one— I can tell from the workmanship on the filigree.

Shakky asks him to show us some of the jewelry while they discuss their price, and the proprietor shrugs and obliges by pulling out a heavy sack. He dumps it on the countertop and we are suddenly staring at a pile of silver rings, ranging in size and weight from the cheapest tourist pieces to highly carved, heavy objets d'art. My favorites are the seals. These rings were functional, which is lucky because many of them are too huge to wear. The center stone is the seal itself, cut from lapis, carnelian, or another semi-precious stone, about an inch across. It's set in an ornate carved silver or even brass base, the bezel of the ring sometimes a half-inch thick. To put one of these rings on makes you feel as though you are sliding your hand into history—you cannot help wondering what important documents were legitimatized with this impressive jewelry, even if the truth is that it belonged to a clerk or was used for the books of a household.

The seals are expensive, but this man's prices are still insanely good. Compared to some of the jewelry stores we've seen them in, with price tags of $600 or more, the $150 we might pay here is much more reasonable. We pick out a couple of rings for friends, and then make our way onto the main street.

Wending down this relatively empty cobblestone road, we pass a set of thousand-year-old baths. I am, courtesy of Shakky, possibly the only woman who has ever been inside this male-only establishment (at least, that's what he tells me). Shakky snuck Greg and me in once, just to see the turquoise walls, the almost Spanish curve of the roofs. It was dank inside, filled with the humidity of the liters of water that have been heated, used, and swirled into the drains over the past millennium. Luckily, the baths were also empty, or I'm sure Shakky would have gotten us all into serious trouble. But this is the luck of the "bad kids"— we have never gotten caught and don't intend to. Across from the baths is a marvelous stained-glass window that forms part of a synagogue or church, and next door is the most run-down shack of a place. Shakky claims you can buy the best stewed fava beans in Egypt here; despite my trepidation about eating local food from unknown origins, as we passed it the line was out the door and my curiosity got the better of me.

We skipped the long queue, as is typical of Shakky, and wormed our way into the place, Shakky and the proprietor exchanging such warm greetings as to make it obvious that he was family, and therefore entitled to line jump. Behind the counter, plates of brown fuul (pronounced "fool") and warm pita puffs were pushed towards us. Shakky set about doctoring the beans as he usually does, adding cumin, a dash of mild cayenne pepper, salt, and the juice from a local lemon, which are closer in size to a key lime and taste more like a lymon. The beans were warm, the bread—soft and fresh in our mouths—the perfect complement. The only non-locals in here, we were given a few curious glances but no one seemed to mind our presence.

*   *   *   *   *

After the jewelers, we join the rest of the group at Naghib Mafouz Restaurant. Some of the Khan's restaurants have been in the same spot for over a hundred years. Naghib Mafouz, the Nobel laureate writer and a revered Egyptian native son, used to sit for hours every day, writing in the restaurant that now bears his name. The food here is excellent and, as at the Mena House's Khan restaurant, a house specialty is roast pigeon stuffed with rice, nuts and raisins.

Given the prevalence of pigeons, it is no wonder they serve them stuffed and roasted. Once while we were visiting the Sphinx, it was swarmed by a flock of pigeons. They landed all over its pharaonic head and face, lending one of the world's most iconic images the look of the pox, as if it were bravely standing sentinel despite being quite under the weather. We had a chance that day to speak with a man painting a chemical on the Sphinx to protect the vast statue from acid rain. He was also undertaking work to cure the Sphinx of pigeons without harming them, by using ultrasonic sound. On subsequent visits we have seen pigeons fly over, but not so much as a drop of birdshit land on the great statue. I hope the sound waves are not too much of an inconvenience for the little guys.

Naghib Mafouz Restaurant has low tables where you can buy shisha and a coffee in their charming little front room, and a cozy main dining room with tables tucked into alcoves. As soon as we are seated, the waiter throws down the typical bowls of Egyptian mezzes with a clatter.

Carter looks taken aback when the food begins landing in front of him. Rose looks at him, concerned. "Don't you like it?" she asks in a light, Eastern European accent.

Carter's eyebrows go up. "Well, I had it yesterday!"

Lyra laughs. "Get used to it. This is what the Egyptians eat all the time! It's delicious!" She scoops some tabouli onto her plate. Rusty reaches across Greg for a bowl of tahina. Greg, his mouth full of bread and the flavorful sesame dip, shakes his head and points to the one on the other side of Rusty.

"Get your own," he says, when he finally swallows. Everyone laughs, and the conversation dies down as we concentrate on moving the delicious appetizers from our mouths to our bellies. Our main course is a set menu of vegetable stew or grilled half-chickens served on a bed of chopped parsley, with a side of pommes frittes. Whoever decided that French fries were the ubiquitous accompaniment to Egyptian main courses certainly was catering to the American palette. I prefer the rice: buttery, coarse granules, shot through with broken strands of thin brown noodles, a yummy (if superfluous) addition.

Stuffed again, we head out into the Egyptian sunshine to continue our search for trinkets.

*   *   *   *   *

On her second Spirit Quest Tour, a guest brought an article that appeared in her local paper, about the "Alley of the Tentmakers," and we asked Shakky to make a special stop. It proved so popular that now we always go. Tucked away behind the Khan, blocks from any tourist traps, we make our way through a typical Egyptian market street. Each of the vendors sells only a single line of product: there is the baker, the woodcarver, the shisha manufacturer, the saddle maker. We walk by them all single-file, sharing the street with the traffic as there is no sidewalk, and trying to keep close to the cars that line the side of the road. The security man, our constant companion, is truly earning his keep, as the drivers come so close to us we are almost grazed by a few vehicles. Two blocks, three, finally we come to a corner with a lovely mosque along the side of the road and a giant arched gateway. Shakky points in the opposite direction and we see a block of shops on both sides, straight out of nineteenth century artist David Roberts' paintings of the Khan. In fact, the wooden roofs of the Alley's buildings are mere feet away from Bab Zuweyla, the southern entrance gate to the city, which has protected the city for over 700 years and is the subject of one of Roberts' most famous works.

We walk through the Alley, only about a block long, enjoying the handcrafted quilts and pillows. The patterns are myriad and colorful, as each man is an artist as well as a craftsman. As we pass they call to us that their wares are the finest, the most rare. There are no women. We are here for the textiles, but their mainstay is tents for weddings and parties (out in the desert, toss up a tent, throw a party), as well as sails for fellucas and dahabeyas—the smaller boats that cruise the Nile. One sail maker explains in detail the construction of the quilts, each piece hand-measured and cut into a floral, geometric, or abstract pattern, then sewn by hand. While we might pay a thousand dollars for something similar to this in the States, the most expensive, largest quilt we see in any of the stalls is around $300. I buy a toy-sized tent, complete with camel, for around $5. Our shopping lust is sated, for at least a few hours.

RELIGIONS OF THE WORLD

Every day we leave the hotel in our traveling coach, sitting two-by-two as we cross the Nile and head out of the Giza plateau and into the depths of Cairo. The traffic is dreadful everywhere, but we barely feel it on the bus, cooled by the air-conditioning and distracted by the process of getting to know one another. Lyra usually sits with her roommate Rose, but sometimes comes to talk to Greg and me. We learn she's from California, and she tells us stories of her family and her spiritual journey through life, the first such tales I've ever heard. Carter sits in the rear, next to Rusty, the only two single men in the group, and I can often hear his loud laughter as he shares an anecdote. Rusty is quieter, but he seems to really enjoy Carter's company. Vivian sits with Eleanor, and these ladies are especially suited to each other. Eleanor is younger than Vivian by fifteen or twenty years, but they both have a gentility that works well together. They would prefer to be roommates, but get on well enough with the ones their hosts have assigned them. My mother, Judith, sits in the company of whoever she's talking to that morning; like several of the other women, she has already made a good many friends.

Today, on the way into Old Cairo, we stop for an hour at the Ar Rafai Mosque, known as the Mosque of the Healers. It is also called the Mosque of the Snakes, as the queen who commissioned it did so to thank the Sufi master who healed her son from a snake bite. The Muhammed Ali mosque and the adjoining Citadel are nearby—we pass them on the way—a site more popular with the touristses, more famous, but now only a museum as prayer services are no longer held there.

Standing at the front of the bus, microphone in hand, Shakky tells us the story: "There was a group, a caste, you know? Of high-born Turkish slaves, the Mamluks, servants to the Egyptian rulers from the eighth century to the middle of the thirteenth. They were famous and everyone was afraid of them, because they were bad fighters, you know?" Shakky makes a fist, his face twisting into a grimace. "They took power for themselves for the next three hundred years. When Muhammed Ali, who was Albanian, became Pasha Kabir—that means 'the Big Boss'—at the beginning of the nineteenth century, he knew he would have to get rid of the Mamluks." Shakky makes the same gesture again. It's going to be bad for the Mamluks, I can tell. "In 1811, he ask-ed all the most important Mamluks to a party, a celebration—nearly five hundred of them. He bring them inside the Citadel, through what is now called the Red Gate. As the Mamluks come through, Ali's soldiers slaughter them all!" Shakky makes a sweeping move with his arm, like a scythe cutting through grain. "Then, they found and kill all the rest of the Mamluks and their families. Some few escape to Sudan, maybe, who knows. But that was the end of the Mamluks!"

This explains why the Egyptian royalty of the last century was all so fair-skinned. None of them was Egyptian; they were all Turks. Listening to the story, I am reminded of the massacre of the Templar Knights, 500 years earlier. Shakky tells us Ali also destroyed all the old magnificent palaces of the Mamluks, which Napoleon's scholars had described only a few years earlier as the most beautiful sites in Egypt, despite their decrepit condition. So much of history is lost to us as it is rewritten by the victorious in their ego-driven efforts to reign supreme.

At the entrance to the mosque, we remove our shoes and hand them over to be put into a small wall of shelves. The women have all worn long pants or skirts, long sleeves, scarves and hats, and the men have eschewed shorts for the day, although (typically) no one cares what the men wear so long as the women's bits are hidden. We move silently across the thin carpet that covers yards of marble, looking up to take in the huge stained-glass dome above us. We hope to see the call to prayer, but it is silent and empty in here. I am surprised. We are the only visitors, and I feel peace as I walk—I suppose, not what I was expecting in a mosque. It feels like God's house, if I believed in that sort of thing.

After a short lecture, Shakky tells us we are in for a treat. We follow him out the back of the mosque, where he greets a small man, bowed and gray-stubbled, leaning on a thick crutch. He seems quite elderly, especially from the way he walks, but as I get closer I see that he is only in his forties; his body is twisted underneath his galabeya and he must walk assisted by two crutches, each a different height, which he relies on heavily. Shakky tells us he is an Imam—a priest—of this mosque and a Sufi master. The Imam's job is to sing the Muslim call to prayer, and the sound pours throughout Cairo five times a day as hundreds of Imams echo each other. The Imam, Mahmoud, painfully makes his way to an enormous thick wood door inlaid with a beautiful geometric pattern, and produces the largest brass key I have ever seen. He unlocks the door, which makes a great echoing click, and Shakky helps him to push it open.

We enter a mausoleum with three tall, intricately carved tombs inside. These are the wives of the Khedive Ismail, the last king of Egypt; elsewhere in the mosque are buried King Farouk, King Fuad, and Reza Pahlevi, the last Shah of Iran. We stand in front of the tombs, like little flat-roofed houses sprouting from the marble floors, the columns sticking up like chimneys. The middle tomb belongs to Ismail's Christian wife, nearly identical to the others except for a Christian cross on the tomb. Inside a second door, equally heavy and ornate, lie another two tombs; here the Khedive lies next to his mother for all eternity. These choices, the relative proximity of the women in the Khedive's life, speak volumes about the structure of Islamic society.

Inside the interior chamber, the Imam shuts off the overhead light and closes the door behind us. We all sit on the marble floor or lean against the wall, unsure of what will happen, but expecting a meditation of some sort. As we close our eyes and begin to breathe, Mahmoud throws his head back and begins to cry it into the vast height of the mausoleum, a private performance for these lucky pilgrims. His voice is throaty, somewhat rough, perfect. It is as if angels are singing right through him and we feel the music wrap around us like a blanket of comforting sound. Somewhere in the middle, Shakky starts to clap, very slowly, perhaps only every eight beats or so, and we pick it up; the slow, ritualistic clapping emphasizing his soaring melodies. The Sufi master sings to Allah: "Allll-AHHHH…uwh! Allll-AHHHH..uwh!" the sound of the word for God, a glottal stop at the end added for emphasis. We pick it up, and soon all of us—Christian, pagan, Jew, agnostic—are chanting to Allah and it is beautiful and lovely and right.

When we open our eyes, many of us have tears in them and some are openly weeping. Judith keeps wiping her eyes and shaking her head, astonished. Vivian, recently widowed, is particularly moved, and as the others come forward to shake the Imam's hand, pressing $10 or $20 bills on him in gratitude, she hangs back, barely holding onto her sobs. Coming forward last, once everyone else has left the room, she tries to give Mahmoud money but he pushes it away. This last kind gesture undoes Vivian; overcome with emotion, she bawls into his shoulder, her hand resting on the top of his crutch where it sticks out a little. He is exquisitely patient with her, and as her sobs subside, the Imam pulls her to him and tucks her face down, whispering a blessing into her forehead.

We walk out together, and I support Vivian a bit as she is still shaky and emotional. After a few moments, she starts to speak.

"My husband. Lost him. Six months ago. And my parents. All in the last two years." Her words are halting, the sentences stopping in the middle as she draws tremulous breaths. "Today, just now, I was able to say goodbye to them all. I grieved, I cried —for the very first time!"

We pause for a moment and retrieve our shoes at the front of the mosque in exchange for a pound. Then we walk to the bus together, my arm around her petite shoulders. Vivian smiles, her tears drying up. "They died, but I hadn't cried about it. I had to be responsible, I was the executor of all the estates." She tosses her head and laughs, the peals coming easily from her throat. "I never cry. I actually feel lighter." All of a sudden, she looks ten years younger.

We get off the coach again near the entrance to the ancient Coptic City, strolling past several souvenir shops, one of which sells antiques and tchotchkes. Mother bought me a hanging Moroccan lamp here, ornate and delicate, which I hand-carried home on the plane. Descending a wide stone staircase, we enter the main door of Coptic Cairo, the site of the oldest synagogue and church in Egypt, which sit right next door to each other.

We visit a church, arriving at the end of the service. I make eyes at a little Egyptian girl in her mother's arms, and the young Christian mother instantly comes over and thrusts the toddler at me. As the rest of the group moves through the church, I am treated to a cultural exchange. The women and young girls surround me, as well as some of the men, their enthusiasm and interest almost overwhelming me. As word catches on, no fewer than twenty people gather, concealing me until I worry Greg will think I have disappeared. The Egyptians are warm and friendly, all wanting to shake my hand and practice their English on me, giving me so many babies to hold I feel like a politician in the last hours of the campaign trail. I find it curious that in this tourist capital there are so few opportunities to meet us, but they act like a chance encounter with an American is both celebration and celebrity. It is fifteen minutes or more before I feel comfortable enough to hand the last kid to his mother and make my excuses, rejoining the group as we leave the church.

We stroll through tight-walled medieval streets, occasionally passing a romantic old wooden door at the top of a few stairs or the twists of a wrought iron door screen, and make our way towards the Coptic Church. Copticism is the major form of Christianity in Egypt; the word Coptic comes from the Greek word for Egyptian. Tradition holds that it was the apostle Mark who began preaching Christianity in Egypt. More recently, scholars have thought the origins of Egyptian Christianity come from the Jews of Alexandria, living in the century after Jesus. Either way, in the fifth century, the Christian church was torn apart, most Egyptian Christians choosing to side with a group that claimed Christ has one nature, a human who became divine. In 451 CE, a group of "learned men" convened to debate this issue—the Council of Chalcedon. They denounced the doctrine, saying that Christ was dual-natured—both human and divine. Today, the Coptic Church still affirms Monophysitism, a significant difference from the mainstream Christian beliefs of the Trinity. This means that whole religions think that their opposition won't get into Heaven because they believe a man became God instead of that same man being partly God already.

All of it is so removed from what could possibly have been intended by those who created these religions. It reminds me of the dudes who invented Facebook. If you had grabbed one by the arm and said, "Hey! Someday soon people in the Middle East will use this program to start revolutions!" he probably would have laughed at you. A lot like Facebook, all religions started as good ideas and intentions, and then developed a life of their own as they became successful. I think you should believe what you want to—whatever works for you—and you shouldn't get in anyone else's way, so long as they don't hurt other people over it.

It's easy now to say that at heart I'm a deeply spiritual person. But growing up, I would never have identified myself as such. Religion and spirituality were inextricably tied, and both were denied me before I was old enough to think. As a child, I always felt slightly at sea not being a part of a religion, like I had no real place to call home. I used to suspect there was something wrong with me, as I was also my father's daughter: an atheist born and raised to reject religion, and unable to distinguish for myself what I believed.

When I was about five and we lived in Germany, I brought home a drawing I had made in Religion Class: "Kane tötet Abel" (Cain killed Abel), and proudly showed it to my parents. My dad took off from work to meet my teacher and explain what an atheist is, and after that, I had to spend each week sitting outside the classroom, in the wide hallway with the cold linoleum floor, while the other kids learned Bible stories inside.

While now I both appreciate my father's reasons, and might even have done the same thing to my kid, that pretty much describes how I always felt about religion after that... like I was sitting outside the room, in the hall. Is it a coincidence that my name, Halle, in German means "hall?" Maybe not. Eventually, I called myself an agnostic, because I had no better word.

Like Judy Blume's heroine in my favorite children's book, *Are You There, God, It's Me, Margaret*, I examined and discarded each religion as not quite a fit, though I appreciated pieces of each. For example, I loved the ceremony of the Jewish traditions. I'll always be grateful to our next-door neighbor, Pearl, who knew we were Jewish (once a Member of the Tribe, always a member) and made sure to include us in Passover and Hanukah ceremonies. And while I thought the Catholic ceremonies were too long and boring (wedding vows could easily take over an hour, which was forever when you're a child, and only a little shorter as an adult) Midnight Mass struck me as extremely cool, and not just because you got to stay up so late. I guess, looking back, it was the traditions of all of them, the ceremony of belonging, I craved.

Yet part of my uneasiness came from religion itself. From not really believing, even though I wanted to; from the prejudice that comes from how people treat you when you're different, when you're outside their easy point of understanding. You could see the radar scanning... Catholic, Protestant, Jew—got it, check. Halle—whoop, whoop! Setting off alarm bells, have no label for "mixed-up agnostic!"

When I was about eight or nine, I came home from school with words that would strike fear into the hearts of parents anywhere: "Susie says I'm going to hell."

"Why?" my dad asked.

"Because I don't go to church."

So off we went to church. To be specific, a Catholic church, a Presbyterian church, and the largest synagogue in Washington, DC (because my dad used to date the rabbi's daughter, and he remembered the place as spectacular). I guess in those days, Dad couldn't imagine us choosing to be Muslim. Or Buddhist. He was very good about it. He asked friends from work if he could bring my younger sister and me to their church. Of course they said yes, and over the next month's weekends, we visited all these places, so we could pick where we liked best.

I sat in those services, wanting, needing, to believe. I listened to those good men talk about leading a moral and blameless life,

God, Salvation, Heaven and Hell. I was always stumped by my logical mind, which told me something was missing, that this was not for me, no matter what arguments I mounted in favor of their beliefs. But I was certainly willing to go, willing to try, yearning for something to strike a chord.

I remember talking with my dad about God. Dad said, "God to me is like a ghost in the closet. If you say there is a ghost in the closet, I can say, 'Prove it to me.' And in every case, no proof, no ghost. But not with God."

"So," I asked, "why is it different?"

Dad shrugged. "I don't know, but it is. In God's case, if I can't prove God exists, that doesn't matter, and I'm just wrong about God." That was too hard for his logical mind to accept. Simplistic, but at ten years old, none of the nice men behind their podiums could outwit that reasoning to my satisfaction.

The last visit was to the Jewish synagogue. The stage was draped in red velvet and trimmed with gold tassels like an opera house, and the plush chairs were all rockers (as opposed to the Presbyterian Church, which was gray and austere, and where we sat on hard benches. My delightful ex-Presbyterian friend Eloise calls this denomination "The Frozen Chosen"). Afterwards, the whole congregation was invited downstairs for milk and cookies. This was our downfall. My sister and I decided we liked the synagogue best. Because of the milk and cookies. But when my dad asked if we wanted to go again the next Friday, we said, "Naah." Apparently, the risk of eternal flames couldn't compete with the hell we felt sitting through religious services, even cushy ones offering such heavenly rewards as cookies and milk.

Our group arrives at the undistinguished Coptic Church during communion and take the bread, blessed by the priest. In another departure from the Catholic Church, Copts believe you are eating the actual body and blood of Christ when you receive communion. The priests physically transubstantiate it before it is passed out to the worshippers. I am surprised tourists are allowed in here, let alone able to participate in this most sacred rite. Eleanor, ahead of me, reaches for the bread with her left hand and the priest says, in perfect English, "Please give me your right hand, because the left hand is unclean." Judith informs me later that the reason our society shakes hands with the right one is that Muslims wipe with the left hand and eat with the right. It's why in some societies the punishment for thieving is to cut off your right hand so you are shamed forever, because you have to wipe your butt and eat with the same hand. In these days of antibacterial sanitizer, perhaps we're all taking things a little too seriously, but Eleanor smiles, embarrassed, and switches hands immediately.

Afterward, we get to witness the baptisms. The babies are dressed both bizarrely and garishly, some as baby popes wearing both headdress and miter (a miter rattle, I presume). After they are baptized, these babies are carried in a swift, almost running, parade around the interior of the church, and the women war-whoop like Indians, ululating a LooLOOLAA sound that raises the hair on my arms.

Our last stop is the oldest existing synagogue in Cairo, which was refurbished and reopened several years ago. The ornate balconies and Middle Eastern carvings on the wood make it the most local-seeming place of worship we visit; most of the others appear more Italian and Baroque. My favorite thing here is a postcard they sell at the front. For me, the key to peace in the Middle East is contained in this simple postcard, if only the two sides would recognize it. There is only one word on the card. It says *Shalom* in Hebrew; turn it upside down and it reads *Salaam* in Arabic.

We go out into a small empty courtyard on the side of the synagogue and look through carved wooden doors that, though locked, have enough room for Shakky to jiggle them open a little. Inside there is a dry area where you can step down—he tells us we are looking at the place where Moses was found in the bulrushes. Then we continue around a corner to look at an ornate well cover, the only place that still indicates the presence of water where there was once the mighty river Nile. I am disappointed. Moses and the bulrushes and all I can see is a well cover? I want so much more—perhaps Charlton Heston to part the Red Sea for me, or at least point his NRA-sanctioned gun at those who would fail to acknowledge such an historic site. But all is quiet as we make our way out of this ancient city.

WHERE WE LEARN THE CONSEQUENCES OF IGNORING INSTINCTS

The Egyptian Museum, or as it's formally known, the Museum of Egyptian Antiquities, is familiar to most people these days. Right in the heart of downtown Cairo, the distinctive orange brick building is adjacent to Tahrir Square, the epicenter of the recent Egyptian Revolution. It contains the largest number of pieces of Egyptian art and archeology anywhere in the world. The government is actually building an entirely new Egyptian Museum on the Giza Plateau, about ten minutes' drive from the Pyramids. The new locale looks to be at least twice the size of the current museum, and it is rising out of the sand right in the middle of nowhere. The Department of Antiquities has so many artifacts they can display only a small percentage simultaneously, so after its opening they will continue to use the current museum site, a classic building set off by a lovely sculpture garden (when it's not at the edge of an entire country's political upheaval).

The museum has definitely evolved since we started coming to Egypt. The main hall used to remind me of a garden party for statues. About fifteen enormous sculptures, some forty feet tall, were shoved higgledy-piggledy into a two-story room, facing each other at odd angles as if having a conversation. I almost expected an ancient priest serving stone drinks to appear. Sadly, it was more like a warehouse for these magnificent pieces, since it seemed there was no reason for the placement of each sculpture, except the room might have been the only one tall enough to fit them. Thankfully, a lot has changed during the ten years I've been visiting, and the Egyptian Museum now seems peaceful and orderly, with the central hall showcasing, rather than merely housing, its largest artifacts.

I'm intrigued by people's reactions to the museum, especially their initial experience. Greg got a terrible headache and had to leave after an hour, overwhelmed and exhausted. Now that he understands why, he describes it as a hundred radio frequencies all trying to broadcast simultaneously to the receiver in his head. I think what he and many of our guests sense is a psychic discomfort in proximity to so many statues that were ripped out of their consecrated homes, brought here without concern for the energy which resides within them. The only real example we have found of a statue sanctified to a god, whole and in its original place (other than perhaps the Sphinx), is the Sekhmet statue at Karnak Temple. People feel completely affected in her presence, and she is just a single statue. All these pieces together in one place, each carrying a tremendous amount of energy, amplify that power and sensitive people react to it.

Most people visit the museum because they want to see the treasures of Tut Ankh Amun, which (when not traveling the world) are housed almost in their entirety in the Cairo Museum. The King Tut exhibit is the reason to try to get there as early in the day as possible, because it gets so crowded. They used to charge a separate admission fee for the exhibit but now everyone gets to go. Unlike the rest of the museum, which is usually temperate due to the brick and extensive marble, the King Tut artifacts are kept inside freezing cold air conditioning, so when it's 95° F outside, it's delicious—like walking into a large glass icebox full of gold.

The Tut exhibit, while not vast, contains many intriguing pieces, including the famous inlaid headdress and several oversized pure gold boxes in which the King's mummy case was transported. One of my favorite articles is a thin, hammered gold collar in the shape of a bird—a kite or a vulture, perhaps. The collar seems too big to be worn comfortably, but it's a typical example of the kind of magnificence the pharaohs chose so that they could be set apart from their people.

Although I love the pantheons of gods in Egyptian lore, I believe the pharaohs were merely great men who built important things, accompanied by their outlandish egos. A pharaoh like Ramses II, with his dozens of wives and over a hundred children, is more an icon than a real person. I do not care for the presumptuous way the pharaohs would ascend the throne and overwrite the name, and often the likeness, of the previous king, or of gods they didn't favor, making history that much harder to decipher.

But I forget my judgments as I stand two inches away from the iconic mask of Tut Anhk Amun; the gold is gleaming, winking at me in the light; the iridescent lapis and rich carnelian remind me that these are not merely colors, but the stones themselves. When I look at the eyes of Tut's mask, they are so large and sensitive-looking, I can almost see them wet with the liquid of life. I fleetingly feel as if I am staring at the live Pharaoh. I unexpectedly envision myself a part of the ancient way of life—the kohl makeup, the throne, the ceremony. In this environment, it is easy to give yourself permission to slip across centuries and stand for a moment in the ancient world.

Gliding perhaps a little more regally than necessary, I pass from the icy air into the stuffier main hall and make my way up into the room of ushaptis (where Harry Potter would surely go if he visited the Cairo museum). This unassuming space features row upon row of glass and wood cases filled with the tiny mummy statues that accompany the dead to their new life—the Egyptians thought of everything concerning the Great Beyond, which they also referred to by many other names, such as the "Field of Offerings." These statues acted as a substitute for the dead, in case something in their afterlife required manual work, like plowing a field. I imagine a dead dude in a Barca lounger made of reeds, sipping on hibiscus juice while these little figurines scuttle around him doing his bidding.

Apparently, ushaptis were somewhat expendable, or else the dead were expecting frequent requests for hard labor, because there were often at least a hundred found with every mummy. Of course, it's possible they were expecting some of them to refuse to return to work eventually (perhaps they would hear about the revolution and go on a ushapti strike) and since the afterlife is, well... *forever*, they anticipated the possibility of running out of proxies. Ushaptis, which can be mere inches tall, were often made of faience, a fired quartz ceramic that is bright cobalt blue and looks like lapis lazuli. The combination of small size and valuable material made them popular with thieves, and though there are hundreds in the museum and dozens more can be bought, thousands have disappeared into the pockets of greedy tomb robbers.

I join Greg and Lyra in a room containing four statues of Akhenaton, the heretic Pharaoh. Akhenaton was the foremost monotheist, the earliest Egyptian pharaoh and known ruler to embrace a single entity as God. Akhenaton, which means "spirit of the sun," taught his people to worship the sun, not as a god, but as a representation of the one God. This was considered blasphemous in a culture that worshipped (among other things) cats, crocs, and hippos, but his monotheism arguably found flower in both Judaism and Christianity.

Akhenaton apparently ordered a shift in artistic interpretation during his reign. Rather than the highly stylized triangular shapes of costumes, the almost comical cliché—half-profile, half-frontal, arms akimbo, *a la* "Walk Like An Egyptian"—Akhenaton asked for things to be depicted realistically during his reign, everything drawn, painted, or sculpted as in real life. And so it was, except it creates a few head scratchers. For example, Akhenaton and his wife Nefertiti are fourteen feet and ten feet tall, respectively, in all the art of the period. Akhenaton is severely pear-shaped and has magnificent Negroid features, with enormous, heavy lips, high cheekbones, and lidded eyes. Nefertiti, who has delicate features and is quite beautiful by our modern cultural standards, is often depicted wearing an elongated headdress that sticks out a foot or so behind her head. However, in the statues I have seen of her sans headdress, what it's covering is her giant head, which is shown bald, her skull egg-shaped and over a foot long. Without their headgear, they both simply look like aliens with elongated brain cavities.

This new idea awakened an awareness for me of creatures coming from other worlds to hand down technology; perhaps that's where some of Egypt's most complex information came from, since no evidence of it developing over time has yet been uncovered. Several schools of thought wholly support this idea, but not the current antiquities administration, which likes to perpetuate the idea that all Egyptian creations came from simple tools and the "can-do" attitude of the local workforce.

Akhenaton's statue room also holds a finely wrought bust of his lovely wife Nefertiti, and a small statue of Akhenaton sitting with one of his six daughters in his lap, the little girl staring up at him adoringly. The most impressive pieces in the room are four nearly whole statues of Akhenaton, each originally fourteen feet tall. Lyra, Greg and I go up to the most complete statue, which is in the far right-hand corner of the room.

Lyra taps her forehead between her eyes. "Dredj, Halle, put your third eye against the statue." Puzzled, I watch as Greg does what she instructs, placing his forehead onto Akhenaton's body.

In case you are as unaware as I was about these energy centers, your body has seven central shakras. If you start at the very base of your crotch (your root shakra) and stretch your hand out so your pinkie finger and thumb are splayed apart, you'll approximate where your second (the sex or sacral) shakra hits just above your pelvis. The third one is at the base of your solar plexus, the fourth at your heart, the fifth at your throat, and the sixth between the eyebrows—this shakra is called the third eye. The crown shakra is right at the top of your skull, where the fontanel closed up when you were a baby. Each of these shakras corresponds to one or more ancient temples, and you can visit the temples with the intention of opening and aligning that energy center. Come on, you align your car tires, right? Trust me, your shakras get a lot more use than your car, so you should probably be taking better care of them.

The third eye shakra is good for second sight—seeing things in your mind's eye—which is why Lyra wants us to put them against Akhenaton's statue. Our third eyes reach Akhenaton's thighs, which are covered by a triangular skirt. He seems cold and smooth, then warm and fathomless. We intone, and I can feel it resonating throughout the statue. *Hello, father*, I tell

Akhenaton. *Hello, daughter*, I hear in response. I feel peaceful; I could stay here a long time. As it is, some touristses come into the room, chattering noisily, oblivious to our meditation. The spell broken, we bid silent farewell to the giant statues.

*   *   *   *   *

One time, we bring a large group to Egypt and are given a private after-hours tour of the museum, which is delightful since the normal daily traffic is over ten thousand visitors. As the museum tour is fully guided by our Egyptologists, and Greg and I have already explored the Cairo Museum several times, we choose instead to join Momo at his full-service barber around the corner. I get my only Egyptian manicure—not the best in the world, but Hannah, the sole female hairdresser, cares so much and I can feel her wanting to do a good job for me. Greg gets a shave, the kind of retro experience they now charge over a hundred bucks for in the States. He is treated to a facial—alternating extremely hot towels and an ice massage with a ball of ice the size of a baseball. They whip the hot towel off his face, pull the ice ball from a marble jar, run it over his skin, and pop it back in the jar to prevent it from melting too quickly while they start the next round.

On a recent trip, Momo, still recovering from his stroke, picks us up at the museum and takes us to his barber again. This time, Momo is a little too sneaky.

"Momo, what are you saying to Hannah?" I ask suspiciously, as his hands have been pointing at me and gesturing to his head. He looks at me so innocently I can tell I've caught him.

"What? Nothing." He bursts into laughter.

"Momo, are you trying to get her to color my hair?" Momo looks at me sheepishly.

"Maybe. How is your Arabic?" He laughs louder, pleased with himself.

"NO!" I roar, a lioness protecting my rust-colored mane.

Instead he insists that Hannah cut my hair, which she does fairly well, though it's the bluntest, simplest cut I've had in fifteen years. Greg is another story. He has been graying gradually around the temples, but he's so blond it hasn't been a big deal;

still, in recent months we have been talking about him coloring his hair. Glad to have a participant after all, Mohamed claps his hands together.

"Dredj," he tells him, "I am going to make you look ten years younger!"

Greg keeps repeating, slowly and carefully, "I'm a blond, Momo. Yellow, okay?" Momo reassures him, "It will be fine! They'll do a good job, you'll see!"

This particular tour ends today, and we have the afternoon off before the farewell dinner in the evening. I am exhausted from working two weeks straight and while I wait for Hannah, I fall asleep in my chair. When I wake up, they are painting Greg's beard with a thick white gel, and his head is already covered. *Well, all right, that looks like regular hair dye, and it's white, so it must be blond.* I doze off again as Hannah washes my hair. Perhaps twenty minutes later, I awaken to see Greg unexpectedly wearing what looks like a fake vaudeville wig, mustache, beard, and sideburns. Not wanting to upset him, I ask nonchalantly, "What's going on?"

"Oh," Greg tells me, "they haven't rinsed the hair dye yet."

As panic sets in, I drop my calm façade. "I don't think it's supposed to be that dark! Get that hair color off NOW!"

Greg yells to Mohamed, who comes rushing in with his barber. When Momo sees Greg's face, he starts yelling in Arabic. The barber whisks Greg off to a sink, shoves his head under running water and frantically washes off all the dye.

Unfortunately, back in the barber's chair, Greg's hair and beard are now a dark brown, his eyes saucers. I can't decide whether Greg looks more like a melodrama villain or Vincent Price in a horror movie. The barber and an assistant scramble around him trying to fix it, but the dye has also stained his skin, lending an even more theatrical look to his hairline. They scrub his face with alcohol, trying to reduce the staining, and the barber begins clipping Greg's beard. Reducing the hair lightens Greg's beard, but the barber is so pleased by his success he keeps going until only a stubble remains.

At home in the States, reality sinks in and Greg decides he can no longer live looking like a day player in a silent film. He eventually sees a professional colorist, who strips, then re-dyes his head, but it is months before his usual silky flax replaces the farmer's straw of over-processed hair. Greg plans to learn a lot more Arabic before he agrees to revisit Momo's barber.

HANGING WITH KOJAK

If you've ever driven in Athens, you've driven in Cairo, five lanes of cars driving on three lanes of streets. The only difference is that in Athens, hordes of motor scooters join the fracas. When the motor scooters get tired of the traffic not moving, they fan out and onto the sidewalks where they terrorize pedestrians before popping down onto the road. Cairo has far fewer motor scooters, but fewer sidewalks as well. It also has camels, horses, donkeys and carts that Athens doesn't. In Old Cairo a few years ago, I saw a man on a motorcycle wipe out on a curb. At least five men ran to help him; in Athens, I'm sure he would have inadvertently been run over before any assistance could reach him.

Cairo's roads are a free-for-all, where everyone ignores the rules in favor of being first in line and cutting off their neighbor, and everyone competes to be the biggest daredevil on the road. Even on the farm roads—that is to say, everywhere that is not a highway—only two lanes means there's a great deal of "playing chicken" with the other traffic, especially when you are on a bus. The cars want to pass the coach, but the driver knows what he's doing and only allows it if he sees they will consistently move more swiftly than he can drive. The big buses have restricted engines that cannot go faster than the posted speed limits, so it makes them quite a bit slower but they have the advantage of being larger and newer than most of the vehicles on the road.

Cairo traffic has gotten tougher in recent years despite the construction designed to fix the worst of the problems, which is only creating more snarls in the meantime. Once, we were sitting in dreadful traffic when a street brawl broke out in front of us. Given the relative lawlessness of the highways, we have seen surprisingly few fender benders or actual accidents, though Cairo certainly has its share of deadly stats. This afternoon, it seems as if somebody possibly bumped someone's bumper? All we can see is that a car and a white van are suddenly at a dead stop because the two drivers are both out of their vehicles, yelling at each other in the streets.

Sen Akam is one of the Quest Travel staff who acts as a tour escort, and accompanied us on our first trip to Egypt. Sen has zero hair, even though he just turned forty, and looks remarkably like a young Kojak (Telly Savalas from the '70s TV show). Enough people have told Sen this that he has taken to sucking on the occasional lollipop, which was Kojak's trademark habit and makes Sen look even more like the great television detective.

Sen has been our tour escort before, but when Momo came along Sen stayed in the background. When Momo had his stroke, Sen traveled with us for the entire two weeks, and we got to know him much better. Shakky, Greg, Sen and I developed a good rhythm taking care of everyone—as with all the Quest Travel folks, there's a mutual respect and appreciation, and we all really enjoy each other's company.

Mohamed trained Sen, who has been working for him almost fifteen years now. I tease Sen that he is growing into a mini-Mohamed, who Sen worships as combination father figure, boss, and untouchable deity. I think Momo's stroke was harder on Sen because he did not consider it possible that Momo would fall ill, let alone struggle to create some new variation of normalcy afterwards. Everything Sen does at work, he does to please Momo; his intentions are pure and honorable because that's what Mohamed would expect. I don't see how Momo could ask more of his own son.

When the fender bender happens and the fight breaks out, our security guard is first into the street. Sen and I are talking to

Greg, but it kind of trails off as we all turn to watch the proceedings. Our security guard talks to the irate drivers, trying to find out what's going on and how quickly the cars will be in motion again. All of a sudden, the driver of the white van reaches into his cab, pulls out a CB mic and the attached cord, swings it around his head like a lasso, and cracks the other driver in the head with it. That's when Sen gets off the coach.

We've seen a lot of things in Egypt, some crazy and many exotic, but this is the only act of violence I've witnessed (the recent revolution aside). I am more than a little shocked, especially because I notice our security man unhook the button on his holster, his suit flapping open so I can see his gun each time his arm goes up. Sen's a fairly tall fellow, about 6'1" and big, with the same build as Kojak. Now he moves quickly into the fray, his broad chest leading.

The whole group comes to the front of the bus, leaning in the aisles or over the seats, craning for a better view. We stare through the front window as the lollipop comes out of Kojak's mouth and he starts gesticulating. We can't hear anything, but we can imagine the threats he is making, backed up by our security guard, who is packing the only weapon unless you count the CB mic.

The tension is palpable and we hardly breathe, waiting to see what happens. Abruptly, Sen points at the two drivers, still talking, and gestures towards the vehicles. Within five minutes, the drivers are in their cars pulling into traffic, and Sen and the security guard return to our coach amidst a round of well-deserved applause. It might not be crime-solving in New York City, but our Kojak has saved the day.

Sen and I sit together on the bus and talk about all sorts of things; he calls me his sister, and although he's a couple years younger than I am, Sen feels a lot like the big brother I never had. Our cultural distinctions are fascinating and entertaining. Here is a typical conversation:

Me: Jeez, I hope we stop for lunch soon, I'm starving.

Sen: It will be an hour. Do you have something to eat?

Me: Just some protein bars Greg has. I hate all that stuff. Protein bars, protein drinks, they taste awful.

Sen (wrinkling his nose): I agree. How Dredj can stand things like this? How they make them, anyway?

Me: Make what?

Sen: Protein bars. Protein drinks. How they get the meat in?

Me: Huh?

Sen (serious): They are protein. So they have meat in them. But how they get it in? Especially raw?

He wrinkles his nose again, as I burst into laughter.

Sen has also taught us some fun Arabic. A few years ago, Greg wanted to make it clear to the vendors that he's not a tourist. Sen taught him how to say, "Enta f'kearny abeet?" (It's phonetic, but there are no vowels in Arabic.) It means, "Do you think I'm a sucker?" He also taught him, "Enta f'kearny ah-bell?" Which is, "Do you think I'm an idiot?" Both of these phrases have been committed to memory and conjured up many times when the vendors are asking ten times the worth of something. The typical result is a dropped jaw, followed by a mighty Arabic or English protestation to the contrary, and a rapid cascade in price.

I have picked Sen's brain more than a few times about Egyptian men and women and their relationships. Whenever he has an argument with his wife, Sen thinks he's the only person in the world who has that issue, or at least that Egyptian men are the only ones with these problems. Of course, they're fighting over all the normal stuff: who's cooking dinner, who's paying more attention to the kids, etc. Sen's wife is extremely beautiful, and Sen is a little jealous, since she is also a tour escort and often takes groups out. Of course, his wife is jealous, too, which is kind of charming. Sen is a great guy, and quite devoted to her in his heart, but he thinks of her as a different species entirely, and he doesn't understand why she wants him to help around the house or with their children.

I suspect Sen is similar to most Egyptian men—woefully uninformed as to women. To many Egyptian men, women really are from Venus, a completely foreign planet millions of miles away where they can never hope to go. I thought this was merely the backward attitude of some, but over time I've realized it's ingrained through thousands of years of history, and unlikely to change any time soon. In Egyptian men's minds, women are still the sole operator of the domicile, whether it's cooking or cleaning or looking after the children; the woman might work, but the home is her responsibility and hers only. Shakky says, "The man is the head, but the woman is the neck." I had interpreted this to mean the man can't function without the woman, and though that is true, to them it also means that the woman supports the man—that's literally what she is there for. What's the neck's other job? To change the direction of the head. The neck may get tired, but in Egypt, the work of the neck and the woman is never done.

I ran across an article in an Egyptian magazine recently—a young college girl had been raped and murdered. Though that goes on in America with sad regularity, it was clear from the article how unusual it is in Egypt. But I was amazed at the slant the article took. It was an outcry against the media, a public response thrashing the irresponsible reporters who had jumped to conclusions prior to getting the facts straight, daring to report that the girl was not a virgin and that she was mixed up in drugs, reasons which sounded as if they would have made her murder somehow justifiable. It was clear from the story that even in death her reputation was more important than her demise. The contrast between the U.S.'s lackadaisical approach to celebrity excess and the moral code of the Egyptian press was clear. Equally obvious was the pedestal women are put on in Egypt, and the consequences of falling from grace. Then the murder would have been seen in a vastly different light, and it might have been considered by them to be, if not appropriate, at least more "understandable."

Recently, I have done a tiny survey of Muslim women I know well enough to ask about their personal lives and relationships. It was riveting. For a man to kiss a woman they must be engaged; though I'm told kissing sooner is not unheard of, it's usually limited to the cheek. Of the hordes of young modern Muslim women in Cairo, perhaps 90% will be virgins when they marry, and most of the rest are pretending so that they fit in. If a woman divorces, she must leave everything behind. However, she can ask for a divorce, and three months after it is granted is permitted to marry again. It's permissible to have been sexually active inside the marriage, but you should still be engaged to your next husband before he is allowed to kiss you. Living together before marriage is unacceptable, as is sex prior. Despite coming at the question from multiple angles with several women, I was not able to budge any of them from this position so, at least as far as my informal survey is concerned, it's the truth.

An unmarried young Muslim woman once told me that she had taken a lover. After getting over my initial shock, I asked her to define the word "lover." To my relief, also a little to my dismay, her definition was more like that voiced by the naive young wife in George Feydeau's great 1907 farce, *A Flea in Her Ear*: "To flirt. To hold hands and cast longing glances across the room, to share my better parts, my heart, my mind. But to sleep with you? What do you take me for? A prostitute?"

Momo, who is enlightened in many ways, teases me about being a "good Egyptian wife." The reality is that I'd be a terrible Egyptian wife. In comparison to the U.S., Egypt is in about the 1930s as far as women's personal lives are concerned. Work-wise, it's the late 1960s, creeping towards the women's lib movement of the '70s, as witnessed in the recent revolution when women took to the streets as equals, perhaps for the first time. Trying to behave more appropriately in the culture, even for a couple of weeks, brings out my most domineering qualities as I rebel against the chafe of restriction. Quashing my instinctive smart remarks, snappy comebacks, or knowledge of a topic so I won't riposte with my usual quick wit, gives me a bit of a headache. Luckily, as a Western woman I can snap back to myself easily, and the men laugh and give me the leeway to be among them, to be treated as an equal.

*　　*　　*　　*　　*

At the hotel, a few of us have expressed a desire to horseback ride, as we have heard you can do so right near the Pyramids. Recently, I rewatched *Death on the Nile* while I was actually on the Nile. There's a scene where the hero (later revealed as the villain) and his doomed fiancée ride horses out on the Giza Plateau. Not only do they appear to ride right through the Sphinx enclosure (which is physically impossible), but they take the whole place at a gallop which seems belied by the sand.

However, I learn that while we cannot ride as close to the Pyramids as they did in the movie, it *is* possible to gallop through the sands of Giza. We witness this several times while on our own horses as groups of four or five young locals come barreling through, whooping with delight, their horses thundering past us.

We rent our horses from Gamal, a somewhat swarthy, gray-bearded gentleman whose establishment is at the end of Stable Row behind the Sphinx enclosure. We saddle up, then are slowly led clip-clop down the street, past fat-bellied horses who stand beside horses so thin their ribs stick out prominently; many eat huge armfuls of alfalfa, while near other stables their troughs or feed bags are empty. I wonder if the state of the horses represents their masters' current level of financial fortune or ruin, but it would be impolite to ask. At the far end of stable row lies an enormous mound of garbage, perhaps a hundred feet in length, on top of which skinny goats and dogs sniff around for remnants. Our horses carry us past all this teeming, abounding, squalid life and out onto the sands of Giza.

For a while, Gamal's young men lead us on horseback, wearing head scarves and galabeyas, guiding our beasts past dozens of small rocks and the debris of garbage strewn for almost a quarter-mile. It makes my stomach churn to know what carelessness and ignorance we humans are capable of. But the desert is patient; it will be here long after we are dust. As we finally clear the leavings of stable row, we see the Pyramids in the distance. Only now do our guides release our reins and allow us to ride on our own. I am a little concerned about Rusty, because of his leg, but he is fine on a horse, once a stable hand has helped him onto it. Lyra's roommate Rose is a surprise. Neither young nor fit, she gallops past me as soon as we hit the sand, looking like she was manor-born.

"Hey, Rose!" I call to her. She slows, wheels around, and comes trotting up next to me. "Where did you learn to ride?" She shrugs, but I can tell my question pleases her.

"I spent a lot of time in Wyoming. I learned as a girl and I've kept it up. I love riding!"

"Yeah, I can see that," I say to her posterior. She's already galloping off across the desert, and I don't blame her.

It is only my second time on a horse in Egypt, and I love it. The freedom, the wind in my hair—the sleek brown horse knows exactly where he is going and what he is doing. While I am too much of a novice to go quickly, I do let him pick up the pace to a slow trot, which makes me feel much prettier than surely I look. I sense that the horse and I are keeping separate rhythms, that I am kind of klunking along like a slouching city slicker at a dude ranch. After a while, racking my brain for memories of riding (few) and books where heroines learned to ride (several) I recall that you are supposed to post; sitting with my back rigid, I hop up and down a bit on the horse. This works immediately, and the horse responds so quickly I can tell we now have a whole new relationship. Pleased, I jounce around, holding my posture erect and enjoying the thought that the horse now recognizes me as a rider, not a passenger.

On the few hills, the horse seems as sure-footed as on the flat ground, his hooves stepping easily through the sand. Though several of the group are near me, I feel like I have the whole place to myself. I wonder what treasures we might be skimming over as we pass, since they say you can hardly dig anywhere in Egypt and not uncover antiquities. I look across at the Sphinx, and then as we make our way onto the Giza plateau, I see the Pyramids in the distance. My heart gives a little thrill as my horse and I traverse this sacred land. Greg sidles up next to me on his mount, a dappled gray, the reins held easily in one hand.

"How you doing?" he grins, and I recognize the happiness that spills from him as my own.

I squint up at him through my sunglasses and grin back. "Apparently, not as good as you are, Dredj. Are you sure you didn't take riding lessons sometime?"

Greg shakes his head and shrugs, accepting the compliment, as his horse falls into an easy pace next to my animal. It would be romantic to be able to hold hands, but not practical, so I give up the idea, satisfied to be riding next to him and for the few moments of privacy. We amble along in silence. A short while later, Gamal comes up, gesturing that we should all join him.

As the group gathers, I reluctantly get off my horse (helped by a guide who runs over for this purpose) and join the others. Eleanor slides off her horse as if she were slipping into a pool; I envy how collected she looks. I am panting a little from the heat, even as the desert cools quickly into evening. Lyra and Judith ride up together, a Bedouin holding fast to Judith's reins. He helps her off the horse, but Lyra refuses his proffered hand and jumps to the ground easily. The riding skills of my new friends remind me that there is so much about these people I can't possibly know yet. I am intrigued, enjoying these traveling companions.

Coarse wool blankets materialize from saddle bags, their Bedouin patterns reminding me of Mexican serapes. Gamal's workers spread them on the ground and then invite us to sit and watch them work. In the setting sun, the Pyramids in the distance, he and his helpers light a fire. When it is hot and strong, the flames licking the deepening night sky, they make tea.

We sit as evening descends on the Giza Plateau, sipping sweet Egyptian tea from glasses they have kindly packed out here for us. Greg and I lean against each other, watching the Pyramids fade into the dwindling light, and think there is no place on earth we'd rather be at this moment.

ALEX

Alexandria is about three hours from Cairo by coach, through desert largely claimed by homesteaders, and—increasingly—builders creating communities out in no-man's land, as Shakky predicted. This is distance that once would have taken days to cover by horse or donkey. We didn't get to go during our original tour, but since the opening of the Alexandria Library, it has become a much-requested day trip.

On the way to Alexandria, Sen tries to entertain us with jokes.

"A man is driving in a Peugeot on the Cairo freeway. The car is going faster and faster. His three passengers are getting worried. The first man tells him, 'You are going too fast. Let me out.'

"The driver asks him, 'Do you know anything about Peugeots?' The man says no. The driver tells him, 'Be quiet.' Now the car goes two hundred kilometers per hour.

"The second man says, 'I am scared! I want out!'

"The driver asks him, 'Do you know anything about Peugeots?' The man says no. The driver says, 'Be quiet!' The car is going two-hundred-fifty kilometers per hour.

"The third man says, 'I've got to get out! You're crazy!'

"The driver asks him, 'Do you know anything about Peugeots?'

"'Yes, yes!' says the third man.

"'Then tell me how to stop this one!'"

We get out for a pee break and to stretch our legs at what probably started as a gas station, but is now a full-service rest stop with several stores that sell jewelry, handbags, and boots, a Coffee Bean and Tea Leaf franchise, and a large café that serves omelets—the Coffee Bean's competitor for the latte traffic. There's a snack shop that also sells myriad kitschy souvenirs; if you want a lighter where the flame comes out of the center of Pharaoh's head, or a shot glass in the shape of a god, or some real English McVities biscuits, this is the place. Outside, a music kiosk blasts funky Arabic disco fusion. My favorite place is a small glass-enclosed stand that sells everything from Macadamia nuts to roasted squash seeds, all served warm. Your purchases are given to you in a canvas shopping bag printed in Arabic. Though I can't read what the bag says, the message on the stand is clear. In foot-high English letters so all the touristses can understand, it reads: Get Your Nuts Hot!

On the bus, after naps and munching and long talks with whomever we have not yet made friends, we arrive in Alex (as it is known to the locals). Many of the buildings in this city—by far the most European-style locale we visit in Egypt—date back only to the Victorian era, and the result is a lovely cross between Paris and San Tropez, a beachfront bordering the Mediterranean Sea, where you see no more than occasional Egyptian touches: a mosque, shisha smokers at an ahwa, older women wearing burkas, their bodies swathed in yards of black fabric. Alex is principally cosmopolitan and uniquely Mediterranean—it sits right on the sea and has always served Egypt as a port. When Greg and I wore our galabeyas to Alex, all the locals looked at us as if the hicks were in town. Now we know better and wear Western clothes, and the looks we get are mostly approving. Occasionally I will see an old lady wearing a head-to-toe burka glowering at me, but I choose to believe she is jealous of my modern dress, my relative youth, or at least my red hair.

We stop at a beautiful boutique museum that contains Greek and Roman artifacts, along with several finds from an underwater cache that was discovered offshore a few years ago: coins, statues, and vases, the unexpected prizes of a dive. We can get through the museum completely in an hour-and-a-half, so on the last few trips, while our guests are enjoying the site, Greg, Sen, and I walk down the street to a local ahwa where you can get coffee, shisha, and the company of the nearby residents.

There is never a vacant seat inside the ahwa, but the owner is always happy to set a table up for us in the alley and to bring us hot chai and shisha. On our earliest visit we have my mother in tow, back in Egypt for her second tour. In the wide alley, we meet a local old man, his five year-old grandson, and their family of cats—an orange tabby devoted to his mate, and three kittens. The alley backs onto an enormous construction site with a huge modern building going up, and I am initially afraid for the cats. But it is clear the grandfather cares for them all very much. He tells us the orange male is "Mesh-Mesh," which means "apricot," and he continuously feeds them by hand as we watch. He is solicitous with Judith, and inquires after her in halting English when we come the next year without her.

The proprietor brings us steaming glasses of tea, fresh milk, and packets of sugar about the length and width of three toothpicks, all on a tin tray that he sets down noisily on our tiny table. Next comes the shisha; the hot coal at the center already has the tobacco giving off puffs of smoke. In these little ahwas, you don't get the crazy shisha flavors—mint, maybe coffee, usually apple—and enough shisha for all of you, including the service, is one U.S. dollar. I draw on an end of the pipe and pass it to Judith, then sip my milky tea. I love watching my mom—she's so damn cool, dragging on the shisha like it's something she does every day. She crinkles her eyes at me and we share a giggle; it feels like we're teenagers playing hooky.

Outside the ahwa, we see a street vendor, his open donkey cart smothered in fruit. We leave Mesh-Mesh and his kitten offspring playing under the cart and head to the coach with armfuls of small, fresh bananas. As we listen to stories of what everyone enjoyed most at the museum, we hand everyone a sweet banana, a welcome snack since we have another big stop before lunch.

Our destination is the Alexandria Library, which opened in 2002. An amazing building with soaring ceilings and a planetarium that reminds me of the Death Star, the Alexandria Library is one of the few places in the world that claims to have a comprehensive copy of the Internet. However, it suffers from a dearth of books. A shelf I saw, for example, held only five books under one point of the Dewey decimal system, including "Celebrity Horoscopes of 1972." Who knows where the other years were? The library houses many of its books electronically, and digitizes every book they get, possibly in an effort to ensure that there can never be a repeat of the historic loss suffered when the original library was destroyed.

Contrary to my romantic notion of Huns or Visigoths sweeping in, it seems to have been partly razed accidentally while Caesar was burning up his own port in the first century CE, and then several times in subsequent centuries, ending with a final showdown between Christians and pagans (watch Darren Aronofsky's excellent film *Agoura* for all the gory details). In any case, we lost all of those texts in a time when many were the only copy, which is easy enough to avoid now. Also, don't set fire to the building.

On our tour, which is given by a self-possessed young Muslim lady who speaks excellent English, we visit a rare manuscript museum. Inside, there is an application that allows you to view a dozen different books, many several hundred years old, translated from Arabic into five different languages. We also see a rare permanent exhibit: sketches and stills from huge films designed by Egyptian native son Shadi Abdel Salam, who claimed to be a direct descendent of the pharaohs. Through his movies, which included an important Hollywood-style film on Akhenaton, Salam strove to revive the people's awareness of their ancient Egyptian heritage. The production values look as if they would give the Liz Taylor *Cleopatra* a run for its money.

After our tour, I go downstairs to the Ladies Room, where a group of college girls, all Muslim, are adjusting their tarhas, the head scarves they wear with their blouses and jeans. Each of them is so modern looking, their blouses various prints, their jeans Guess or whatever else is popular. Except for the scarves, they could be girls in any city in the States (presuming American teens would stoop to wear polyester). As I go in to the stall, they watch me out of the corners of their eyes. By the time I come out, they have had time to steel their nerves, and surround me, so curious, the bravest ones peppering questions at me. "What is your name?"

I smile. "Halle."

"Where are you from?"

"America."

"How old are you?"

"Forty-two." (Mother always taught me to tell the truth.)

"Where are you staying?"

"Cairo."

"Do you believe Mohamed is the one true prophet?"

???

If I answer this wrong I could set Middle East relations back by fifty years. I consider my response carefully. "Well, I believe Mohamed was a prophet, like Jesus and others were prophets, too."

The girl who asked me this nods, satisfied, and launches into an explanation of Muslim religion that I only half-follow. She is clearly well-informed, single-minded, and the leader of this pack, as they all listen with rapt attention. I remember when I was twenty and every word I spoke was a justified pearl. I'm grateful I've passed the test, and will not be run out of the Ladies' Room on a rail by an irate group of militant Muslim college girls.

If you ever want to feel like a celebrity, stand outside the Library on an Egyptian holiday. A crowd of students and little kids gathers around you, building as the word spreads among them that you are here and a willing subject. "Photo, please?" they ask shyly, again and again. In a moment, you are Brangelina. They stand on either side of you—not touching, but close—and grin while their friend snaps off three or four shots on a phone; then they huddle in to look at the pictures and run off happily to show them to their friends. Then another request and the process repeats itself. A woman in our group—petite, pretty, blonde—is surrounded by teenage Muslim boys trying to get a group picture. As the closest teen touches his cheek to hers, a collective "whooooo!" goes up and the group immediately swells to twice the size. When she does not demur, he grows even bolder and, as the camera snaps, turns his face and kisses her on the cheek. The sound turns into a collective cry of surprise, and I can tell a stud has been born. This boy will have no trouble for the rest of high school getting girls to like him; he has photographic proof of his prowess as a man.

Heading to lunch, we drive down to the Corniche (which is what they call the coastal roads here in a nod to the French), then stop at the Qaitbay Citadel, so everyone can touch the Mediterranean Sea. The fort, built by the Sultan of Egypt in the fifteenth century CE, reused both the exact site and the stones of the famous Alexandria lighthouse. One of the Seven Wonders of the Ancient World, that lighthouse was sadly destroyed by water and earthquakes over the course of several hundred years.

My dear friend Eloise is with us on the trip, and she goes to the water, walking across the concrete slabs that bridge the boardwalk and the ocean. The waves break against the thick blocks. It's particularly windy, and her wide silk scarf ripples around her neck. Several young Muslim women are out here, dressed exactly like the girls from the library, and they surround Eloise the way the others encircled me. I watch as the girls show Eloise how to wear her scarf in the Muslim manner; when she gets on the bus, she is grinning, her long face framed by her scarf, the material cleverly tucked under her chin so her neck and hair are gone.

We lunch at the Seafood Market restaurant, right on the harbor, sporting a terrific view of the Citadel. We go up to the third floor, then walk past a long display where the fish is all laid out like a fishmonger's, so fresh they seem ready to jump off the ice; you can choose your exact meal if you want. When I coo over the fresh crab, unusual in Egypt, Momo orders it for everyone, along with whole grilled local snapper and fantastic fried calamari.

The water is turquoise below us, and many small fishing boats are starting to pull into port after a day's work. The restaurant is bustling too, the waiters running to and fro providing unending fresh bread puffs. By now we know what to expect, and Shakky sends back the first round of bread because it is at least five minutes old and no longer warm enough for him. When he is satisfied with the steaming baskets of bread they place in front of us every three feet, he encourages us to try some of the new mezzes the waiters are tossing down in little plastic bowls. They have a taramosalata-like dip, a garlic aioli whipped until it's fluffy, and a sun-dried tomato paste as well, none of which we have seen before. We exclaim over the food like we have been lost in the desert for weeks, and almost everyone stuffs themselves, knowing that true Tourist Eating means you'll never be able to get this meal again.

On our initial visit to this restaurant late in the trip, the group presented me with a huge citrine ring, set in 18 karat gold, as a gift from them. I never take it off. Every time I return to this restaurant, I remember that afternoon, my tears of joy and gratitude, the generosity and kindness of those people. My feelings mingle with the sunlight and the blue water when I am here, the delightful smells and tastes, making this restaurant a true favorite of mine.

After a satisfying lunch, we discover the Lebanese pastry shop outside the entrance to the restaurant. We go in, just to peek at the pastries, then come out a few minutes later carrying string-tied boxes full of cookies and Turkish Delight, sufficient to tide everyone over on the long coach ride to Cairo. Tourist Eating again.

WHERE I GET THE YELLOW FIRE

At the crack of doom we fly to Aswan, in Upper Egypt, to board our cruise ship. I'm just over the jet lag, starting to settle into this distant and wild time zone, and now we have to pack up and leave the hotel at an obscene hour. Thanks to the porterage, we just leave our bags outside the door to our room the night before, and they magically appear at the bus for our viewing before we board, but it still feels like hard work (of course, I am particularly whiney at 3am).

Unfortunately, this morning I wake up with something called Pharaoh's Revenge. You may have heard it called Montezuma's Revenge in Mexico or Emperor's Revenge in China—perhaps it's even the Queen's Revenge in England, but I doubt it, since the food is so bland. What it actually should be called is, "the Yellow Fire," since (sorry, I know this is mighty personal) that's how it looks and feels as it rages mercilessly through me.

Despite a diet in Egypt of macrobiotic, organic fresh food, this issue affects a small but consistent percentage of our travelers, so over the years we have come to be smart about it. We discovered a wonderfully effective medicine called Antinol, the Egyptian equivalent of Cipro, sold over the counter for five Egyptian pounds ($1 U.S. for 12 pills). Greg and I stock up every time we go, and we make a big announcement at the beginning of the trip that anyone who feels the need can ask us for some. After the trip is underway, we hand boxes out like candy; it's a much more welcome gift than a Spirit Quest Tours T-shirt, even though it doesn't last as long. If the Yellow Fire is caught early enough, no one misses a beat. Wait a few hours, and you'll be down for a day at the most as you recover. But the first time, we were helpless and ignorant, and since I don't go around discussing my bodily functions with strangers (well, not until now, at least) I keep quiet and miserable and hope it will subside.

Which it does not. I spend the ride to the airport going in and out of the bus bathroom; Greg is extra-solicitous of me. I spend the hour waiting for the plane hovering near the Ladies' Room. On the plane, Mohamed, with whom I have exchanged nothing more than a hello at this point in our lives, pulls Greg aside and asks if I have an upset stomach. Greg likes discussing potty functions less than most squeamish teenage girls, so when he sees me approach on what has to be my fifth trip from the bathroom he neatly sidesteps and invites Momo to ask me directly. I nod, embarrassed, and he smiles kindly at me. "Don't worry. As soon as we get to the ship, the doctor will take care of you!"

A doctor! At the thought I start feeling better, and luckily, there's a bathroom on the bus from the airport, too. By this time, thank goodness, my body has expelled whatever seemed to be bothering it most, and I am able to stay in my seat during most of the ride. The doctor visits our cabin about five minutes after we check in, politely prescribing Antinol as well as chicken broth and white rice he has the kitchen send up, and I feel normal within a day. The house call costs $50, which would buy many boxes of Antinol, but was more than worth it.

Aswan has a tropical feel, as does that whole area of Upper Egypt, and the difference from Cairo is distinct. I see plumeria, oleander, hibiscus—except for the unending sand, if I squint I can convince myself I am in Hawaii. Everywhere, the feeling is of lightness and warmth—except the weather, of course, which is insane. Shakky tells a story about a Chinese woman he guided who was irritable in the heat, and yelled at him every day in her strongly accented English, "It's fyking hot! It's fyking hot!" And of course, it is—126 degrees Fahrenheit is the hottest I have ever experienced in Upper Egypt. And yes, you really can fry an egg on the sidewalk. As they say, "It's a dry heat," and it's a part of the experience, so we settle in and try to enjoy it.

The coaches are cushy and well air-conditioned, which is important if you ever truly feel you're going to pass out from the heat—you can run into the cool of your bus. As we drive the Corniche past cruise ship after cruise ship, I realize the scope of Egyptian tourism; this is a serious operation. Fifty or more vessels are docked, each larger and more beautiful than the last, although none is the size you would see with the big international cruise lines. The Nile is on average only about a mile-and-a-half across, and at points on the cruise varies from a quarter-mile to over four-and-a-half miles, so the ships have to be able to navigate the narrowest passages. Our boat, the *Sonesta Sun Goddess*, has three levels, and about eighty rooms.

A word on the difference between boats and ships, in case you are either a Mariner or a grammatical stickler: according to the Historic Ships Committee, they have designated a vessel below forty tons and forty feet in length as a boat. This makes most of the ships on the Nile, well, ships. But I worry it might get boring using the term "ship" repeatedly, so I hope sailors around the globe will forgive me.

Boarding the cruise liner makes me feel fairly disoriented. They are designed to embark on the side, amidship. Recalling old episodes of *The Love Boat*, I think this is fairly standard. But there aren't enough docks to allow all the cruise ships a private berth. The ships line lobby to lobby, sometimes as many as four or five deep, and you walk through the lobby of each until you get to yours. So I go through one glass atrium after another revealing the sky above me, without grasping that we're walking through multiple vessels, since you can only see one cruise ship when you're on the dock. It appears to be an extended lobby, where the scenery keeps changing and ship's personnel bow and greet us as we all troop past. The other fun thing is that each ship is decorated in its own style, and many have small shops in their lobbies; you can pick up a souvenir or some jewelry on another boat as you pass through. The staff is all friendly, and it's quite entertaining to nod to the crews as we traverse four or five ships to reach our own.

Along with our group of forty, on this trip the Sun Goddess is hosting assorted travelers from various countries. They include a group of Australian men in their eighties who had fought in Egypt during World War II, and a small group that call themselves the Sun People, who dress wholly and exclusively in white.

A couple of weeks before we left, I received a call offering us an upgrade to a suite, and I had taken it to surprise Greg. It turns out this is one of the only two suites onboard, and we are both thrilled when we see our room. The suites, across from each other at the end of the lower deck, are twice the size of the regular cabins. The other suite is occupied by Momo and Shakky, which means we pass them regularly as we go in and out, especially since they often leave their cabin door open. The upgrade is clearly the right choice; our bedroom is a standard cabin, and we also have a huge corner living room with a lemon-colored sectional sofa, silk drapes, and a guest bathroom. Our main room has a wraparound picture window that overlooks the prow of the ship. All the cabins have balconies with sliding glass doors. Each morning we throw open curtains and lie in bed watching the banks of the Nile drift by. We start calling this, "The Egypt Channel! All Egypt, all the time!"

I've never been on a transatlantic cruise ship, but I hear the average rooms are nothing to write home about. Like Vegas in the '80's, the theory is: make the rooms as small and unwelcoming as possible and folks will spend more time in the casino and in the bar with their wallets hanging open. Plus, smaller rooms mean more of them, so you can pack in more people. On this boat, however, all the rooms are reasonably sized. Come to think of it, the cabins are larger than some New York or London hotel rooms I've stayed in, where the only way to turn around is to enter the minuscule bathroom first, as if you're a car executing a three-point turn in a tight driveway.

Mohamed stops by to tell us that we will see some extra security measures. Just as Greg and I get comfortable, waiting for the ship to sail, enjoying the view and talking about how excited we are to cruise up the Nile, a few soldiers begin to mill around in front of our window. There is a flurry of movement as we watch the soldiers and several sailors drag Gatling guns onto the bow and mount them—right in front of our living room. We watch as they finish their work, then leave a couple of soldiers for the first shift. We lament the loss of the unobstructed view but are thankful for the ground support; the Egyptian government is taking no chances with our safety. Imagine our surprise when a bored soldier starts primping in the reflection from our mirrored window. It's as if we have a very vain peeping Tom, except he can't see us. Later on in the voyage, there will be hair combing and nose picking; really, it's practically our own private reality show.

This trip is unusually important to the Egyptian government, because we are the only large group to come in six months, a gap that would have been unheard of only a year earlier. If something happens to us, it would be an almost insurmountable impediment to tourism because of what has already occurred: on November 17, 1997, six months earlier, there was a terrorist attack and massacre at the Temple of Hatshepsut, in the Valley of the Kings. Egyptian extremists, in the middle of a campaign to overthrow (now ex-)President Mubarek and replace him with a strict Islamic government, snuck into Hatshepsut dressed as guards and opened fire on Japanese, German and American tourists, killing fifty-eight (plus an Egyptian tour guide and two policemen). As intended, it practically also massacred the tourism business in Egypt for several years. Egyptians had been relying on tourism for about a fifth of their economy and for months after that, no one came to see the pyramids or the temples. Some sites were even shut down before our visit, because they had been empty for so long.

It was very difficult for everyone. The hotels suffered, the waiters and the Temple Guards suffered, many lost their livelihood. So though our trip was a happy occurrence, it was also vital that it come off without a hitch. The plan was to travel on the boat all the way from Aswan to Cairo, about a ten-day journey. All boats sail only from Aswan to Luxor, the southernmost third of the river. The ship was to undergo repairs in Cairo, which is the only reason this route was even possible. But to get there, we would have to travel through the middle of Egypt, which at the time was home to many nationalistic opinions, and the police were afraid we might also come under attack; hence the Gatling guns, as well as a full security detail assigned to our group.

Several years later, Momo finally told Greg and me the story: he was negotiating with the government and the Egyptian police right through the day after our cruise started, to get us permission to take the whole trip. That earned him Greg's nickname "The Surgeon," because he's always orchestrating beautifully organized and detailed experiences unparalleled in the travel business. Shakky is "The Magician" for his ability to get us places and enabling things that are seemingly impossible, as well as recreate the magic of the temples by invoking the memory of their power. So with The Surgeon and The Magician, and the Yellow Fire under control, the boat steams off on what would famously become known as "the Long Cruise."

WOO-WOO TIME

This first morning on the ship, after the Yellow Fire has subsided, I am still vaguely nauseous. So despite our plan to visit some temple or other, which name I cannot recall despite having been told it at least five times this morning, I decide to stay home. As soon as the group leaves, though, I suddenly feel better.

I unpack, gazing out of the windows at the startling tranquility of the Nile, which laps below our cabin. As usual, my thoughts drift to Greg. We were drawn together inexplicably, and I am conscious of an ache when he's away from me. It's as if we were planets, lost in the universe, and no matter what interesting and distinctive stars we found to distract us, we were never in orbit around something until we met. Now we are a double star, rotating around each other. It's not that I am dependent on him, although I am. I am also independent; sometimes fiercely so. It's just that my life didn't mean anything until we were together. Through almost insurmountable odds, Greg and I have both stayed because we have always known somehow we belong together.

We met when Greg cast me as Fern in a theatre production of *Charlotte's Web* he was directing. Only a year earlier, my husband and I had moved to Houston (whenever I mention my wusband now, Greg gasps and says, "You were married before?") Things had been rocky even before we got there, and I admit I was looking for an affair—something to keep me occupied while I lived my life—you know, the one that was starting to not turn out the way I thought it would.

Initially, I couldn't have cared at all about Greg. He was kind of distracted, mispronounced my name, and looked about as "white bread" as you could get—soft, bland, no crust. Then about three weeks after I met him, I had a dream. This was unusual, because in my whole life, I have had perhaps five dreams that I could remember when I woke up. This time I had, and still have, total recall of this dream: we were in a car together, driving across a bridge, talking. As we crossed the water, he reached out and held my hand. That's the whole dream. But when I woke up, I had a crush on him. It was inconvenient, especially since I neither particularly liked nor knew him well, but there it was. And over the next few weeks, my crush got worse… and bigger. I started noticing how blue his eyes are, the curve of his biceps where his T-shirt stopped, how his blond hair falls in curls and waves, how the combination of his facial hair and his gold earring make him look kind of piratey and very sexy.

As I started trying to get his attention, my hemlines got shorter and my necklines got lower. I wore makeup after the show, to walk to the parking lot. I started flirting, started asking around. To my intrigued surprise, I discovered that Greg was a serial Lothario. Married right after college, he took one mistress at a time, starting several years earlier with the woman who was now playing Charlotte the Spider to my Fern. She was happy to fill me in on all the details, to assure me that Greg was a good person trying to assuage the nagging feeling that he, like me, might not be happy in his marriage. Actually, he had been about to leave his wife when she got pregnant. He recommitted to the relationship and made a real effort to make things work. When I met Greg, his daughter was only a couple of weeks old, which was the main reason he was so distracted. I know… I'm a monster, taking a husband away from his wife and his new baby. That's sure one way to look at it. But in his heart Greg had left his wife long before we met, as I was on my way to leaving my husband.

Once the baby was sleeping more regularly, and Greg had settled into his new routine, he took the time to notice that the woman he referred to as "Rebecca of Sunnybrook Farm" was more than a little interested in him. I was hardly the good little girl Greg imagined I was. I had recently lost weight so that I could get professional theatre and film work; in combination with my vivid red hair and enthusiastic personality, men were now quite interested. I had been married about three months when I ran into the first man I was drawn to since my husband, dashing my hopes that "I do" would stop the revolving door of attractions I had enjoyed before marrying.

There had already been signs my marriage suffered from a terminal illness, even if I was doing my best to ignore them. My husband liked to make love about half as often as I did, and while I was still in warm-up mode, he was often already done and drifting off. He smoked behind my back and lied to me about it. Hint: if I smell smoke on your breath, it's not because you were near someone who was smoking (unless she had her tongue in your mouth, which would be a different problem). There were money issues, stemming from our disparate approaches to finances. And I was already feeling like I had an itch to scratch, if only I could find the damn thing. While Greg didn't know it when we met, I had already had two brief affairs.

After a couple weeks of prancing around in front of him, I invited Greg on a picnic so that I could ask my burning question: Is it possible to have regular sex outside of your marriage and still stay happy inside your marriage? Somewhere in the midst of cold Tandoori chicken and salad, he suggested we conduct a real-life experiment so I could find out. We agreed up front on some ground rules. Rule One: no falling in love.

It turns out Greg is a serious romantic, and after a few brief months of secret rendezvous, love poems scrawled on scraps of paper, and breathtaking sex, he fell down the rabbit hole and I jumped in right after. Things got harder and harder for us, and we became blindingly obvious in our affair. We had started a multimedia company together, and his wife and my husband worked their jobs while we stayed home with his daughter and built our brand-new baby business. We both left the theatre, and began working about a hundred hours a week, since multimedia was fledgling at the time and we were inventing new things almost daily. We were inseparable, entirely besotted, and at times incredibly stupid. We also started breaking up nearly every week.

The conversation would go something like this, every time: Greg would say something jealous and laden with testosterone, such as, "I saw you looking at that guy at the taqueria."

I would respond, clueless: "What the hell are you talking about?"

He would presume I was posturing. "Don't try to make me believe you didn't. The tall dude, the one with the dark hair." (Never, never tell the one you love, who is blond and of medium height, that your ideal man is tall, dark and handsome. Don't mention it even once, even if he asks. Big mistake.)

"Wait a minute." A vague recollection of the big fellow blocking the poster I was trying to look at on the wall. "You mean the guy standing in front of the concert poster?"

Greg thinks for a moment. "What concert poster? You were flirting with him—I saw him wink at you!"

And we were off to the races. Greg, in a bizarre twist on the idea that imitation is the sincerest form of flattery, thought that because he lusted after me every single second of every single day meant that everyone else did, too. Admittedly, before Greg (It feels a little ponderous—B.G, "Before Greg") I could spot a prospect at twenty paces and ensure he was interested in me at ten. But wholly unexpectedly, "A.G," the vacuum I had felt inside of me my whole life, the hole in my heart that had kept me on an aggressive manhunt for the last several years, closed up, never to reopen. No affairs, no interest, no attractions. My roadshow had unaccountably found its permanent theatre, eight performances a week.

The divorce rate in the U.S. is above fifty percent; couples split up no matter how their relationship started, no matter what their initial closeness. But after twenty years, Greg still makes my heart beat faster, the simple act of him taking my hand still sends shivers through me. Why is this? Was I really good in another lifetime to deserve this love that twists and winds, but continues forward in an unbroken line? Early on, we nearly split up enough times I lost count, so what kept us—keeps us—together? I believe it's simply that we are soul mates. Greg says there is a

Halle-shaped hole in his head; when we're together, it's gone, and when we're apart, he feels the tug of the empty space. It's easy to mistake passion for love, with so many different types of love and varied levels of feeling. Maybe the divorcing couples are still in search of the soul mate who will fill that void inside their heads, their hearts. I loved B.G. But A.G, I left all the others behind.

Unfortunately, there was nothing I could do to convince Greg of that, plagued as he was by his incandescent fear that I would leave him. The fights got worse, escalating to the point where we were both screaming and crying. One of us would try to storm out, never to return, but the other would restrain the deserter, by physical force if necessary. In hundreds of fights, neither of us ever got out of the room. Eventually, the latent escapee would get so worn down—we both would—that we would calm down for a bit and start to talk things through. There was only ever one thing at the bottom of these fights: though we were having an affair, both of us cheating, *he* didn't trust *me*. In vain I struggled to convince him that I loved him, that I would gladly leave my husband if only he would be willing to tell his wife. Since he was afraid she'd take the baby and he'd never see his daughter again, that wasn't an option he would risk. Ground Rule Number Two: The baby trumps everything and everyone.

Three long years, we fought the same fight over and over. We moved from Houston to Seattle with our growing business, taking houses within five minutes of each other and carpooling to work so we could spend as much time together as possible. Finally, like some great descending knock on the head, Greg decided to deal with the consequences of his feelings and risk everything to tell the truth. Ground Rule Number Three: No more ground rules.

It didn't go exactly as planned. We each told our spouses shortly after Thanksgiving, and my passive-aggressive husband acted as if everything was still hunky dory. He was supportive, kind, and understanding. After all, he had told me several times he believed we had moved to Houston just so we would meet Greg. Greg's wife was not only told about me, but to Greg's credit, also about the many other notches on his headboard. She said some interesting things to him about me that night. Years later, Greg finally confessed her words: "How can you be in love with Halle? She's fat and hairy." Now, I admit I had gained about twenty pounds since we had met, which is what working every waking minute will do to you, and if I don't wax for a few weeks, I get a tad bit hirsute, but still... She also told Greg that she was staying put—either he would get tired of me, or I would get hit by a bus. I couldn't argue her logic, since he had gotten tired of all the previous paramours, but I did call her some impolite names when I thought I couldn't be overheard.

This is all so hard to justify, looking back: Greg stayed, my husband left, the deep friendship his wife and I had inadvertently enjoyed ended abruptly, and we all stayed like that, frozen in limbo for years, except for his daughter, who kept growing. Of course, he and I kept seeing each other, now finally out in the open. The fights, believe it or not, were getting worse. After a few months, my wusband had switched from passive to aggressive, and now I had no spouse at home to occupy the time when Greg was with his family; therefore, in Greg's mind, I could be off doing God-knows-what with who-knows-whom.

Early on in our relationship, Greg and I took a Meyers-Briggs personality test, and we scored almost exactly the same: I was an ENFP, which makes me an Extroverted, iNtuitive, Feeling, Perceiving person. He was the same, except for that pesky first letter, which was an I. That stands for Introvert. Now you may ask why an introvert went into the theatre, but supposedly Dustin Hoffman, movie star, is the shyest man you'll ever meet. The difference is that where I can walk into a room and get energy from everyone there—it's almost like they recharge my batteries—an hour with the same bunch of people, even ones he likes, will utterly drain Greg. So he begrudged my desire to be out in a crowd, to attend parties without him, to have the active social life I craved. It was the last thing he wanted us to do together, either. This was a further source of our fights, of his jealousy, as I chafed against his concerns and resented his feelings.

As much as I tried to be understanding when Greg would fly off into his jealous rages, he fought dirty, and he would say whatever he could to push my buttons and I, I am ashamed to say, would slap him so hard across the face it would make my hand hurt. When he could control himself, he would respond verbally. When he could not, he would shove me, although he never struck me.

Of course, there was that time in Boston when we had dinner with my ex-boyfriend from high school, who had a hairline receding so fast you practically noticed a change during dinner, but a sharp, clever personality, which was what I had been attracted to initially. By the time we made it to the hotel room, Greg was working up to a righteous boil. We had our usual fight, then the whole thing ended up in the tiny bathroom, where I slapped Greg, and he tried to throttle me on top of the toilet tank. I knocked him off after about five seconds, but it was long enough for my brain to get the bizarre notion that this was not the first time Greg had tried to kill me. I gasped out, "You tried to strangle me! Here! In Boston!" Unusually, this remark succeeded where none of my angry outbursts had; it killed the fight. That was when I realized we needed to see someone. Now.

At home in Seattle, a friend recommended her ex-husband and we decided to give him a try. Comparing Kevin Connor to a regular shrink is akin to comparing Superman to Clark Kent, but Kevin certainly looked the part of a mild-mannered therapist when we met him. We explained the problem quite simply: "The argument doesn't justify the fight that occurs, the feelings seem to be deeper than they should be, and we are thinking about splitting up because although we are deeply in love, we're also dangerous to each other's health." Kevin agreed to see me alone, then both of us together, since Greg was reluctant to share his issues with a stranger.

I had never been in therapy before, but I had seen it on TV. You're supposed to lie on a sofa, tell the therapist your life story and your problems, and listen to their advice. I should have known I was in for something different; Kevin didn't have a sofa. What he did have were some radical techniques, which included hypnotherapy and past life regression. Hypnotherapy is simple. You sit in a chair, you are told to relax a few dozen ways, and then to test that it's working, the therapist might ask you to do something simple, such as raise your arm. The funny thing is, you want to, in the worst way, and you are cognizant of everything going on around you, yet you cannot raise your arm even the teensiest bit. You're sitting there with your eyes closed, your brain is going, "Come on, arm, move!" but it's not happening, until the therapist asks you to pretend you are tying a balloon string to your wrist and that the balloon is slowly floating up. Then you realize your arm is suddenly up over your head. The good thing is, you don't have to take hypnotherapy on faith once this type of example proves to you that though you won't quack like a duck, you are hypnotized.

Kevin got me under, then talked me through a past life regression where I went back in time, in my head, to a fight Greg and I had, the earliest altercation I could remember. It was as if I was seeing a home movie from far away, like the TV I was watching was in another room. From the dress I was wearing, from the cars, I could tell it was the 1930s, it was San Francisco. I could see my shoes as I walked up the steeply angled street. My name was Veronica, and I was this flibberty-gibbet of a girl, vapid and self-centered. I could physically feel what it was like to be her, so wrapped up in my clothes, my looks, my boyfriend. I told myself I was hypnotized, that Kevin was making me see these things, but he was only asking me questions, and I was telling him what I saw, what I sensed. At some point, I laughed, and I actually reached over and put my hand on Kevin's knee. The ego part of my brain, the Halle part, was thinking, *What the hell??* But Veronica knew just what she was doing. Veronica was trouble.

Kevin asked me to step forward in time to my death. It was a sunny day, not too much later, and I was coming home from church with Biff, my boyfriend, who I recognized was Greg in this lifetime. Yes, I know Biff and Veronica sound like characters from the *Archie* comics, but I had never done a past life regression before. Maybe it was the same as this book— most of the names were changed to protect the innocent. Biff was big, husky, and mad. I had flirted outrageously with another man, right in church. I was wearing a bright red dress, something in chiffon and silk, and we stepped into the kitchen of our apartment.

I knew I was wrong, I knew what I did in church was disrespectful, but I didn't care. I was full of my triumph that this man had flirted back, and I kept laughing, kept rubbing it in. Then Biff hit me. So hard he knocked me across the room, and I fell and hit my head on the chair, cracking my skull as I dropped to the floor. I lay there, dying, and I could feel myself rise above my body and hover for a moment, watching the red chiffon dress on the black-and-white check of the linoleum tile. Then I was gone. Veronica's last thought was that she didn't blame Biff, that she had deserved what she got, then I was in Kevin's office again and he was bringing me out of the hypnotic trance.

Well, that answered at least a few questions. Then Greg came to the next session, and the strangest thing happened. When Kevin hypnotized Greg, he nonchalantly said, "Oh, hello. It's you." It turned out that in some former life Greg had not only known Kevin, he had been his teacher; as Kevin started working with him, he asked if the techniques he was using were okay, then began applying different methods, guided by Greg. I knew for a fact that Greg didn't know anything about past life regression or hypnotherapy, but there he was telling Kevin exactly what to do.

Under hypnosis, Greg said there were things he and his wife needed to work on together, which was why he hadn't left her yet, things he needed to teach his daughter which he could only do if he were there. Yeah, he could have been lying, could have been pretending to be hypnotized, but too much came up that day. Also, I come from a weird family. My mom left my dad when I was seven, he raised my sister and me, and my dad's been openly gay since I was sixteen. Yet my parents never divorced. And now they're best friends. So I can live with unorthodox, as long as I know I am loved without reservation. Greg has always shown me that, no matter how hard we fought. In all the time we've been together, I never stopped loving him, not for a moment.

Past life regression should have cured any doubts I had about having a soul, about the existence of an afterlife, of whatever type—after life, more life! But I wasn't sure if I should trust my regressions, if I was simply manufacturing them in my mind. People remember repressed memories all the time that turn out to be created from their imagination. I wanted so badly to believe in something, maybe I was just making this all up? My logical mind demanded more proof, something concrete and definitive. Something that couldn't be taken away from me the further I got from the actual experience, as it took its place among my many memories.

At this point, I find people are usually divided into two camps; people who read "past lives" and say, "Wow, cool," and want to know more, and people who drift off towards the exit, wondering vaguely if I am a nut or hoping they can skip to the travel bits of the book. I have always straddled the fence between being intrigued and highly skeptical, but this trip would answer all the questions that past life regression left dangling.

*   *   *   *   *

After the group returns, I go on the top deck to see everyone milling around. Rose and Lyra are talking together. "How was it?" I ask. They both give me the thumbs up, but are obviously in the middle of a debate. I head over to Eleanor. "How was it?" I repeat.

"Amazing," she smiles, tossing her short hair. "Everyone had a great time."

I glance at all the people. "Have you seen Mother and Greg?" Eleanor nods.

"Judith went to have a shower and a nap, and Greg is right there." She points through the crowd. I follow her finger to see Greg standing with the Sun People, who I recognize from their white clothes.

On the way over, I run into Carter and Rusty. Carter gives me a look. "What?" I ask in response.

He shakes his head. "Ah don't trust those people," he informs me.

Rusty laughs. "Carter, man, you have an opinion about everything." Carter nods in agreement.

"Ah shore do."

I smile at both of them and shrug. "I like them. Besides, that's where Greg is." They part so I can pass more easily and I traverse the length of the deck.

The male leader of the Sun People is English, slight and compact, with a shaved head. His wife practically towers over us all; sporting big buckteeth and even bigger bosoms, she conveys the impression of a formidable woman. Yet there is something deeply nurturing about her as well. She is called Helena and he is Argon. As I approach, they are gathering their followers around them. Argon waves his hands for silence.

"Wasn't the temple incredible?" Argon asks. Everyone nods, smiling and happy.

"We had the most powerful epiphany there," Argon continues genially. "We are the re-embodiments of Isis and Osiris!" Who are, of course, the best-known of the Egyptian pantheon of Gods, roughly corresponding to the later Zeus and Hera in Greek mythology.

"From now on," Argon tells the other Sun People and all those in earshot, "we are to be known by these names alone!" The bizarre idea that Isis and Osiris are walking among us as divine reincarnations is a lot to swallow, but their group seems perfectly comfortable with the change, so we shrug and go along. The group breaks up into little conversations; the announcement apparently requires some discussion.

I give Greg a squeeze. "Hey, Dredj. I unpacked."

"That's great!" He's a little glassy-eyed, sweating lightly and obviously enthused.

I ask, "How was—what's the name of the temple again?"

"Philae. And amazing. I had an incredible meditation there!" This explains the glassy eyes; I've seen meditation cause some real shifts.

"Cool. I can't wait to hear about it. So what did—I can't remember the name again. What did it look like?"

Greg smiles. "*Philae*," he emphasizes the word for me, "was beautiful, a temple on an island in the center of a lake."

I sigh. "I'm sorry I missed it." I turn towards the Sun People. "Argon—I mean, Osiris—have you been to—aah!" I look at Greg. "I'm so sorry! I can't keep the name of the temple in my head!"

Osiris looks at me. "What happened there?" He claps his hand to my shoulder.

I have this instant flash of being killed, and I stammer out, "I —I died there."

Greg turns towards me, looking incredulous and agitated, but just when I expect him to make fun of me, he agrees: "You were struck with an axe, right—there!" and he points at the place in my shoulder I have just visualized cleaved in two. As I nod dumbly, Greg looks a bit horrified. Osiris turns to me again, and asks me the name of the temple.

"Philae," I say immediately.

And I never had trouble remembering the name again. A few years later, visiting Philae Temple for the first time, now leading a group for a private visit, Shakky asks me to bring the party inside. As I hit the ground, I have an overwhelming urge to take off my shoes and I walk barefoot, in the black of predawn, all the way to the inner sanctuary, knowing instinctively where to go. To this day, Philae, dedicated to the mother goddess Isis, seems magical to me.

And that, folks, is my original woo-woo experience in Egypt. A word about the word "woo-woo." I mean "spiritual" when I use it, and I think it's appropriate and sweet. Some people find it offensive, but it's not intended as such. For people who are uncomfortable with my transgressions of vocabulary, consider that I'm doing my best, just as you are, as we all are...

I eventually had another past life regression, which told me that Greg and I had been together, over and over, always as lovers. This is unusual, because most people, I believe, go around in these little soul groups and trade off: mom in one life, husband in the next, son in the lifetime after that. But that experience had been difficult to get to, and I had to be hypnotized, as I was in my other past-life work. The moment on the deck was different. It was a blinding instant of pure clarity, and it happened several times for me in Egypt after that, all perfectly lucid moments. At home, I can get there, but in Egypt, it's as if I am plugged into the information directly.

AFTER A WHILE, CROCODILE

The big cruise ships reach Kom Ombo in clumps—usually, at least four or five simultaneously—and the only way to get any solitude is to go when they aren't all docked at the side of the Nile. My initial visit to Kom Ombo was both searingly-hot and singularly unmemorable, except to make me truly appreciate our private temple visits. Since then, we have had many delightful experiences visiting Kom Ombo when we are guests on *The Afandina*.

A few years ago, Momo built a private cruise ship he dubbed *The Afandina*, which means The Old King. The dahabeya is designed like the boats of old. Before the advent of the motor, these sailing ships were part transportation, part houseboat. Cleopatra and Caesar honeymooned on one; archaeologist Howard Carter spent winters in Egypt going from salon to salon, not in homes, but on the dahabeyas that his English patrons rented to cruise the Nile. *The Afandina* has hosted several major politicians and movie stars, and the eight well-appointed cabins, two decks, living room and dining room with private chef, are the most pampered way I can imagine to travel the Nile.

Private cruising enables us to sail at a wholly alternate schedule than the big ships. Though when we arrive at Kom

Ombo it's usually the middle of the day and fairly hot, we often have the place to ourselves. When you are on the big ships, you park at the main dock, and go up to the compound through a pleasant garden oasis. The shops here sell exactly the same tourist trinkets that everyone else does, but it's very attractive, surrounded by greenery and bougainvillea, palm trees and shady roofs of dried grass to keep the sun off the visitors. A cold Coca-Cola beckons either before or after your temple visit.

When we dock on the private ship, we enter Kom Ombo from a different direction—walking up a rather desolate sandy stretch, past a couple of security guards who only stop talking long enough to say, "Saba el nur" (Good morning) to us, and into the main ticket office. At the top, we can see the roofs of the shopping lounges and the palm trees below, then we turn in the opposite direction and go into the turnstile security area where Shakky has secured our tickets.

The many touristses who swarm Kom Ombo make it hard to move around. Kom Ombo is dedicated to two gods: Horus the Elder and the crocodile god, Sobek, and the temple has two magnificent crocodile mummies, each over six feet long, encased in glass. They sit side-by-side in a room so small it can barely hold three visitors simultaneously, creating a long line; as a result, people give up and leave without visiting these creatures, magnificently preserved for thousands of years. During our tour, Kom Ombo is silent, peaceful, the experience entirely different.

With no one around to crowd it, the temple seems much bigger than in previous visits. The sky is brilliantly clear and all I can see is Kom Ombo's outline etched in the middle of that great expanse of blue; it looks like it has landed here temporarily, and might just as quickly take off again. It's as if the visitors have been Photoshopped out of my view, and all I'm left with is the monumental structure and the shape of the world.

We don't know how long it will be before the next flood of visitors, so we quickly hit all the highlights while we still have the place to ourselves. The main temple is made of beautiful Ptolemaic columns, tall hieroglyph-etched pillars topped by wavy carved leaves that make it appear that the columns are sprouting. At the far end of the main temple, a rectangular carving two feet across depicts surgical instruments: forceps, pincers, knives, scalpels, even a sponge—all sitting in a surgical tray sculpted into a back wall. This isn't incongruous, as Kom Ombo is half-dedicated to the god Horus the Elder, who has been referred to as "the Good Doctor," but it is unexpected, especially the sponge—you can see the little indentations, almost as if the artisan pressed an actual sponge into wet cement, but on closer inspection, it really is carved stone and therefore that much more impressive.

We continue past the image of the physical activation of the god Horus the Younger—like the statue of Pharaoh in the Cairo museum, Horus stands between two other gods whose hands hover about six inches away from him, their energy activating the hawk-faced deity. We walk past the beautiful renditions of the gods Isis, Hathor, Horus, and Set that grace the walls of so many of these temples, and cross the open courtyard to look into the crocodile pit. In ancient times, crocodiles were kept in this deep stone well, but now there is only a small amount of water at the bottom and a set of curved stairs disappearing into the depths. It doesn't look the least bit fearsome, more like a dried-up culvert somewhere, but when I peer over the side I can imagine the crocodiles below, their long tails thrashing, snapping for their meal—a terrified lamb or goat—their tiny brains oblivious to the concept of worship.

The crocodile god Sobek was both revered and reviled by the Egyptians, and the ancient Greek, Strabo, perhaps the foremost travelogue author, wrote about tame crocodiles hand-fed by priests at the temples for ancient travelers' amusement, and told stories of local crocodiles being hunted and killed. The god Osiris' penis was supposedly eaten by a crocodile, and after that tale got around, the beasts gain a reputation for being virile, and were hunted almost to extinction by several cultures that began to use ground crocodile penis as ancient Viagra. Despite his sense of humor, I have not seen Shakky The Magician handing out any ground spices, claiming it is powdered "crocodile thing."

Last, we visit the setting of the ancient Kom Ombo initiation. A drawing in Drunvalo Melchizadek's *The Ancient Secret of the Flower of Life* shows the ritual ceremony, part of the great mystery schools that thrived at so many of the temples and now are all but lost to us. You dove into a tank full of crocodiles and swam underwater to the other side of the tank. When you got most of the way across, you would abruptly encounter an underwater wall. "Fight or flight" instincts fully engaged, you would immediately surface, thinking this was the end. But to pass the initiation, instead of coming up you had to dive further down, deeper into the water, where—at the bottom of the wall—there was an opening large enough for you to swim through, but too small for the crocodiles to pass. Reaching the crocodile-free side of the tank, you passed the test. This initiation takes you past the fear of failing, since it includes the possibility of drowning, death by crocodile, even just a panic attack; these experiences were not for the faint of heart.

I don't know who figured these things out, but given my own experiences, I suspect they simply "remembered" it. Some of the magic in Egypt is determining what each part of the space was used for, given that the landscape, topography, and buildings may have changed over the centuries. For example, because of building the Aswan Dam, Philae Temple has been moved in its entirety, stone by stone. At Luxor Temple, there is a mosque three stories in the air now, because ground-level sand used to come up that high. Here at Kom Ombo, with the stones in ruins, we can now stand in the base of what was once the deep crocodile tank.

As we chant and perform our group ceremony, I am reminded of my original visit here—the experience when Lyra invited Greg and me to join her personal initiations. She had recently met Shakky (on a tour in Bali, of all places). He persuaded her to join this Egypt trip, and she had been given specific journey instructions by the gifted spiritual writer and teacher Barbara Hand Clow. In each temple she was to do an initiation in a special place; for the most part, we still do them in the exact locales she showed us a decade ago. Lyra shook a small wooden rattle around our heads and we intoned the vowel sound for the chakra of that temple: at Kom Ombo—the sacral shakra and the chant "Ka." Being here the first time, at least in this lifetime, was powerful. However, spatially I was a bit disoriented, as the only thing remaining from the crocodile tank is a flat stone floor and a small narrow wall at one end, making it hard to visualize what the initiates would have seen and felt.

Now we finish meditating and toning, sounding the single vowel sound "Kaaaaa" to open the sex chakra. Afterwards, I scootch into a round opening in the only remaining wall, popping up to sit in the base of a short tunnel—perhaps the place from which initiates dove into the tank where I was just standing? It makes an excellent resonating chamber. I sing into the stones, which echo and reverberate around me, the timeless warmth of smooth masonry taking in my sound, absorbing and reflecting it in the very atoms of the rock. I feel content, cocooned.

Eventually, I hop down and head out of the cool shadows and into the midday sun. No touristses have come to shatter the peace we feel, and I take a last look at this ancient temple floating in the modern world before we amble over to our boat for lunch and an afternoon nap.

AS THE HAWK FLIES

We sail on all afternoon, passing mile after mile of green fields, palm trees, and narrow sandy beaches, arriving in the evening at Edfu, home of the Temple of Horus. This site is also dedicated to two gods: Horus the Falcon and Set the Jackal, his uncle—a singular locale depicting both the light and dark of the human psyche. Edfu is a strange place, and I find the energy of this city of sixty thousand people to be jagged and disturbing. Along the wharf are a dozen or more shops, each a single big room where the ubiquitous galabeyas, jewelry, trinkets and Egyptian souvenirs are on display, spilling out into the street through the open shop fronts. The racks of colorful galabeyas, placed outside to entice customers, have faded in the sun until they all look sand-washed and colorless; for me, the proud display of flat monotone is emblematic of the town itself.

On our first visit to the Temple of Horus, we came through the old entrance on a blistering oven of an afternoon. I found a fossilized rounded rock, which I fantasized had been used in ancient games of football or as a temple-building tool—I nicknamed it "the Eye of Horus." It is hugely old, the baseball-sized stone almost perfectly shaped, parts of the rock gleaming dully, polished over so many years by the hands that held it. It is expressly forbidden to take any artifacts, but once I picked up the warm stone I found I could not put it down, and carried it all afternoon. We are like that rock, each lifetime smoothing us a bit, polishing us so the next one is a little easier. We can't usually see what made us this way, the lives that touched or changed us; we merely see the surfaces. But we can sense the connection to something older and deeper, to another time and place.

Nowadays we visit the Temple of Horus at night, venturing out after dinner on the five-minute bus ride. It's cooler that way, for one thing, but the temple seems to have many more secrets to explore in the dark. Like most temples, the entrance has now been moved, and we are dropped off in a new parking area surrounded by the standard tourist stalls and shops. This late, they are closed and we are the only visitors, so the space is quiet except for the occasional dog barking or the sound of policeman's walkie-talkie. The group moves quickly through the entrance turnstile; despite the presence of security, the tourist police, and metal detectors, we are rarely stopped and our bags are only infrequently checked. In this police state, they actively practice profiling: "American tourists? Move right on through."

Inside the grounds, we are lit mostly by the moon; consequently we pick our way slowly over the cement walkways and up a short flight of stairs, the risers so low you hardly sense you are going uphill. We pass an outer temple with carved scenes of Horus' wife, Hathor. Now we face the towering main walls, still off in the distance. At night, lit from below like footlights at the edge of a stage, the temple is eerie and powerful —a great malevolent castle.

Greg waits behind our group and as the last person passes in front of him, he begins to speak, his words sending chills up the spines of the listeners. His voice is slow and theatrical, unspooling the tale of Osiris and Set, the two brothers whose story is so similar to Cain and Abel, and of Isis and Nepthys, their two sisters who were also their wives. These gods are the four offspring of Geb, the Earth god, mating with Nut, the Sky goddess. They are the precursors of Zeus and Hera, who became Jupiter and Juno, the new religions swallowing the old.

"Osiris, the god-ruler of Egypt, was a popular king," Greg begins, his voice echoing across the wide courtyard, "and Set was jealous, plotting against his brother. He threw a great feast to which Osiris was invited. At the height of the festivities, Set brought out a magnificent, ornate casket and declared that it would be given to whomever it fitted. All the guests tried to fit in the casket until finally, the god-king Osiris stepped into it, unaware that Set secretly had the casket made to fit his brother's exact measurements. Once Osiris was inside, Set slammed down the lid and sealed the casket with lead. Then he threw his brother's coffin into the Nile and usurped his throne, ruling the known world.

"Isis, devastated at the loss of her husband, searched everywhere for her missing lover, brother, king, and god. When she finally found the casket, it was inside a tree whose trunk had grown up around it, sheltering it and protecting Osiris. Isis brought the coffin back to Egypt, but Set found out, and he dug Osiris up from where Isis had buried him, chopped his brother's body into pieces, and scattered the parts throughout the land. Wherever a piece of Osiris fell, Isis had a temple built, the same ones we walk through thousands of years later. Isis sought the parts of her husband, and eventually found all but one—the 'male organ'—which had been eaten by Sobek, the crocodile."

Greg narrates that Isis reassembled Osiris and wrapped him in bandages—a story of early mummification. She also had a golden phallus made, which was attached to Osiris. Isis breathed life into Osiris' body, then turned into a kite (a female hawk) "and hovered over him, taking her dead husband's essence up into her body and becoming pregnant with Horus. After Horus the falcon-headed god was born, he was hidden, concealed from Set and the displeasure of his jealous and wrathful uncle. Only after he came of age did the young Horus go out to battle his uncle Set and avenge his father's death. They fought for many years—Horus lost an eye, Set lost a testicle, but neither ultimately could prevail over the other. Eventually, Osiris was declared king of the underworld, Horus was made king of the people, and Set ruled the deserts as the god of chaos and evil."

Many pieces of this story resonate through the ages—the eye of Horus is usually shown singly and is iconic to the Egyptians; the immaculate conception of Horus the Younger predates the story of Jesus' birth by four thousand years. But to the spiritual seeker, the most important part comes when Greg talks about Horus fighting Set. He tells of "mastering" Set, not beating him, but man mastering the darkness within. This is the struggle—and the Egyptians did not think in terms of evil versus good, but of light versus dark; simply, man working against the forces inside that might swallow him up: depression, guilt, sadness, anger, pride. All these tales are really about man gaining purchase over his dark side and coming into the light, and that is why we are all here, to experience this growth.

For me, the darkness I had to master was my fear of death. For some it is a fear of success, or of living too much—that Marianne Williamson quote comes to mind: "We ask ourselves, 'Who am I to be so brilliant, gorgeous, talented and fabulous?' Actually, who are we not to be?" For others it is a fear of not having enough, or not being loved. Set—who was eventually called by another name: Satan—is not to be destroyed, but to be overcome as we let in the light of our newly found wisdom, the best part of ourselves.

After the story, we pass into the outer courtyard, and then the main temple itself with its huge hall of columns. In front of us is the "Holy of Holies," the sanctuary. Shakky explains that these sacred spaces are laid out according to the body of man—the outer courtyard is the legs, the inner courtyard with its columns are the ribs, the sanctuary is the head. Then he shows us some holes way at the top of the walls. These cavities had curtains attached to them, Shakky tells us, which were used to cover the gods and goddesses on the days when the public was allowed to visit, since they were not allowed so much as a glimpse of the consecrated carvings. Fewer and fewer priests, each more powerfully ranked, could access each space, until inside the sanctuary only two priests and the pharaoh were granted admittance to the Holy of Holies.

Passing through each room, I notice different aspects—the hieroglyphics on the walls, the tiny side rooms (one of which Lyra, Greg and I ducked into on our earliest visit to perform our temple ritual), the birthing chamber off to the right of the Holy of Holies. The staircase going up to the roof on the temple's left side is straight, whereas the flights of stairs on the right side turn at ninety-degree angles, again and again until they reach the top. I go up and down, only vaguely aware of this, navigating across steps so worn with the footfalls of the ancients that they sag like old mattresses and shine like glazed pottery. Then Shakky explains that the Egyptians made these staircases to model the hawk, who flies up in circles borne on the lift of the thermal air currents, and then zooms straight down to nab his prey. It is clever and subtle, a standard example of Egyptian invention and romantic storytelling, but also an engineering feat typical of their attention to detail in every last stone of the cavernous temple spaces.

Shakky has a tremendous respect for these architects of spiritual intentions made manifest as buildings, and I find myself marveling at the power of these structures and the tantalizing clues we have been left as to their original intentions, their age, and their value in the lives of the men and women who walked here when the temples were created. Just to be in this place now, to glide silently in their footsteps wearing my galabeya, imagining their daily lives, is shifting me, making me aware of forces so much larger than I have ever contemplated.

BROADWAY SHOW REFERENCES

In Edfu I sometimes buy Egyptian shoes, hand-stitched leather that costs only a little and lasts about as long before the seams burst open and I have to repair them. When Greg and I started leading tours, we ventured out together to try to make friends of some of the local shopkeepers. We try to prescreen everything our guests do, and though with Quest Travel as our partner, that's usually not necessary, in the case of a little side shopping we need to check things out ourselves.

After dinner, around 9pm, we go out into the street. All the shops are open, as well as an ahwa where locals are smoking shisha. No other boats are docked tonight, so there are few other tourists. Proprietors who seem to feel that they cannot draw another breath unless we come into their place of business anxiously bombard us. "No buy, just try!" they call. "Lady, lady!" Always appeal to the woman; for these vendors, the man is merely the woman's wallet walking around on two legs.

We meet Ahmed, a tall, bespectacled young fellow who reminds me of the character of Motel from *Fiddler on the Roof*. I keep expecting him to tell me he is really Jewish, and he and Tzeitel have settled here to open a tailor shop. Ahmed earnestly tries to sell us many things, though we explain we are window shopping on behalf of our future groups. Now, I don't want to reveal all my secrets, but the two greatest words in Arabic are English, and they are "tour leader." They mean: "Thanks for offering to sell me all your stuff at tourist prices, but I come here all the time, so therefore I don't need it, and I know how much it's worth, so don't try to pull any of your regular hustle on me." The best part is it works every time, as long as you actually are a tour leader, because they will test you. You have to know what the merchandise is worth, and it helps if you already have three of everything at home because you really have been to Egypt that many times. Ahmed, to his real credit, backs off and tells us he hopes we will bring our groups to see him.

Down the way, we meet a character out of a different Broadway show: Ali is the Artful Dodger from *Oliver*. This little man is about fourteen or seventeen—somewhere in there—so smarmy and cocksure it's funny to watch him talk. Cigarette dangling from his lip, he explains to Greg that he owns his own shop, that he has worked since he was seven; his parents died and he took over, and he is the youngest proprietor in Edfu. Now the truth about Greg is that he is so sweet he is a bit of a pushover, but I have no reason to think this fellow is telling us less than the truth; all I know is that I don't care for the kid. So I bargain for a pair of shoes—pale orange leather stamped in hieroglyphs, toes pointed like genie shoes—and then I go to bed, leaving Greg to shoot the bull with Ali.

At 1am, I wake up and look around our cabin, realizing Greg has never returned. Thoughts of kidnapping, or at least an accident involving a ditch, race through my sleep-addled brain. I quickly dress and go out into the street to look for him (my paranoid fantasies notwithstanding, it really is that safe). Despite the late hour, most of the shops are still open; the only problem is that we had passed up and down the two blocks so many times I can't remember which place belongs to Ali. So I start at the left end of the strip of stores, and walk from place to place looking for my errant man. A few of the Egyptians, recognizing me from earlier, smile and wave to get me to shop, but at the ahwa, my concerned face leads the owner to ask if he can help. He invites me to sit, bringing me a glass of the requisite mint tea while he sends a child out to look for Greg. It is a practical solution, since five minutes later the boy is back, speaking rapid

Arabic to the man. The ahwa owner turns to me kindly and asks me to follow the boy, who will take me to Greg.

I thrust a sweaty twenty-pound Egyptian note into his hand (about four times what the tea cost) and trail the kid. All the way down at the end of the second block, lights blaze in a shop, and the boy points up the stairs into the wide-open storefront as we approach. I don't see Greg, just a few Egyptian boys sitting around smoking cigarettes and laughing uproariously. Leaning against a column is an Egyptian wearing a galabeya, his head wrapped in a turban; the boys are laughing at something he has said. As I come around the corner, I realize this Galabeya Boy is really Greg. He looks surprised, then sheepish, a cigarette in his hand and an, "Uh-oh, I'm in trouble with Mom," look on his face. The boys laugh even harder at this turn of events, and Greg slinks towards the boat.

Out of earshot, he apologizes profusely, and explains that this Ali kid wanted to do business with Shakky. "Our Shakky?" I ask, more than a little surprised. Greg explains that he has offered to introduce Ali to Shakky as a favor, to help this enterprising young man get on his feet. The rest of the conversation apparently involved sex. With a cooperative American male under their microscope for a few hours, the Egyptian boys wanted to know everything about American women—what they wanted, what they were like, even what Greg did with me in bed. He swears he didn't tell them, but I suspect that was only for my sense of propriety, since I had walked in on the group and he didn't want me to feel embarrassed. I was mostly relieved that Greg was all right, and agreed that the next day we would take Shakky to meet Ali.

I've had a similar conversation myself a couple of times, as Egyptian women are curious about American women and Egyptian men are curious about women in general—unable to talk to their peers about it, let alone their own wives or sisters. Egyptian women aren't supposed to enjoy sex, or at least not speak of it after marriage, and Sex Ed consists mostly of watching animals "doin' what comes natur'lly." They still have arranged marriages in Egypt, even among the relatively young and hip in the big cities. The marriage bed is still examined the morning after for signs of consummation, and it is not unheard of for a man, even in his late twenties or thirties, to lose his virginity on his wedding night. So everyone's ready to discuss whatever they can with whomever might know more than they do.

I have learned not to be too surprised at how different things are here, both in practice and knowledge. The boys often do engage in sex, just with each other. I found this out after inquiring about the multitude of young men wandering around two-by-two, holding hands or arm-in-arm. Unlike in Europe, Egyptian women never seem to touch each other, nor have I heard tales of any lesbians. But for the boys, I was told that everything is permissible until they are around sixteen. Personally, I find it difficult to believe that most adult men are involved only in heterosexual activity, since the women are so sexually restricted.

Most older women have been circumcised—that is to say, their clitorises have been removed. Although Egypt was the first Arab nation to outlaw it, is still practiced heavily in the villages. After all this time, I have come to some interesting conclusions about myself:

1) I'm tolerant of everything, as long as I believe there's a good reason for it.

2) I'm very open to new ways of doing things and unfamiliar practices.

3) Once I love someone or something, I will forgive them their trespasses as much as I can, knowing we're all doing our best, even if our best is lousy.

So my opinion about sexuality in Egypt is colored by my tendencies to want everyone to be right. Greg calls this my "defense attorney" mechanism—that I can always see the other side of the argument. But I have a hard time with centuries— let's face it, millennia—of pederasty and sexual repression. I also don't know how long it will take for significant change, since like all traditional behaviors these seem ingrained to the point of institution. The women in the streets at Tahrir Square were not fighting for their clitorises, but effectively for the right of their daughters to keep theirs. Meanwhile, I am merely an outside observer of the lifestyle, as curious as Ali and his friends, but unable to effect a shift by my attempts to discuss the subject.

Shakky thinks Egypt's sexual mores are humorous. He says he asks every man: "When you were a boy, were you a doer or were you done?" He says in all the years he's been asking, no one was ever "done," and this strikes him as especially hilarious. I hope, for the sake of the boys Greg met that night, society has broadened, but I suppose that is me being a Pollyanna again. In any case, their conversation was one-sided, so all Greg could tell was that they were a bunch of horny, uneducated youths, and he was more than happy to give them the information they eagerly requested.

The next morning, over breakfast, as Greg tells Shakky about our evening's adventures, our friend pays close attention, not saying much of anything. Shakky's been around the block so many times he doesn't remember his own address, but he's never forgotten where he's from. Whatever he might have been thinking about Ali, he keeps it to himself, listens politely, and agrees to visit the shop with Greg. Of course, when we get there, it is a different matter entirely.

Most of the conversation takes place in Arabic. Ali pulls his smug strutting routine on Shakky, who asks him a few questions but then starts to yell at him. Ali gets increasingly uncomfortable, finally starting to squirm like a moth poked by The Magician's pin—no matter how he tries, he can't get away. Greg and I are confused until Shakky finally turns away, grabs Greg around the neck (giggling in his gleeful, childlike way), and pulls him out of the store. I follow, listening hard.

On the way to the boat, Shakky schools Greg in the art of the Artful Dodger.

"You have to trust me," Shakky explains, his hand on his chest for emphasis. "I know this boy. Dredj, I *was* this boy."

"So he doesn't own the store?" Greg asks. We are both starting to catch on. Shakky laughs.

"Not only that, of course his parents are both alive! Ali was trying to be a—what do you call it—'big shot' because you are rich American!"

Greg snorts. "More likely because I paid attention to him."

"That, too." Shakky nods. "You were too nice to the boy. I fixed him!" He chortles some more.

It was charming in hindsight, and Greg had a laugh about it when he repeated the whole story to our group. "Enta f'kearny abeet?" Greg teaches them. "Do you think I am an idiot?" But I notice now, each time we are in Edfu he looks out for Ali, careful to avoid him. He doesn't want to let the Artful Dodger pick his pocket again.

*　　*　　*　　*　　*

Happy to leave Edfu behind, we stop next at Esna, where we wait for the locks to be opened. The old locks, which have been closed for several years, used to take only one boat at a time. So the boats would wait their turn, sometimes sitting all day. You could get to Esna at 3pm, and your boat could go through at 9am the next morning. For the cruise ships, this dreaded possibility could delay their schedules and cause the passengers to miss a planned event to make up the time. At the new locks, larger and smaller ships can go inside together, even two wide cruise ships, which barely fit end to end. This effectively halves the wait, and it's decreased again by the addition of a second lock. Depending on the time of year and the number of cruisers, you can still idle for quite a long time, and those ships captains who can manage it cross at odd hours in an attempt to avoid the rush.

The forced delay in Esna has caused the town to create an unusual floating enterprise. On the Long Cruise, the local kids would stand on the side of the lock, as close to the water as they could get, waving and yelling to grab the attention of the people up on the decks watching the proceedings. Then they would throw film canisters onto the decks at us—they had to have terrific aim, since they were trying to get these plastic bits up to you two stories away. The canisters were empty so you could fill them with change or a tightly wadded bill. It was a little game, the kids down below pleading "baksheesh, baksheesh" and then winging the canisters up at you; you picking the kid you want, making eye contact, and then throwing the receptacle back down, hoping your own aim was comparable. The flying canisters inevitably hit the ground and the kids scrabbled around to catch them, opening them triumphantly, hoping for a U.S. dollar instead of an Egyptian one-pound note.

The new locks have changed all that. There were issues of the children's safety before, and the current locks aren't at all close to the shore, therefore a new capital venture has sprung up. Now boys and young men ride out to the ships in open rowboats or feluccas, the small sailing boats so prevalent on the Nile. They bring scarves and galabeyas, which they fling onto your boat. The item is wadded up and lobbed at you, landing somewhere on the deck, hopefully at your feet. The prices are phenomenal, too —perhaps twenty percent of what you would pay in a shop—but you have to hope something in your color or size lands in your vicinity, so I wouldn't suggest this for any planned shopping. Still, passengers who already have three lovely galabeyas and had no intention of buying more are rapidly running for their wallets. This shopping method is on the honor system, since once the enterprising boys have thrown the galabeya to you, they have no way of getting it back should you choose to take it "as a gift." Of course, everyone is grateful for this new diversion and the fun things they are able to buy, and many dollars are exchanged in the most unusual shopping experience we have ever had.

The last time we traveled into the locks was on *The Afandina*, Momo's ship. He accompanied us on that trip, which was highly unusual. Mohamed normally does not have the time to travel with his groups unless they are so large they require his full attention but, because we were filming an ad for *The Afandina* on this tour, he chose to supervise as well as get some much-needed vacation time. *The Afandina*, which is perhaps thirty percent as long as a standard cruise ship, and a full-size ship sat comfortably together in the locks. We were finishing dinner on the far side of the lower deck, when all of a sudden, a spotlight hit our boat. Not just any spotlight, either—we became a stage spectacularly washed with light that made it bright as day. Everybody was curious, so we ran to the top deck to get a better look.

Momo and I stood squinting into the spotlight. All we could see was brilliant illumination—blocking out whoever was behind —and the outline of the cruise ship in front of us. Way at the top, on the third deck of the big ship, we could tell there were several people gathered around, peering over the side at us and the lock crossing.

The Afandina's purser was standing as close as he could get to the other ship, screaming at the top of his lungs and frantically waving his arms to get them to turn off the spotlight and stop interrupting his boss' dinner.   At that point, several of the women on the boat were looking at the curtains that hung around the cabana on the upper deck, looking at the spotlight, at our captive audience, and thinking… floor show?

I'm sorry to say that after a couple minutes, the crew of the cruise ship deigned to turn off the mega-wattage, which killed our growing impetus to burst into song and dance.   Instead we began a cultural exchange with the passengers of the other ship, which translated into this basic question: "Where are you from?" Unlike our group, these folks were from all over—France, Germany, Spain, Italy, Switzerland—they spoke a Babel of accents, English prevailing.   So we waved, we smiled; we made sure there were no hard feelings about our purser yelling.   As Momo and I went down to finish our lovely meal, the gates opened and we sailed out of the locks and onto the Nile.

IN THE VALLEY, IN THE VALLEY OF THE KINGS

If you're very lucky, one morning in Luxor you can get up at 4am and take a sleepy walk to the dock, where a water taxi will take you to a van, and the van will take you out into the desert to experience a fabulous balloon ride over the Valley of the Kings.

Prior to this, my experience with balloons was limited to watching *Around the World in 80 Days* and seeing ads for picnics in Napa après landing, but the balloons are delightful. What surprised me was that the baskets were big enough to hold many people. And then there's the fire. Flaming plumes of propane gas are shot into giant sacks made from the same type of material as the parachute pants everyone wore in the '80s. Even with Plexiglass covers to protect the passengers, it tested my "fight or flight" instinct to know I was going to be that close to the gouts of hot red-yellow flame that the crew has to blast into the balloon periodically to make it rise and keep it aloft. Yet, everyone has a glorious time.

We climb into the waist-high basket, which houses twenty of us snugly in six wicker compartments; it looks like they are designed to hold wine bottles for a giant's picnic. I am sharing a corner with Judith, Greg, and Eleanor, my favorite Texan, and the rest of our group is evenly distributed throughout the remaining compartments and a second basket. I look across to see how everyone's handling the new situation. Vivian and Rose are thick as thieves, as usual. Carter has positioned himself in a corner of the other basket, where he can observe everyone. Rusty talks to Lyra and some other women in our group. I catch Lyra's eye and she smiles and waves to me.

The suave-looking captain saunters over. He's young, his English is excellent, and we can tell he is our captain because he's wearing a uniform that looks as if he's about to set sail on *The Love Boat*. He's very sure of himself. The captain directs us to take a crouching position, holding tight to the leather straps that are at waist level along the side of the basket. This is our eventual landing position, where we will have to stay for ten to fifteen seconds at the ride's end. The captain tells us there are three kinds of landings over the desert: an Egyptian landing is soft and easy, an American landing is hard and bumpy, and an English landing is somewhere in the middle. Everyone laughs, and the balloon lifts off so smoothly, you can barely feel it leave the ground; then you look down and notice the land is below you and falling away.

Over the valley, we soar higher and higher, sailing over the Temple of Hatshepsut, Medinat Habu—the palace complex of Ramses III—and the Village of the Workers (still occupied by those who dig or excavate in the valley). I expected thrilling, but instead it is peaceful, gentle… and miraculous. I feel like a character in *Harry Potter* or *Chitty Chitty Bang Bang*—I get to ride unexpectedly in a flying car. We see the tops of people's homes, many of them without roofs, like some crazy science experiment: a bird's eye view of the daily activities of Egyptian farmers. Our roofless research reveals goats inside, or people still sleeping, sometimes both in the same rooms. I do not know how goats get upstairs, but if the experiment's data is correct, goats enjoy hanging out on the top floors of as many buildings as they can. Shakky hates these balloons, feeling that they are an invasion of people's privacy, and after I catch sight of my second naked person, I agree he has a point.

We sail over field after field of neatly sown crops. We see corn, alfalfa, and closer to the Nile, rice paddies. But we're not supposed to be this close to the Nile—we're supposed to be going the other way. Recall *The Wizard of Oz* and you'll realize how off-course one can be blown. Since you can't control the balloon's direction, we go with the flow, and on this fine morning sail right across the river, which is beautiful and glassy, like a shiny ribbon. It is made even more lovely by the reflection of the many balloons in its waters as other baskets join our drifting revolution.

Now we are over Luxor's St. George hotel. We sail over the city's roofs—even some more rooftop goats. How they got up six stories is something of a question, but surely they can get down the same way. Further and further we sail, until we are once again in green fields, east of downtown. Now the captain's voice is urgent and he sounds less certain—as we are safely past the tops of the buildings, he must land the balloon in one of these fields.

Little boys wearing their school uniforms wave and shout up at us. I don't understand what they are saying, but I suspect it is something like, "No—don't land here! This is Daddy's field!" but it could as easily be, "Welcome to Munchkinland!" The captain calls to us to take our landing positions. Crouching as instructed, I can no longer see over the side of the basket, but there is a hole at my eye level in the thick rattan weave. I peer out and watch the field as it rises to meet us. The captain is shouting in rapid Arabic to his small crew—they are both excited and determined; this little band of travelers will not be the ones to break their accident-free record.

We crouch for over a minute, and I glance at Mother and Eleanor on either side of me. Eleanor is wide-eyed, alert, but Judith's eyes are squinched up tight. I nudge her in the ribs and she giggles. My legs are starting to complain when the peephole fills with the rushing green of alfalfa and we begin bouncing along the ground. Two, three, four big bounces, and a good deal of dragging in between; this is one crop that will likely never see harvest. Then all is quiet for a moment, and the parachute-like folds of the balloon settle toward the ground.

The captain gives us the OK so we stand up, not even really shaken, as the landing position has braced us thoroughly. We climb out into the verdant field, happily greeted by the young boys, whom I suspect are thrilled to be late for school. The farmer makes his way out onto the field. I ask later, and am told he is paid for his damaged crop and the inconvenience of having a house-sized basket land on him. We walk out of the field on a mud ridge, right past a scarecrow. I look around, hoping for a Tin Man or a Cowardly Lion but instead, at the end of the row is a dirt road where our transportation already awaits us.

The vans take us back to the dock, where a water taxi ferries us to our boat. By 8:30am, we are all attacking a huge breakfast of omelets, sausage, falafel, and fuul, the omnipresent fava beans. The talk is all about the balloon landing and what might have happened if the captain hadn't been on the ball. Everyone is enormously pleased with themselves; having cheated tragedy is one thing, but having glided right past it is cause for celebration.

*   *   *   *   *

After breakfast, we enter the Valley of the Kings, home to many tombs of Egyptian pharaohs, most notably Tut Ankh Amun. His tomb now costs extra to get into but ironically is the least interesting, as almost all his artifacts now live in the Egyptian Museum or spend time touring the world. Nefertari lies here in the neighboring Valley of the Queens, and I have been lucky enough to be in her tomb. Nefertari should not be confused with Nefertiti, who was considered the most beautiful woman in the world and was Great Royal Wife (chief consort) of Pharaoh Akhenaton. Nefertari was Great Royal Wife to Ramses I. He seems truly to have loved her, if you believe the poem on her tomb wall attributed to him:

My love is unique—no one can rival her,
for she is the most beautiful woman alive.
Just by passing,
she has stolen away my heart.

The Valley's tombs are one of the few places where you can see the original wall color, a hugely popular feature. Nefertari's tomb is not often open to visitors because our very breath decays the gorgeous paints of ground lapis, carnelian and jade that make the walls so vibrant. No photographs are permitted; these days cameras are surrendered to security at the front of the Valley.

The whole Valley is a well-organized museum for the tombs that have been found, but more importantly, it's a permanent excavation site, continually turning out more treasures and information about the lost past. On a budget that would pay for a mid-range secretary in the United States, the Theban Mapping Project hires a whole team of locals, at double the going rate, to assist in excavating the tombs as they discover them. Kent Weeks, who has been the director of the project for many years, is responsible for everything from the 3-D acrylic model of the whole Valley, showing the descending passages into the tombs, to the new visitors' center which houses it, to the trams that take people up from the parking lot—now outfitted with batteries, since the rumble of the engines had the unfortunate side effect of caving in the tomb excavations.

It is through the Theban Mapping Project that a comprehensive map of the Valleys of the Kings and Queens, formerly known as Thebes, is finally taking shape, and that several newly discovered tombs are being excavated. Dr. Weeks estimates that possibly twenty percent of the tombs have been uncovered, which is mind-boggling when you see the Valley—it means that nearly every cave opening all the way up into the hills is probably a burial chamber of some sort. Not that much of a surprise when I start to think about it—look how tombstones quickly crowd a cemetery, and those are areas with only a few hundred years of dead people. If I had an extra fifty grand lying around annually, I would happily double the budget of the Theban Mapping Project.

On our earliest trip, we see Seti I's tomb, full of amazing color, then we enter the tomb of Ramses II. Shakky wants us to be able to meditate inside, so he simply kicks out all the other tourists. He bribes the guard, of course, and tells the waiting guides that the tomb is closed for twenty minutes, due to some concern about air quality. Then he starts shouting into the long mouth of the tomb, "Out, out! Closed! The tomb's closed!" His voice, reverberating and amplified, carries deep into the tomb's main chamber. Then when the touristses don't move fast enough, Shakky reaches along the tunnel wall and shuts off all the lights for a few seconds; when they go back on, the people scatter like roaches scuttling out to avoid fumigation. Not really fair, but terrific for our group. I vow to try to be less selfish in my next lifetime, presuming I have one.

After The Magician clears the tomb, he rushes us all in, past the glorious painted walls and down into the tomb. We arrange ourselves around the black granite sarcophagus. You can tell what Ramses thought of himself by its sheer size. Designed to hold graduated mummy cases (think Russian stacking dolls lying on their backs) it still doesn't explain the vast mass of rock Ramses wanted to be buried in. But from what we see of his ego elsewhere, I'm sure logic was not his gating factor. (You've got to make a fairly big statement in life for a corporation to decide, thousands of years later, to name a condom after you.)

Once we are seated, he yells up to the guard to shut off all the lights again. We sit there, in the pitchest of pitch black, oming and breathing for about ten minutes. It is kind of fabulous, as long as I don't open my eyes, but when I do I realize it is equally dark no matter which position my eyelids are in.

I'm new to mediation and my mind tends to drift, which I understand is fairly typical of the Western brain. Deep Breath in, Deep Breath out. Deep Breath in, Deep Breath out. *Wonder what we're having for lunch? What was the name of that god again? Uh-oh. I'm not meditating, I'm thinking.* Deep Breath in, Deep Breath out... etc. In the middle of this ping-pong process that I pass off as a meditation practice, I suddenly remember the terrifying end of a movie I saw when I was a child.

My dad and I would curl up together almost every weekend to watch the old movies he grew up on. This film was called *Land of the Pharaohs*, and it starred a young and fabulously glamorous Joan Collins as a real bitch-kitty of a queen named Nellifer—surely some studio head's idea of a ridiculous "Egyptian-glam" name that would appeal to a '50s audience. Nellifer plots to take over the kingdom by killing her husband and succeeds. She is about to triumphantly savor the victor's spoils, as soon as she finishes this pesky burial procession and Pharaoh is interred in his tomb. Nellifer leads the long funerary line of priests and slaves inside, and gives the order for the tomb to be sealed forever. The priests hit the stones, the doors grind closed and the sand starts to pour in. Nellifer realizes she has been tricked and is trapped inside, and the head priest tells her this is the price for her treachery. As I recall, she asks him if he, too, is not terrified to die, but he points out that all these other men happily give their lives to go with their beloved Pharaoh to the afterlife, whereas evil Nellifer is freaking out and trying desperately to get out. The men stand there implacable, stoic, and she runs around screaming to all the sealed exits, tearing at her bosom while the sand piles higher and higher. Roll credits.

In the middle of my meditation—which now sounds more like, Shallow Panting Breath in, Shallow Panting Breath out—I am thinking about this scene, and this tomb, and the black that just goes on forever. I open my eyes to see… nothing. I fight down my panicky feelings, trapped inside this tomb, trapped for all eternity, not being me, not being anything any more. I am scared, angry, and I have this tremendous petulant child's voice inside my head screaming, "Not fair, not fair!!" I know Ramses' sarcophagus is right there near me, and I want to reach out to touch it—it's solid and cool, and I hope this will help. So I stand up in the middle of the group, but then I realize I can't see to reach it because it is that black. Is this what eternity will be like? Standing stock still in the middle of a room trying not to trip over anyone? Oh, no, wait—that's if I'm still me. But I won't be. I will be like the immobile stone itself, and Halle will be gone forever. *Not fair, NOT FAIR!!!*

I am so panicked I want to scream, and this meditation, which is about ten minutes long, feels like freaking eternity. I suck in a deep, shuddering breath, and some of the electric tension goes out of my limbs. I have to calm myself, to reason with whatever rational bits I can command. If I am going to spend all eternity as "not me" it will at least be peaceful. There's a tranquility in the tomb of Ramses, and a coolness. I slow my breathing down, until the panting, wet dog sensation is gone. I have almost gotten a handle on it when the lights come on again and it's time to head out.

I walk up the long ramp to the surface slowly, breathing evenly, and say nothing to anyone of the incident. Greg and Lyra smile at me as they pass, chattering about the drawings on a tomb wall. Judith touches my hand as she walks by, but she's in conversation with Vivian about her experience in the mosque, and neither notices my discomfort. No one can help me, not really.   This is my most private fear, and I am too ashamed to speak of it.

When the conversation on the ship turns to our experiences in Ramses' tomb, I laugh along with the rest as Greg mimics Shakky, "The tomb's closed! Everybody out!"

HOT CHICKEN SOUP

Greg likes to learn to curse in whatever language he can get someone to teach him. He's shooting for sixteen languages, and so far he knows at least twelve. Cursing in Arabic is definitely his favorite. For example, the translation of one of the best American curses ever: "Fuck you and the horse you rode in on," in Arabic becomes: "Fuck you, and your camel." He has also gotten a ton of mileage out of "ibdn mitnaki," which is roughly the Arab equivalent of "motherfucker." No Egyptian who ever heard Greg use this phrase has failed to laugh and clap him on the shoulder, almost as if proud of him for bothering to learn how to insult them. I initially learned it wrong—I thought it was "ibdn mc-nacki." Momo cracked up when he heard me pronounce it. "It sounds like a person," he said, laughing so hard he collapsed into his office chair. "Mr. McNacki, Mrs. McNacki, and all the little McNackis!" I coldly informed Momo he was acting like Mr. McNacki, but he just held his belly and roared.

One afternoon on the cruise ship, after we had all known each other for years, I was napping in our room when Greg came in, obviously uncomfortable, and sheepishly sat on the end of the bed. "Are you awake?"

"I am now."

"Shakky grabbed me," he said.

"What do you mean?" I asked, still sleepy.

"I mean he grabbed me. He grabbed my crotch."

"What on earth did he do that for?" I asked, still a little skeptical but now fully awake.

"I don't know," Greg said, "but it seems like it's an Egyptian thing. Maybe men 'crotch shake' each other here. He grabbed me, and then he said, 'Oh, it's so big!' and then he slapped his hands together and giggled, you know the way he does."

I did indeed. I shrugged. "Okay, no big deal, I guess."

At mealtimes, Greg and I often sit at the ship's crew table with the Quest personnel. As we came over, Shakky looked really happy to see me. "Wow," he said. "You are a lucky woman!" I looked at him quizzically.

"Because of the Greg," he continued.

"Because of Greg," I agreed.

"No," he corrected me. "Because of THE Greg." He made a clarifying hand gesture.

"Ah," I tell him, catching on. "The Greg."

"Yes," Shakky agrees. "When I go out of town, I tell my wife I am leaving 'my thing' at home with her. I tell her I leave my thing on top of the refrigerator, so she will know where it is, and she can have it any time she likes." Greg and I are both laughing by this time. "Now, when I leave, I am leaving her 'The Greg' on top of the refrigerator. She will want that even more." He is cackling wildly, and we can't help but join him. Like any good disease, Shakky can be infectious.

That afternoon in the Valley of the Kings, Shakky leaves the group for a moment and calls to Greg. "Dredj, come here! There is someone I want you to meet."

I watch as Greg ambles over, dressed almost identically to the Valley guard standing next to Shakky. The guard nods. "Masa al khir," Greg greets him ("Afternoon the good"). Shakky speaks briefly with the guard in Arabic, gesturing at Greg. The guard's hand darts forward and he grabs Greg's crotch. Greg recoils, shocked, and then reaches out and smacks Shakky hard on the shoulder. "Ibdn mitnaki!" he reprimands Shakky. Shakky, who all of a sudden seems six years old, stares at Greg for a second, and then he and the guard absolutely split their sides laughing. Apparently grabbing a tourist's picnic basket happens about as often as that same tourist cursing you out in Arabic.

After that, it becomes almost a ritual, with Shakky parading his protégé around while they perform their vaudeville routine for the unsuspecting guards. The Magician tells the guard about The Greg in Arabic and invites him to check out the goods, the guard grabs Greg's crotch, Greg yells, "ibdn mitnaki!" and whacks Shakky, then everyone laughs as if it's the highlight of their week, which it probably is. This gets so popular it begins to substitute for the baksheesh Shakky would otherwise have to hand out, so Shakky is extra-pleased. By the time we reach the temple at Medinat Habu, Greg's reputation has preceded him. The guard greets Shakky, and then turns to Greg and says, in English, "The Greg!" as he surreptitiously grabs a handful. Then he turns to me and says, "Oh, lucky! Ramses Two!"

To commemorate this running joke of theirs, Shakky eventually gives Greg a small black statue of a god with an erection almost as long as the statue is tall. The little man has only one arm and one leg, but his giant phallus is intact. This is the god Min, who was once merely an old man left in charge of a village when the other men were off fighting. However, when they returned, every woman was pregnant. So they cut off his arm and leg to punish him, but not his penis, which *seems* the logical choice. Eventually he was deified, and now looks like he shouldn't be able to stand up, what with the one leg and the counterbalance. It makes for interesting conversation when people come across the statue at home in our living room.

*   *   *   *   *

After the tombs of the Valley of the Kings, we head to Hatshepsut Temple over the hill. Hatshepsut was an unusual Pharaoh. Though her reign was long, peaceful, and rich, and she oversaw a lot of growth and building, what distinguishes her from other Pharaohs is that she ruled as a man—a king not a queen, thousands of years before the likes of Bodicea or Elizabeth I. She must have been fairly power hungry because when her husband, Thutmose II, died and her son became king, she ruled as regent only a short while before deciding that she should be Pharaoh in name as well as in fact. Since she was often depicted with the beard and forelock of a man, historians scratched their heads wondering why her name was erased, especially from the famous (and otherwise fairly comprehensive) Wall of Kings at the Temple of Seti I, until they figured out that she was a woman. I suppose later generations of priests didn't care for the whole disguise, angry that a woman would have been supreme ruler of the land, but now she exists as an enigma, a preeminent example of what one woman is capable of in a man's world.

These days, the only thing we have a hard time with is her name. Sen tells us that it's easy to pronounce: you say "hot chicken soup" really fast. It is enough of a mnemonic that people begin to remember her name.

Hatshepsut Temple is set into the mountain behind it. To the right of the structure, you can glimpse a thin white road that leads all the way up over the mountain and directly into the Valley of the Kings. Though I have never seen a person traverse it, the way looks quite intriguing, and I imagine a young boy or a priest leaving this temple, walking the road for an hour or more, and arriving at the burial places of so many pharaohs. On a recent trip to the Valley of the Kings, an ambitious Galabeya Boy talked a whole family into climbing the other side of that ribbon of road, all the way to the top where they could see down into the Hatshepsut complex. Despite the fact that it made our entire group over a half-hour late, I was proud of the "bad kids" choosing to see what was at the top of the mountain, and I am inspired to sneak off sometime to see it for myself.

Recently, Shakky told us a heartbreaking story about a guard at the Temple of Hatshepsut on duty the day over seventy people were massacred, in a rare attack on visitors to Egypt. The gunmen were Egyptian, they were in the middle of their desperate act of violence, and one of them confronted this particular guard, who was protecting a Japanese woman. The sniper yelled, "Get out of the way, I don't want to shoot you, you're my brother!" But the guard refused to move, and eventually, the terrorist opened fire on both the Japanese visitor and the guard. At the last second, the guard rolled his body over the woman's to try to shield her, taking the full force of the bullets in his arm. He is still a guard in the Valley of the Kings; after telling us this story, Shakky introduced us to him. That guard is the only one-armed worker in the Valley of the Kings, and he saved the Japanese woman's life; terrible bravery in the face of misguided cowardice.

From the parking lot, we take a little electric train to the base of the long staircase. Then we walk up fifty or more steps to the main entrance of the temple. It's no longer than the walk at some of the other sites, but you can see the temple from the parking lot, almost all on a single level, so it seems farther away. This is a good solution for the touristses who are often not given much time there; but for me, the little train is simply incongruous in the Valley of the Kings—the Disneyfication of a solemn burial ground. I suspect more than one Pharaoh would raise his (or her) eyebrows at the changes made to all the temples.

Hatshepsut's Mortuary Temple, as it is called, is beautiful. It has a lengthy set of wide stone staircases leading up to it—possibly a hundred shallow steps up to the top—with the temple way at the back, set into and almost carved out of the mountain. We go in the middle of the day, when it is quite hot and fairly crowded, and walk around the front of the complex. There's a beautiful little courtyard dedicated to the goddess Hathor on the left side. On the right is the small area where the massacre took place. I've seen the site since. There's actually a bloodstain more than ten years later. When it was new, we weren't able to go into that part of the temple, but we did a prayer circle there for all the people who died and were wounded, as we now do each time we go.

I have only been inside the actual temple on one occasion, as there have always been other diversions for me: the outdoor café with its unusual souvenirs and five-dollar Cokes—at twenty-five Egyptian pounds, the most expensive local soda ever; the location of the massacre; the temple to Hathor on the left side of the main building, each column ending in the goddess' features —her sweet, heart-shaped face, sharp nose and cow-like ears turned in each of the four directions.

On the way out, exhausted from all the walking and confused as to which of the dozens of tour buses is ours, the vendors pounce. At Hatshepsut, they are ruthless, determined that you buy your souvenirs only from them, and, though that can mean bargains, it sometimes seems to mean bargaining without end.

Inevitably, we end up with three or four guys crowded around the front door to the bus, holding up their carved soapstone cats and their wide cotton scarves, calling to us that they have the cheapest price, that this is real alabaster, or, my favorite: "My mother made this scarf. And it's my last one!"

Eventually, Shakky the hawk ambles off the coach and steps amongst them. If he feels something is worth buying, he brings it into the bus and offers it to the group, somewhere south of forty percent of what they were originally asking. If it's postcards or bookmarks, which we can get anywhere, he will shrug and say, "For mercy!" In other words, we—and our wallets—might take pity on them and get these items. To be perfectly honest, I have often seen the best bargains here, and the vendors may collect a hundred dollars or more, because the prices are so much lower than what we have been hearing everywhere else. It's hard to resist another beautiful scarf, another carved statue. So we buy, we buy, and we buy some more. For mercy.

MY NAME IS
OZYMANDIAS

The Colossi of Memnon always seemed stuck out in the middle of nowhere, sitting by their lonesome on a length of deserted road, with only a dusty tourist shop to keep them company. The towering, man-shaped statues were originally built to guard the mortuary temple of Amenhotep III, and are both sculpted in his likeness. For centuries, they are all that remained of this enormous center, reputed to be bigger than Karnak, which currently holds the title of the largest temple complex in the world.

You can see them from quite a distance away, because they are huge—measuring sixty feet in height—and are surrounded by flat desert. But that's about to change. El-Colossat, as the locals call them, are now known to stand at the front entrance to a temple similar to Abu Simbel in the South. The ruins behind the massive statues were recently uncovered and now, when you are up in a hot air balloon, you can see the full extent of the dig site and the crumbled structures they are excavating. Sadly, they keep them as covered up as possible, to ensure that no one can take pictures and spoil the Antiquities Office's rights to this magnificent find. Later, they will sell the rights to the pictures and then we will finally get to see what lies beneath the tarps. When I heard the news of the dig, I thought, *Well, of course!*

Anyone can see the Colossi look exactly like the ones at Abu Simbel or at Luxor Temple, guarding the complex... Yet I didn't see it, and neither did anyone else.

It's a minor miracle that the Colossi manage to remain standing when the rest of the buildings behind them are completely gone. An earthquake in 27 BCE broke a Colossi statue in half, but in the second century CE it was reassembled. Over the next fifteen to thirty years, Egyptologists will finish digging up the remains of the temples and lucky travelers will be able to visit the site during restoration. Then Egypt will add another magnificent jewel to its priceless collection.

For now, the Colossi are the kind of attraction where you halt the bus, get out, snap a picture, and get back on. There is nothing other than the two statues, but ever since Ancient Rome, tourists have made this a must-see stop on their itinerary. During the part of their tenure when the statue was broken, it was reputed to whistle or sing—as does one of the Colossi at Abu Simbel—and it was said to be good luck for travelers who heard it. But joining the two halves, courtesy of a well-meaning king bent on restoration, put a stop to the singing; now the only excuse to visit them is that they sure are big.

Once, Greg took a small group to Egypt on his own, rooming with a dear friend of ours, a unique individual called Largo—a graphics designer who had created iconic album covers and posters for movie studios and musicians. He was now living the life of his dreams up in the Hollywood Hills with his wife, children, and a garage full of antique cars. Largo had come to Egypt because he was inexplicably pulled to it ever since he was a boy. Egypt is experienced according to each person's sensitivities, and people on our trips often come for spiritual work, not an ordinary vacation. In the context of our mundane daily lives, this can create a dichotomy that is hard for some people to handle. These days we are careful to help people with "reentry" to ease their way, but there can be exceptions. Largo was more affected by Egypt than anyone we ever took before or since, and his personal experiences were so powerful they entirely overwhelmed him. When Greg initially returned from Egypt, without the benefit of re-entry assistance, he sank into a deep depression, yet it paled in comparison to what Largo went through.

Their first morning at the Mena House, Greg came out of the shower to find Largo getting dressed in the dark. Since it was already midmorning, Greg walked over and opened the curtains to the room. As the light flooded in, Largo screamed, "My eyes, my eyes!" and promptly fell on the bed, clutching at his face. He told Greg afterwards that the light in Egypt was so specific that the moment he beheld it he remembered another lifetime as a sculptor to Akhenaton, working on a magnificent statue. He hit some sort of fissure in the rock and it exploded in his face, throwing bits of stone into his eyes and blinding him.

This was the beginning of Largo's strange and unusual voyage in Egypt. He was constantly going up to the locals, handing them his business card, and saying, "I love you! You are my friend. You will come to America and stay in my home." The Egyptians are incredibly friendly and tolerant of travelers, but even they were baffled by Largo's quirky behavior.

At the Colossi of Memnon, the little group got off the bus and Largo went straight for the statues, as if to have his picture taken with them. You can't get that close, of course, because they are roped off, but it's not a problem for tourists since they are so large. Even with fifty other people milling around (and there usually are), it's easy to get a shot of just you and a Colossus. But Largo didn't seem to notice—or maybe care— that the statues were off-limits. He ran over, jumped the flimsy rope, and began to scale a Colossus.

Shakky may be a bad kid, he may enjoy doing all sorts of illegal things, but this does not include potentially desecrating an important monument. He yelled, "Get him off there! Dredj, get him off!" Greg and Shakky raced to the bottom of the statue, and each of them grabbed one of Largo's legs and pulled him from the Colossi. Then everyone re-boarded the bus. Ever since, when we visit the Colossi of Memnon, I am always on the lookout for impassioned guests from our intrepid band of pilgrims who might try—should I be foolish enough to look the other way—to climb a monument.

There is an evocative Shelley poem about the statue of a great king:

And on the pedestal these words appear:
My name is Ozymandias, king of kings.
Look on my works ye Mighty, and despair!

The irony of the poem is that the pedestal and the feet of the statue are all that remain, and it sits in a barren desert—the rest of the statue and the king's other constructions are gone, carried off by time or later generations. Shelley's inspiration for Ozymandias was perhaps the impending arrival in England of an actual Colossus, that of Ramses II, which the British Museum obtained in 1816 from Giovanni Belzoni—he of the tomb-raiding and adventuring. Shelley's poem comes to mind every time we see the Colossi, though it is possible that, looking at the great temple being brought forth again from the sand, all they had to do was dig to find the remains of the once mighty king.

*   *   *   *   *

The last thing we visit in the Valley is one of the dozens of alabaster factories. The Valley contains deep cores of alabaster, and the Egyptians here live with their houses built partly into the hills, so it makes sense that they would discover the alabaster and then create things from it. The quality varies from cheap imports to the most exquisite hand-turned pieces. Alabaster is soft, so it crumbles easily and can be hard to sculpt, but when a lovely thin piece is held up to the light, it is a translucent, ochre-veined art—God extracted by man.

All alabaster used to be authentic and worked by hand. Then someone figured out that soapstone—cheaper, easier to carve, and heavier than alabaster—looked quite similar (until you held it up to the light). So now pieces are available that claim to be alabaster, but are its lumpier, machine-made cousin. Then the Chinese came in, offering to make some of the more popular items for even less money than the Egyptians. They created a plastic that looks like an indelicate alabaster, reminding me of a streaked creamsicle. Since it's plastic, it appears somewhat translucent, which satisfies a few touristses. If you look at many of the cheaper souvenir items from Egypt these days, you will see the "made in China" stamp, which has led some craftsmen in Egypt to start using a "made in Egypt" stamp to compensate for their often higher prices. It's no different than coming all the way to California to visit Disneyland, only to find that everything there is made in Asia.

It's a whole socio-economic goldfish bowl here in the Middle East, topped off by the icing on this strange confluence cake: the Chinese invention of white plastic "alabaster"—which was less popular until someone realized it glows in the dark. Now there is a whole section in each shop, devoted to black light and these green, glowing, ethereal-looking statues of the Sphinx, some generic pharaoh, or an elongated Egyptian cat. The irony is that these cheap plastic knockoffs have acquired their own cachet, and often command prices almost as high as the alabaster they sought to impersonate.

Two men sit in the outer courtyard of the alabaster factory, offering demonstrations of the grinding and polishing processes. Around the corner stand bags of rice and other staples, an open oven, and about a dozen pigeons who also make their home there, nesting in little paper alcoves. The cramped area is littered with pigeon droppings and tiny feathers; though it is obviously part of the kitchen, the symbiotic relationship of the family and the birds is long established.

The showroom is big and clean, the wares arranged into various sections on tidy shelves. A large table is set up, behind which the owner holds court and shows off some of his largest pieces. The prices are amazingly low; about a fifth of what you might pay in the States (unless of course you're in the market for some glow-in-the-dark plastic). We had guests on one tour who bought a large, beautiful round vase, and then packed it in their shipped luggage. Though wrapped in bubble wrap, by the time they got home it was smashed into little pieces. The following year, I hand-carried another vase home on the plane for them, holding it in my lap for most of the journey, as if it were an infant. The pieces are so stunning, it's worth it.

Perhaps because he is eager to interact with the locals, they love Greg. In five minutes, they'll be offering him cigarettes or showing him pictures of their children. However, he seems to get recruited into some nefarious schemes. One trip, a man Greg never saw before singles him out and invites him for a "special tour" of the caves near the alabaster factory. Greg loves to make friends with Egyptians, on whom he can try his smattering of Arabic (inevitably, this will include a chance to show off his cursing skills) so of course he leaps at the opportunity. Within a few minutes, Greg is at the mouth of a tomb. Like many of the locals, this Egyptian and his family are living in the caves that are the natural tomb entrances. A kind of integrated grave robber, they can explore the tombs whenever they like, bringing up artifacts when they run across them.

"Look, look," the man tells Greg, bringing out a large stone scarab that he explains was buried in the tomb. The rules about Egyptian antiquities are spelled out in small letters these days, after centuries of French, English, and other countries' enterprising plunder. Greg knows it, the man knows it. Heedless, the Egyptian plunges on.

"I many bebes," he says, holding his hand down at hip level to be certain Greg understands his broken English. "Bebes need shoes!" he explains to Greg. He will sell him this special antiquity for only seventy-five U.S. dollars, which would keep several Egyptian children in shoes for years.

"Only please, you must not tell Shakky!" Greg narrows his eyes and waits, eager to get his hands on the palm-sized scarab. "Shakky will tell the police, and—" The man silently draws his finger across his throat, his eyes bulging.

Greg speaks in broken English as well. He has a habit of modeling the locals that drives me crazy but seems to endear him to them.

"I take," he says, pocketing the scarab in his galabeya. "I bring to my wife. My wife sees." He points at his eyes and then pats his pocket.

The man nods, his finger to his lips.

Returning to the showroom, Greg comes right over, hovering as I negotiate with the owner on behalf of some of our guests. He drags me off by the elbow as soon as he can, and unwraps the "antique" scarab, which is clearly elderly and dirt-encrusted, holding it out for me.

"What do you think? They told me not to show Shakky."

I had been considering whether this was authentic, right up until I heard that sentence. "Go show Shakky. Now."

Shakky is drinking tea and entertaining some of the locals at their own expense. I motion him over. When Greg shows him the scarab, The Magician turns it over and shrugs. Then he takes his thumbnail and scrapes off a little of the dirt. As he scratches harder, some paint comes off the bottom, revealing that the scarab is nothing more than painted plaster left to "age" in the Egyptian earth.

"Take it. Give him—" he makes a swooping gesture with his hand—"Nothing! Give him nothing!" He laughs, and so do we, relieved that we didn't get hornswoggled. Greg wraps up the scarab again.

On our way out to the coach, the men line up outside to see us off, waving and solicitous, as the group has bought a lot of wonderful pieces and spent a lot of wonderful money. When Greg passes the man who lives in the cave, he motions in a sort of underhand wave to Greg, reminding him of his "bebes," his hands at his hip. Greg smiles over at the man, then, as he gets close enough, hisses under his breath, "Kiss Imak! Ibdn mitnaki!" The look on the man's face, the sharp intake of breath, and the round O of his mouth are priceless. We laugh all the way to the bus, knowing he will pull the same crap on the next visitor, but happy we managed to win this round

.

EGYPTIAN PROM

Luxor Temple is visible from the Nile; as your ship sails in and parks along the Corniche with all the other cruise ships, you can see the spires of the obelisk and the mosque (both on the temple grounds), the massive outer walls and the Colossi at the front of the main temple. If you are lucky your boat sails down to the other end of the Corniche, where you can spy the roofless columns of Luxor Temple's soaring central hall as you float past the enormous structure in the distance.

We always visit Luxor Temple at night. We try to go as late as possible; the site is open until 9pm, so we have dinner and then head over, arriving at 8:15pm. This means fewer touristses, who dwindle as it gets closer to closing time. Our goal is to outlast them all and have the temple to ourselves.

Entering from the Nile side, we go through a surprisingly rigorous security check, where they actually look in your bag and send you through a scanner. The temple appears in front of us, its footlights elevating the scene to a theatrical display. To our left is the Avenue of the Sphinxes. A two-mile long walkway that for thousands of years was almost wholly underground, it connects Luxor Temple to the Temple of Karnak farther north. Because this avenue is now almost fully excavated, and stretches out on either side of the main walkway all the way to the old entrance, we can see the entire line of Sphinx statues on their pedestals. Each of these is a ram's head on a lion's body, about six feet long. Underneath each ram's head is a miniature pharaoh, as if the sphinx is protecting the king.

Illuminated like this, the walkway is striking, though never more so than the time we held a private dinner on the grounds of Luxor Temple. We had a large group that trip—nearly seventy-five people—and though there are advantages to traveling with a smaller tour, a group of this size receives special treatment. Mohamed, in his role as Surgeon, arranged a magnificent five-course dinner, catered by the deluxe Sonesta St. George hotel down the road. The private dinner was held after the temple has closed, so we didn't eat until 10pm.

The evening kicks off with a carriage ride from the boat: two people to an open, horse-drawn coach, the roof folded convertible-style. Greg and I, dressed in our richest galabeyas, walk the Luxor Corniche past nearly forty carriages full of the smiling faces of our guests, until we reach our own. As the groups tend to go native after a few days in Egypt, and even the men like to buy a galabeya to wear to dinner and to the temples, almost everyone is dressed in colorful Egyptian finery. I feel like we're the king and queen of Egyptian prom when we pull up in front, with everyone standing around cheering as each couple gets out of their private conveyance.

We walk into the old entrance—the only time I have had the privilege—and descend the steps to the Avenue of the Sphinxes. Young girls in Egyptian costume and full makeup wait on each step, and boys dressed in pharaonic garb, carrying lit torches, flank each sphinx. When we reach the main square in front of the temple, waiters and waitresses costumed as priests and priestesses offer us trays of colorful fruit drinks while we mill around in front of the obelisk and the Colossi, two forty-foot high statues of Ramses II. I suddenly notice that the obelisk is shifted slightly to the left, off by mere degrees from a right angle. As I wonder if this is a trick of my eye, or caused by an old earth movement, I see that the angle of the obelisk exactly follows the line of the building entrance—to what purpose I can only imagine, but it is clearly deliberate.

The Temple of Luxor is enormous and ingenious; a gentleman named Schwaller de Lubicz spent over fifteen years studying it and dissecting its nuances. Before de Lubicz's work, people thought the temple was a slightly sloppy expression of the period: the line I noticed at the top of the obelisk, a statue's foot stepping forward but a matching statue standing with its feet together, the angle of a building changing in the middle—all seemed to point to carelessness. What de Lubicz discovered was that everything at Luxor, down to the last quarter-inch of the workmanship, was deliberately created. For example, the statue where the king's legs are together is showing the pharaoh after he has died, whereas the walking pose indicates the live—or activated—pharaoh. De Lubicz also postulated that the temples of Egypt are built according to the body of man; his definitive works are the *Temple of Man*, and the *Temple in Man*. Considered somewhat heretical in the more traditional scholarly approach to Egypt, De Lubicz has been embraced by most esoteric authors as either furthering their work or as a stepping stone to build upon.

Perhaps not surprisingly, Luxor Temple was often used for other purposes in its long history. Right inside the main complex is Abu el-Haggag mosque, built on the grounds in the thirteenth century CE. At that time, Luxor was buried in sand. When the sand was eventually excavated, the mosque door was left in place, over two stories in the air. David Roberts, the famous illustrator who visited Egypt extensively during the nineteenth century, painted Luxor Temple. If you've ever seen any old watercolors of Egypt, you have more than likely seen Roberts' work. In his day, Luxor was swallowed by sand up to the necks of the Colossi guarding the front. Roberts' watercolor clearly shows the mosque, its door at what was then ground level.

Further along is a relatively new discovery. Through the main hall of columns and towards the sanctuary there is a roofless courtyard, once an interior room of the main structure. While cleaning a wall a couple of years ago, the Egyptians uncovered several frescoes of Roman noblemen painted to look like saints, part of a Roman church inside Luxor Temple nearly two thousand years after it was built.

A favorite statue of mine sits in the main hall beyond the first courtyard. While it has somewhat crumbled over time, it is of the youthful rulers Tut Ankh Amun, of King Tut fame, and his wife Ankh Sen Amun, though poor Ankh Sen's nose was utterly gouged out by someone who either didn't appreciate art or else needed a wedge for something he was building. When you walk around to the rear of the statue, you can see Tut Ankh Amun's bride with her arm around his waist; she is being depicted as both his wife and as a goddess protecting the king. This is typical of Egyptian art, which works on multiple levels concurrently, some of which are surely still unknown to us.

The main hall of columns is a stellar example of the monumental engineering that produced these structures. Sixty-four papyrus-topped columns ring the large square, leading to a hypostyle hall: thirty-two columns grouped together in four rows of eight. This special night, I walk ahead of the others, who are still being toured around by Shakky and Sen. I stand alone in this enormous space, taking it all in and preparing for the group to join me. When they are all finally here, gathered in a square instead of a circle in homage to this ancient hall, I sing a sacred melody. I always sing in the temples, as a way to awaken the energy of the space, but I rarely get to really vocalize at Luxor because of the other visitors, so this is a true gift for me.

The best place to sing in any temple is the Holy of Holies— the sanctuary—but the one at Luxor Temple is usually ignored. Though it contains an altar stone, of all the temples, it is the most trafficked and therefore the least potent; since the sanctuary is open on both ends, people are constantly walking through, perhaps mistaking it for another passage. When I go to the sanctuary I close my eyes and begin to meditate and tone. Within a minute, I can clear the space of the chattering tour guides perambulating their couples or small groups. The only ones who remain are those who want to listen to the resonance, echoing off the chamber walls of the Holy of Holies and carrying out into the next courtyard.

Also unlike most other temples, Luxor has had additional construction in later centuries, and the rear of the temple is now a warren of buildings and walls. In front of the sanctuary, there is only a single room, its front wall directly blocking the line of the doorway. So when I stand at the center of the Holy of Holies and project my voice, it's the only sanctuary from which I cannot be heard all the way to the outer courtyard. Ironically, as the song builds tonight in the hypostyle hall, I realize that the acoustics of this big courtyard, open to the night sky above us, aren't conductive either and the song is still being swallowed. I finish as best I can, and then the whole group strolls out towards the front entrance of the compound to begin our dinner; we have the whole temple to ourselves. I imagine being here thousands of years ago as part of some sacred ceremony, our clothes rich and fine, the power of the day and the moment working on us until we are all half in trance, consumed with the presence of the god we have come to worship.

I enjoy the light playing on the columns, though the juxtaposed McDonald's sign visible between two pillars reminds me what century I am in. As we reach the front entrance, a swarm of bats, part of a colony that lives under the eaves on the side of the mosque, flies past us and alights in their roost, hanging upside down and snuggling together for a nap. Once I was treated to the company of a small white owl, who flew wherever I was and perched a hundred feet up on a column, hooting down at me before taking off and soaring silent to the next spot, often exactly where I was intending to go. The delightful creature was no more than a foot tall, the only owl I have ever seen in Egypt.

On the outer grounds near the main entrance, the view of the lit temple full and unobstructed, the Sonesta staff has transformed bare dirt into a magical feast house with a sky roof. Everyone is babbling to each other, overwhelmed with the food, the presentation, the sheer audacity of the meal being created for us in an empty corner of this millennias-old temple. Greg holds a chair out for me. "My lady?" I sit, staring in awe at the table laid out before us. I think how incredible this evening has been, and we haven't even eaten yet!

We dine on gold and silver, Persian rugs under our feet. The group is treated to five courses of the best European-style food, served exquisitely by waiters who could easily work at a fancy Parisian hotel. The pastry chefs charm us with things that are rouched and truffled, and the cooks have set up a full kitchen behind the wall hangings to cook filet mignon, lamb, chicken, and fish to perfection.

When it's time for dessert, torches are lit anew; a large cake is borne out on the shoulders of costumed Egyptian men and presented to the tour leaders, who make lovely speeches. Then Mohamed stands, his dark Armani suit impeccable, his red tie contrasting nicely with his white shirt and the olive of his skin.

"My fellow Americans," he begins, laughing as we all join him. "I am so grateful to all of you for being here tonight, for making Egypt a truly magical place for all of us." I glance around the silk carpet walls at the smiling staff gathered in the makeshift kitchen, probably more of them than of us. "We are honored you have chosen to visit, we are so happy to have you in our delightful country!" He is grinning now, in his element, as he weaves a preview of the adventure that still awaits. No matter what the Surgeon does for us, it seems he will always create something more to top it.

Greg and I share a secret smile. I take a bite of my cake and look up into the vast night sky. We are the luckiest people alive; for several on this trip, they tell us, this is truly the best evening of their lives.

THE NIGHT MARKET

Often I see someone living in circumstances different from my own and think, *thank God that's them and not me.* Yet the mendicant monk with his begging bowl wouldn't want to change places. It's an ego trip at best to believe myself better off—my ignorance of his perspective. The world has grown so small that it is possible to see and be everywhere without traveling, and distant locales cease to be a yearning. For those who crave America and our vast consumer society, they can have its trappings even if they never step foot on its soil; or like so many, they can throw their lot in the melting pot of the country. But many of these Egyptians wouldn't want to live in my shoes any more than the monk would. They are happy going about their habits and patterns in the streets of Cairo or Luxor.

Shakky invites our group to visit the night market and to experience Luxor through his eyes. This is the real, true heart of the place, where the Egyptian people live, work, marry, and die, many without ever leaving the village where they were born. The trip will be a walk around Shakky's old stomping grounds after he shows us where he lives now, a five-story apartment building that he owns and occupies with his wife and children. It has vast marble floors, beautiful fixtures, and the smallest kitchen imaginable.

His lovely wife, Ament, raven-haired and still beautiful, offers us Coca-Colas. Most Egyptians are Muslim, but Shakky's family is Coptic Christian. We sit around admiring the painting of his hero, Saint George, captured in full-color oils slaying the mythic dragon, complete with gloriously dripping blood. Shakky has mementos from thirty years as a guide—crystals, plaques, wooden boxes, gifts from all over the world brought to him by grateful tour leaders—but the two stuffed birds in the living room are a surprise: the taxidermist has caught them in flight, and their wings are spread forever over Shakky's marble side tables.

Then we walk into the back streets of Luxor—dirt and for the most part unpaved, the dust of thousands of years compressed to a compact surface by the feet that have trod on it. The buildings are low, two or three stories high, made of stuccoed mud brick or more recently, concrete with a metal beam core. They are painted a variety of colors, all dulled by the natural patina of the earth that settles its fine dust over everything. Most of the streets we take are too small for more than one lane of traffic, and many are limited to pedestrians, who bob their heads or smile as we pass them.

We stop occasionally, first speaking to a woman who is raising her two daughters by herself—hesitating, the girls come out of their small front room unveiled, perhaps shyer because of it. They greet us quietly, offering us their delicate hands and smiling out of their beautiful eyes. The mother encourages the girls to talk to us in their rusty English. I can't think of what to say to them, except to comment, "Gemila" (Arabic for "beautiful," and I remember to pronounce the "g" soft since we are in the South). They live in two rooms in the bottom of a three-story apartment building. The door of the building next to them is old wood with an ornate wrought iron window, a beautiful Moroccan pattern that I covet. I imagine taking the door off its hinges, carrying it off down the street. It would look so good in our garden, but I elect not to mention it to The Magician; he would probably take me seriously and the next thing I know, I'd be trying to get it through customs.

We go to many places that night. We visit shops, stalls, stores —people who Shakky has seen and known his entire life. We see the window of the apartment where Shakky used to shinny up the gutter to watch the old man and his beautiful young wife have sex. We stop by a Nubian home where four generations of women, dressed in black and mostly veiled, give us tea and dance for us in a large front room, the walls painted an almost incandescent turquoise.

Shakky has been coming to this house since he was a child. It has long, low benches that we sit on, a toilet with a water faucet that never stops dripping, and a roof open partly to the sky. The Nubian women all seem kind. The eldest, whose face is wrinkled like a dried apple-head doll, is in a wheelchair—she seems too old to be breathing, let alone sitting up, but her eyes crinkle and she taps her hand when the dancing begins.

The women all make sure we have tea, then clap their hands and start to dance although there is no music. The old lady rises from her wheelchair and joins in the dance with the younger women, one of whom is quite beautiful. I have a hard time imagining her taking her turn in the wheelchair in a couple of generations. For the people of this land, there is no fear of getting old or dying, at least none I have ever been able to discern; it's an accepted part of their experiences.

When we rise to leave, we proffer money as a gesture of thanks—as we do with others who are friendly to us, who offer us tea and their time. In the throng of people saying good-bye, the old lady grasps my hand and refuses to let go. I initially take it as a gesture of goodwill, but it goes on and on, and it dawns on me that she wants me to give her more money. I've already given her twenty pounds, as has almost everyone in our group, and I know that we still have a long way to go this evening. I can't stop her from wanting this money, or me from not wanting to give it to her, so I am left wishing we would not return there. Of course we go again to the house almost every time we visit Luxor, but the incident never repeats itself. I have learned to give money freely to the people we meet in Egypt, and to be grateful that I can. I am told the Nubian house is a brothel, a hospital, a home—I'm not sure which story to believe, but I'm certain one of them is true; perhaps they all are.

We continue out on the street, where we are accosted by a ragamuffin group of Egyptian children. It's a different culture entirely—the children run in the street barefoot, muddy, in tatters of clothes—but it's not necessarily that they are poor, though here in the market I'm sure many of them are. Though the average salary of $400 a month seems impossibly low, in this regard, it might not make a difference how much money they had.

On one occasion, we pulled *The Afandina* to the side of the Nile in the middle of nowhere, and got off the boat to go into the homes of local villagers. There were two houses, side by side, making up a little farm enclave. I can't imagine that one family brought home significantly more money than the other, and both proudly showed off their abodes. The first home was neat as a pin, with a cozy seating area, a fairly large modern TV set, and a teal blue painted armoire. The second was utterly filthy, every square inch covered with dirty clothes, the cabinets all hanging open, things shoved in higgledy-piggledy, and goats running around the living room. Each family had several toddlers and young children; however, you could not tell the difference between them—they all looked as if you would have to crack off their crust before being able to bathe them. But they sure were happy little buggers; perhaps we worry too much about keeping our kids clean.

Strolling through Luxor we talk in twos and threes, and I discover Rusty has a passion for Heifer International, a charity he introduces me to as we walk. Heifer is a unique system that buys and supplies breeding animals to villages so that they can grow their livelihood, and Rusty is active in supporting them; Heifer even has a system where the offspring of the animals are handed down to other villages, and I am fascinated by this type of "pay it forward" charity. As he talks, Rusty pulls out an old-school Polaroid camera. He begins to take Polaroids of the people he meets, then hands them the developing picture. They watch, intrigued; as their faces swim into focus on the formerly blank page, they break into huge smiles. It's a gift more appreciated than any other I have ever seen (except perhaps the Obama T-shirts we brought over right after the historic election). Rusty hands out picture after picture that night, and the immediacy of his gift—of this moment captured in time—is striking. The voodoo of the picture developing in front of their eyes is something not even Shakky has seen.

We continue on into the night market of Luxor. The shops and stalls are open late out of sheer necessity, since it's so much cooler, even in the summer, and there's the added advantage that the sun is not beating down on you. The night market is extensive, proceeding for blocks and blocks. Mostly, it's permanent stalls, with articulated metal roll-tops for doors like in any self-respecting barrio in LA or London. But here, instead of a distinct fashion or electronics district, everything is mixed in. You have a micro-market in one stall, selling everything from tobacco to tissues to sodas, and then across from him, a butcher —two slabs of beef hanging from hooks on the front of his shop. Then there's a cell phone shop and a clothing store on either side of the butcher's; as you pass by or shop for T-shirts, you can smell the strong scent of the raw meat, see the flies attracted to the blood, and look at the hanging carcasses, so recently walking around. If someone wanted to get people to shop less in America, they should offer butchers a stand in the local mall—sans air-conditioning, of course. And on it goes, for nearly a half-mile.

Eventually, we find our way to Luxor's tourist market. The streets here all seem to be spokes of a big wheel, joining at the hub in a large central ahwa, its open patio inviting weary shoppers to rest. The ahwa attracts almost as many locals as travelers brave enough to go in and order shisha and coffee on their own. This section is quite similar to the open market in Aswan. I like it better here, even more than the Khan el Khalili in the heart of Cairo. It may lack the history of the Khan, but for pure shopping, it's easier to maneuver (the streets are wider and less crowded), less high-pressure, and has as wide an array of souvenirs as you could hope to find.

The markets all offer scarves, galabeyas, souvenirs, silver jewelry made by the Bedouin, and T-shirts with cartouches on them that spell your name—which you can have embroidered there on the spot. A feature at both the Aswan and Luxor markets is the array of spices. These deliciously scented ingredients are piled high in baskets on the spice vendor's table, the colors deep and vibrant—orange saffron, gold cumin, brown coriander. Don't try to eat the cobalt blue spice—that's bluing for your laundry. I suppose the only reason the spice tables carry something inedible (and likely poisonous) is that it makes such an attractive contrast to the other colors: subtle, but still good marketing.

Eleanor, Judith, Lyra, Greg and I break off from the main group, bringing Carter along for extra protection. Of course it's safe, but our mothers taught us to be nervous in strange situations.

We are looking for wine, expecting to find several stands that sell liquor here in the tourist market. But Muslims and drinking don't go together. Though Egyptians are willing to make some concessions for those who wish to imbibe, the taxes on alcohol are extraordinary. I have personally carried bottle after bottle of duty-free booze to friends who are locals, because it saves around fifty percent of the cost if they were to buy it at retail (our friends are either Christian Copts or Muslim, so they don't drink, but want liquor to give as gifts or to offer to guests; after all, they are in the tourism business). Even wine costs a lot more than it should. It's as if they're saying: okay, you can drink, but Allah doesn't want you to, so we're really going to make you pay to do this terrible thing.

Recently, the Saudi owner of the Grand Hyatt in Cairo ordered his staff to flush all the alcohol in the hotel down the toilets. I'm sure anyone who drank from the Nile for the next few days was drunk—the staff tossed 2,500 bottles worth over $300,000. Now the Muslim owner and the Hyatt chain are locked in battle, as they want to reduce his four-star designation to two stars (the highest rating a hotel can have in Egypt if it doesn't serve booze). It's a continuation of the push me/pull you that goes on in a country relying heavily on international tourism in an expanding Muslim world.

Given the dearth of liquor stores in the market, Shakky gave us clear instructions, which we have now finished following with no wine shop in sight. Unexpectedly, we encounter an eleven or twelve year-old boy who offers to help us and says he knows where the place is. The boy seems friendly, and the streets are open and well-lit.

Judith looks him up and down. "What the hell?" she comments to the rest of us. "Isn't this supposed to be an adventure?" We laughingly agree to let the boy lead us. He runs on ahead, continually turning around to ensure we are still behind him, and motioning with his hands that we should hurry up.

Within a few blocks, we see the wine store, not on the street where we were, but around another corner; it's not likely we would have found it on our own. The wine shop is really more of a wine stand, and I have more bottles of wine at home on my rack than this fellow has in his inventory. An open stall with a low, wooden half-wall across the front of it acting as a counter, its sole furnishing is a refrigerator holding some sodas and a couple bottles of beer. On the far wall's crossbeam support, five bottles of wine are equally spaced.

Judith seems to be enjoying herself. "What kind of wine have you, good sir?" she asks in her most proper English tones. In response, the wine merchant points to these bottles. Carter looks concerned.

"Is this all ya got, fella?" he asks. Greg leans over the stall and looks around at the ground.

He nods at Carter. "I think that's it, cowboy." Carter looks put out. The proprietor still hasn't said a word, but now he talks to the boy in Arabic. The boy shrugs and asks us, in perfect English, "Do you want any of his wine?"

Eleanor steps in. "Well, it's all white." She's got a point.

"Sir, do you have any red wine?" Judith is polite, but we are really trying hard not to giggle at his lack of inventory.

The boy translates and then responds on the merchant's behalf. "White only. More red on Tuesday." Ahhhh, we understand the situation now.

"No wine, not here, anyway," Eleanor tells the boy, who passes it along. The wine merchant nods and waves to us as we walk off discussing what to do next.

The Egyptian boy's eyes light up. "I know where there's another wine shop!" he tells us. "Come? Come!" Our little splinter group is amenable, so we set off after the boy again, occasionally losing sight of him but always catching up as we are led down into the center of the market. This makes us all a little more comfortable, since it's obvious he is not taking us off to be accosted by the members of his criminal posse, lurking in the shadows somewhere. He leads us almost to the end of the market, a good six blocks away, and shows us another stand, far better stocked. Here we are offered four varieties of Egyptian red. We had already tried a couple of brands, so Eleanor picks out the one she liked best, the Cleopatra label. Each bottle costs approximately $30, even buying it here; in a restaurant, it can be more expensive. Eleanor and Carter each buy two bottles, then the young boy accompanies us to the main part of the market.

As we rejoin our group, Vivian is having trouble finding some special scarabs, so the boy offers to help her, but refuses any money. Instead, he rushes off to procure the scarabs; when they are deemed acceptable, only then will he accept a small tip on top of the cost, before racing off with Vivian's money to pay for them. Then he returns to ensure we no longer need his services. Of all the children I have met in Egypt, this boy most impressed me. I tell him, as I shake his hand in farewell, that he is a trustworthy shop owner in the making, clearly a great businessman. He smiles shyly before melting into the night.

On some of the big ships, it's not acceptable to bring alcohol from the outside onto the boat, unless you plan to drink it warm in your room, and then what's the point? They charge you a corkage fee almost as high as the already pricey booze. On our anniversary, the waiters looked the other way when we brought our own champagne. We met some of our group in the upstairs lounge and everyone toasted with the water glasses from our bathrooms. That was the last time we tried to sneak anything on the boat. I still think that champagne had a whiff of toothpaste.

We have wine, now we need some beer—"spirit" has multiple meanings on these trips. Judith suggests the beer, since they like a nice warm one now and then in London. This is seconded by Carter, Rusty, and even Greg. Shakky tosses everyone who wants beer into two taxis and gives the lead driver explicit directions deep into the heart of the city.

A word about Egyptian taxis. As an American, it's hard to fathom driving cars in this condition. I have been in some that are decent, even clean. But mostly they are all elderly vehicles, featuring doors that won't open except from the inside, windows that are permanently rolled down—or up—seats with cushions or leather split open and stuffing hanging out, and a weird smell, like the time I found a desiccated rat in our attic after a hot spell. But when Shakky says go, you go!

We set off in these two taxis, driving crazily across bumpy streets, and finally pull over, our taxicabs double-parking bumper-to-bumper. Shakky jumps out of the front cab and runs into what might be someone's home or office, but that must be a store of some kind, because eventually he comes out with several six-packs, and we all pile into the taxis, which take off again. A mere five minutes later, the lead taxi stops—more accurately, comes to a screeching halt—then we all just sit there. And sit there. Other times, there have been traffic jams, even in the middle of the night, but right around the time we think to send out a scout, Shakky comes over to our cab and tells us the other taxi has a flat tire, though for some reason no one has yet begun to fix it. Now you might expect that we would go on and the other taxi would come when the tire was replaced, but this is Egypt. Cars are parked on either side of us, leaving only enough room for a single lane of traffic, which is typical of a city like Luxor, where the streets are significantly more crowded than they were built for.

Effectively, we're stuck. Not only are we unable to move forward, we can't move backwards because cars are starting to pile up behind us. Within ten minutes, the line of headlights reaches farther than we can see. Over the next half-hour, we sit quietly, watching as various drivers make their way up to us, observe the driver changing the flat, shrug, and head back to their cars to wait it out. Though we feel terrible for causing this roadblock, the locals take it in stride, placidly participating in our flat tire, and then starting up their cars and puttering off when the road is finally clear. A lesson in patience for me.

*   *   *   *   *

One of our must-visit stops in Luxor is Radwan the Jeweler, a corner store featuring a forty-square-foot sales floor on each of two levels. The downstairs features galabeyas of the most elaborate hand stitching, and along with the tourist kitsch, more unusual pieces such as painted copper etchings of David Roberts' drawings. Upstairs is the gold. Egypt is known for its gold, and the prices can be impressive if you know where to look. In Radwan's case, their prices probably aren't the cheapest, but after buying from them for a decade I know everyone goes home happy because the workmanship is so good.

The shop entrance opens onto a large empty marble room. Each wall is covered with gold-filled glass cases on the right side of the room and silver on the left. Every wall also features a long glass waist-high floor case so you can see all the jewelry, but the middle of the room is inexplicably empty. Perhaps this is a safety measure—in case they are ever robbed, they can protect the perimeter where the goods are—but who would be foolish enough to break into Radwan's?

Then you notice the men. Approximately one for every three feet of glass casing. They are tall, short, fat, thin, and vary in age by forty years. They look like an Egyptian dating service... right this way, ladies, we have gold, we have silver, we have escorts... Of course they're all lovely fellows, and most of them are married, but I do find it strange that the only women at Radwan's are the customers.

The cartouche counter is always quite popular, as you can have the oblong gold or silver strips set with hieroglyphs or symbols, and they will deliver the finished pieces to your boat the next evening. This is where my own cartouche came from. It has the hieroglyphics for "Halle" on the front and "Cleopatra" on the reverse (which Greg will kindly tell you is redundant). The gold is thick, the hand-set letters individually carved so that I can see the detail on them; it brings me joy every time I look at it.

Over the years, I've gotten three gold necklaces from Radwan's: my cartouche, the face of the goddess Hathor, and a singular combination of an ankh and a djed (one of the pieces Pharaoh carries on his scepter, also known as the "backbone of Osiris"). I never take any of them off, and they all look exactly as they did the day I got them. I also have a bracelet—small lotus flowers separating two thin gold bands. The clasp is the head of Hathor, topping a "knot of Isis," a simple human-shaped curved symbol that also doubles as a representation of the female reproductive organs. This had to be pointed out to me—I think it looks like a squashed piece of ribbon candy.

Our group fans out to explore, heading for the gold or silver, sometimes for the semiprecious stones with the carved animal totems or Egyptian gods and goddesses. Each year, Radwan's introduces new designs, and a few years ago, Greg sent them a drawing of a sacred geometry piece called the Flower of Life, and now they produce the symbol in both gold and silver—as earrings, necklaces, bracelets. It has proven immensely popular to the esoteric tourists, and people sometimes even buy it without realizing what it is. When we introduced it to our group, they bought out the supply completely. I like our groups to shop until I feel the economy of Egypt rising, as they rely so heavily on tourism for their success.

Radwan's name is misleading because, as I eventually learn, there are three Radwans, all brothers, and Radwan is not their name, but rather their Sufi designation. While I know all the Radwan brothers, I only know to call them all "Radwan," and even after all this time, I don't know which of the other shop staff are related to them.

The one I think of as the main Radwan, since we have known him the longest, took a shine to Judith, and flirted outrageously when they met, until she was giggling helplessly like a teenager. He called on the sun and the stars to dare to shine while her beauty was present; he kissed her hand; he told her he could not live without her—an effusive and unusual display, which I have never seen him repeat with another woman. Several years later, Radwan asking after Mother every time we went in, I called her in London from the store, and Radwan left a poetic message on her voicemail about making himself a pair of golden wings so he could fly to her since she could not come to Egypt.

But we have not seen Radwan in a couple of years now—he was very sick for a while and we feared the worst. On a recent trip, Greg asked another brother about Radwan, and he said, "We are very sad. We miss him terribly. We cry for him every night." So Greg asked Sen if he could help translate his condolences for the loss of his brother. Kojak dutifully walked over to the other Radwan to help Greg out.

He spoke in Arabic to the Radwan for a moment, whose eyes filled with tears. Quite moved, Greg tapped Sen on the shoulder. "Tell him his brother was a great man, that he will never be forgotten." Sen translated, and Radwan looked a little confused, but then shook it off. He took Greg's hand.

"Thank you so much," he said in English.

Greg turned to Sen. "Tell him he should create a gold shrine for his brother!" Sen repeated this in Arabic to Radwan, who now looked even more confused. There was a moment's silence, then a smile broke out on Radwan's face. He began speaking rapidly in Arabic. "Oh!" Sen shook his head. "Dredj, Radwan is not dead, he is convalescing in Cairo. That's why they all miss him—they don't see him every day! He will be home soon."

Greg looked relieved, then embarrassed. "Please tell Radwan I am sorry—"

Radwan interrupted. "No, no. We know you love our brother. Thank you! Thank you!" Greg laughed, happy to know all three Radwans are still with us.

My job at Radwan's, since we have a fixed price, is to help people make decisions, and I enjoy selecting pieces for a friend at home, or assisting someone to choose between two fabulous pieces of inlaid jewelry—my favorite is when the woman's eyes light up and she says, "both!" This helps me continue to develop my abundance consciousness, the idea of always having more than enough. It's lovely to see someone who doesn't think of money as a necessary evil, or worry that they don't have enough of it, but instead sees it as it is meant—energy exchanged in a meaningful way, able to bring great pleasure and circulate throughout the world. Money for me these days is like a meditation: Breathe In, Breathe Out.

Reverend Michael Beckwith, who is the minister of Agape, my favorite spiritual center, says you don't stand on your front porch every morning, trying to take in deep lungfuls of air in case there isn't enough later on. Money is the same. I used to do all kinds of spiritual work around money: mantras, affirmations, subliminal messages, prayer, oh, and lots of begging and pleading. But lately I have released it all. I have great "parking karma," because years ago I set that intention. Now I can find the only empty parking space in a five-story downtown garage on a busy Saturday afternoon. I suppose that money may actually be that simple for me, too. Anytime I have a negative thought about it, I remind myself firmly that I have good "money karma." Breathe In, Breathe Out. There's always money, the same as there is always air. And just like that, it starts to be true. The trick now is to stay in that space, to allow it constantly, not only for a moment, or a day. We are marvelous, human, beings, but we do like to make things more complicated than they need to be.

Eventually, as purchases are made, we migrate toward the seating area, where trays of Fanta, Coke, and Root Beer bottles sit like iced soldiers, steadfastly waiting to revive our flagging stamina with fresh injections of sugar. The fans overhead move the air limply, and we are all fading after a long day and night of shopping. Everyone is patient with the stragglers, but after a while, we all drift towards the door as the last credit cards are being rung up to their very limits. Rose and Vivian, who are about the same age, have tired, and Carter has already gallantly offered to escort them to the ship in a private taxi, which is easily hailed right on the corner.

When we are on *The Afandina*, as a designated "houseboat," it parks on the West Bank of the Nile, near Thebes. To get home, the group walks through the ornately decorated and highly styled lobby of one of the local hotels, and onto their pool deck, right at the Nile. There we have arranged a private water taxi to powerboat us across to the other side of the river. We often strike up a good enough relationship that they agree to meet us whenever we want, so we can split into several groups and still have reliable transportation. As the taxi skims the still water, the only sound its engine, we watch for the blue light that identifies *The Afandina*.

When we are on the big cruise ships, we park on the East Bank of the Nile along the Corniche, and walk or grab a quick taxi ride to the ship, traipsing through as many boat lobbies as necessary until we finally reach our own. The staff of the boat is always there greeting you with a hot or cold towel, depending on the weather, and a refreshment, usually a cold karkady (hibiscus tea) or a hot lemon water. Either way, it's another perfect night asleep on the Nile.

HALLE EAVELYN

TIE DOGS OF EGYPT

The first dog I met in Egypt didn't want to have anything to do with me. That was a surprise. I am by nature an animal person, so drawn to them that I am distracted from anything else until the critters in my sightline are my friends (I will skip the embarrassing story about Lyra and I trying to chat up a wild mule outside a temple). We have three dogs right now, all strays found within a block of our home: a German Shepherd/Pit Bull mix who was badly abused by the asshole who owned him before we did, a Black Lab who adores me, and a butter-yellow Chihuahua mix who literally came running in the front door. You know how hobos make a mark on the entrance to a house that will give them refuge? Greg thinks our house has a hobo dog mark: the redhead's a pushover.

I've noticed each temple has its own dog pack, except Philae, which is a haven for dozens of cats; I have never seen a dog in the years I've been coming. Since Philae is on an island, someone must have brought the animals in originally, as cats are not known for swimming. But now there are many, flea-ridden and crusty; sweet, friendly creatures who will sit and be petted and then are off to greet another visitor. On a recent visit to Philae, two cats accompanied us right into the sanctuary, and as we started our ceremony, began yowling at each other in the most strangulated tones. It was a kitty cacophony as we were doing our ceremony to awaken the energy of the temple. You could almost imagine what they were saying:

"I got here first, dammit!"

"Temper, temper—you're on sacred ground, remember?"

"But this group of legs belongs to me—you can take the next one!"

The dogs are different. I initially noticed the temple dogs at Sakkhara. Despite almost starving, they kept their distance, wary. Greg, Lyra and I had Power Bars—those so-called energy bars that are a cross between a Fig Newton and a Sugar Daddy. We started feeding the dogs bits of Power Bars, which was the only way we could get them to come near us; Greg nicknamed it "Food of the Dogs." Egyptian dogs are vaguely domestic, but half-wild and most have been mistreated in some way or another. Over the years I have seen guards kick dogs, throw rocks or sticks at them, yell and drive them off, but I have also seen others pet them or share their lunchtime sandwiches, even though that is all they, or the dogs, will eat during the day.

The energy of each of the temples may have something to do with the dogs' behavior, (although possibly the guards' as well). At the Temple of Horus I have only heard dogs, never seen them. They keep far away from the visitors, but bark and howl at us. On my earliest trip, I found only one dog who would talk to me, and, like a little child with a black dog called Blackie, I named him Egypt. He was what I came to consider the typical Egyptian male of the species: medium-sized, the color of the desert, and popular with the ladies. I met Egypt the Dog at Karnak, which we visited at dawn.

Karnak is sister to the Luxor Temple complex, connected by the two-mile-long Avenue of the Sphinxes. When we first started coming to Egypt, you could see only the sphinxes inside the temple walls at each locale. Little by little, the Egyptian government is finding the path, buying and demolishing the structures over this sacred ground—digging the sphinxes out and rebuilding the eroded statues. Over the next few years, they will fully restore the unbroken Avenue of the Sphinxes.

Karnak is the most sprawling of the temple sites, and indeed is considered the largest of its kind on Earth. It is over a mile by two miles, and consists of over twenty-five separate temples and smaller chapels. That first morning, when we crept into Karnak to witness dawn, the vastness was camouflaged by the dark and the only hints were the pylons and columns we passed, massive as they loomed upwards beyond the limits of our sight.

Even before we entered the temple gates, Egypt the Dog trotted over, tail wagging happily, and, encouraged by the Food of the Dogs, joined us on our trek through Karnak. He was smart, too, walking over to me, then running off as a guard came by. He had the kind of personality you would expect to see in *Lady and the Tramp*, savvy and cool—I would lose sight of him as he ducked behind a column, then he would catch up right around the next corner, always walking near me, as close as he could. I let my fingers graze his fur, and we would amble together that way until the next guard. Rose and Vivian both noticed him and smiled, and he let them pet him for a moment before returning to my side.

Finally, our group climbed to the top rise at the far end of the complex and welcomed in the morning, Egypt the Dog watching from down below. Karnak at dawn is not to be missed. You can see the whole horizon off in the distance, just a few columns and buildings between you and the edge of the world. The sky dances light and pink, then the sun starts to break through the horizon, and the whole temple takes on a golden color, as if a child giant built the structures out of graham crackers. Ten minutes later, the sun is up high enough that you realize how hot it's going to be, and it's time to start your tour.

Egypt the Dog accompanied me the whole way back, and as we got towards the front of the massive complex, we saw hordes of touristses in front of us, waiting for the gates to open. The guards watched us silently, nodding to us as we passed.

The temple dogs don't seem to live a long time in Egypt, between the heat, the intermittent food, and the general disregard for their well-being by the Galabeya Boys. While my attitude is that we must take care of animals when they cannot fend for themselves, Egyptians and their animals live in a symbiotic relationship that permits coexistence but requires all creatures to be responsible for their own welfare. Ten years after meeting Egypt the Dog, I see his grandchildren or great-grandchildren at Karnak, but there are no old dogs in the desert.

The dogs are friendly and gentle with me—at worst timid—so I forget they are feral and can be wild creatures. They know which guards are mean and bark ferociously at them; they growl at some tourists, and I suspect they sense human intentions quite well. They are also, by necessity, vicious hunters. Once I saw a small bundle, lying near three sweet, placid dogs I had been petting. I stepped closer, curious. It was a fur-covered thing, like a small hedgehog. Coming right on it, I realized it was the head of some hapless desert cat, its eyes in a fierce squint, teeth bared in a last snarl. As I watched, half-fascinated, half-horrified, a dog came over and took the head in her mouth, then lay down, nuzzling and licking it exactly the way my dogs love on their chew toys. At one point, the cat's eyes faced towards me, silently accusing. "Look," his eyes glared. "Look what they did to me."

Over the years, I have found other temple dogs who have befriended me. At Denderah Temple the past several visits, there has been a joyous female, the spitting image of my black and tan Aussie Shepherd who died a few years ago. When I met her, I cried. She was an almost perfect clone of my Flynn Dog and so unlike the other Egyptian dogs I have seen that I took it as a sign we were destined to be friends. The guards tell me her name is Afwan, which is Arabic for "you're welcome," an apt name for this most friendly of critters.

The next year, I was lucky to meet her twice, on two different trips. The second time, after having been truly moved by our initial encounter, I got this crazy idea that if I could get her on the coach, I could take her to Cairo and find her a good home. When it was time to leave, I encouraged Afwan to come with me, enthusiastically egging her on as I moved further and further down the path away from the temple. She came quickly enough, but then as I got near the front gate, she stopped. She hesitated for a moment, looking at me, then took off running in the other direction. It was as if Afwan were telling me, "Hey, I belong here—this is my home!"

On a recent trip, I whistled for her the minute I came into the compound, and she came running to meet me. This time, Afwan's skin was showing in patches where she had scratched off her fur. The sand flies are a terrible torment to the dogs in Egypt; their nasty little bodies, about the size of a horsefly but grayish brown and angular, burrow under the fur and bite at the skin until the dogs are constantly in pain and scratching.

But Afwan was happy to see me, and didn't seem too concerned about the flies. I've discovered that temple dogs want water more than food, so I brought her part of a sandwich and a full bottle of water to drink. It was probably her first time eating smoked salmon and hard-boiled egg on white toast, but she wolfed it down gratefully, and then drank the poured water right out of my palm, her tail wagging constantly. Within five minutes, she had drunk the whole bottle. After chasing off as many flies as I could see, I petted her and scratched under her chin. Afwan stayed for almost half an hour, and then took off running to welcome a group who had arrived at the temple a few minutes earlier.

The next time I saw Afwan, she was better again, and seemed more energetic. She also had puppies, very young puppies who were living with her under some brush in the middle of the ruins. As I watched, she moved them one by one to another area, less out in the open. When it was time to go, I wanted to take her, but I knew she wouldn't go. I thought about taking a pup, but they were far too young to leave their mother. So I left her. I left her to the guards, to the temple, to the sand flies, to potentially starve to death feeding her young. I left her to her fate, as we so often have to leave others, despite what we believe are their best interests.

We all want to control our world, and if you're me, you also want everyone in it to be happy at the same time (because you're the well-meaning puppet master—how could they not be happy?) From a spiritual standpoint, we're all here to learn the lessons we came to experience. But there's free will, so we can resist those lessons for as long as we want, and even die without learning them. What seems like a dog starving and a woman yearning to help, is a lesson on the spiritual plane about giving up control, and it's beautiful when viewed from that angle.

The dog knows her place, better than I. If she wanted to, she could get on the bus. In that moment when she made her choice, something passed between us that told me she understood everything I was trying to do, and the futile efforts I was willing to make on her behalf. It was as if the whole shining path both lay stretched out before us and was traveled to the end; it was not necessary to follow it to discover where the road went. If Afwan dies before I see her again, she will die happy with her lot, and if she's still there next year, or the year after that, I will be grateful.

GETTING SEKHMETIZED

At Karnak, after the sky has welcomed the morning sun, we go to the sanctuary to intone. The Holy of Holies is open at the rear, allowing the sun to stream into the space on the solstice. Karnak is a solar temple, so this certainly fits, but it means there is little reverberation and our toning seems muffled. We wend our way through a few side temples, almost all open to the sky now. Then we move through the main building, well ahead of the other groups who arrive early so they can race through Karnak in time to beat the biggest crowds to the Valley of the Kings. We pass out of the main compound and down a long curving path that started as a flat sandy area; in recent years they have dug it out, forming a real walkway, and have begun excavating small side buildings which are probably other chapels.

At the end of the path a gnarled Sycamore tree's dark green leaves offer the only shade for many yards. As the group walked together on the Long Cruise tour, Momo told us about the tree —though it was over a thousand years old, guards were slowly killing it, pilfering its live wood to keep warm in the winter. The Surgeon and The Magician gathered us around the tree and told us that they were going to buy the guards firewood, and pay them to water the tree. A decade later, Shakky brings our groups to the tree—three or four times its former size, healthy and green, even in summer. He shows us the fruit, inviting us to put the sap on any cuts, as the tree has healing powers in its sticky blood. Thanks to a lot of baksheesh for the Galabeya Boys, this Sycamore can live another thousand years.

Next to the tree is an unusual chapel, a healing temple dedicated to the goddess Sekhmet, the lion-headed goddess, that most formidable of energies—she who heals through destruction, cleanses by fire. Sekhmet's head is a lioness; her little ears and almost gentle face, ringed with a miniature ruff of mane, are enough to disarm a visitor into thinking she might be benign. No such luck. She is the most fearsome bitch ever to grace a carved wall, and she will ruthlessly burn you right down to your core to get to the truth of who you really are. Shakky calls this "getting Sekhmetized" and though we are excited about this private visit, I can feel that everyone's a little nervous, too.

The chapel has two small courtyards; the outer space is long and narrow, leading to the inner, which has a large square altar stone at the center and steps that lead up to a small second-story promenade, perhaps previously used as a lookout's walk. Nothing indicates that either courtyard was ever covered. We make our way to the front, walking in twos or threes; Judith, Greg and I are first, followed by the core group of our closest companions on this trip: Lyra, Eleanor, Rose, and Vivian, with Carter bringing up the rear as he always does. Further in, an oversized wooden door sports a heavy padlock, hiding one of the most sacred sites we visit. Greg is handed the key, an ornate, Victorian-looking metal piece that turns easily. He slides the door open and we peer into the gloom. I feel nothing except the heaviness of the dark.

Inside are three small rooms: a shallow center space and two longer ones flanking it. On the left, nothing remains of the god or goddess statue, now off in a museum somewhere, wreaking havoc with the energies of any foolish tourist who stands too close. In the right-hand room, however, is something you almost never see in Egypt, at least not in the last century or more. It is a statue, still intact, exactly where it was installed thousands of years ago, still crackling with the vibration from the time the priests initially activated the essence of the goddess.

In here it is so dark it takes your eyes minutes to adjust. The room seems empty, but then on your left, against the far wall, you can sense a looming object. This Sekhmet is different from all others. Though she was broken once, early in the last century, apparently by locals afraid she would hurt their kids, she is whole again.

When I enter the Sekhmet chapel, I think, *it's an alien*. The sun disk looks like a head; her curved cup ears—carved in relief at the top front of her head—seem to be the eyes. And then there is this… presence. Rose moves in to stand behind me; I turn to look at her and see the tears flowing down her cheeks. She smiles at me and takes off her glasses, tucking them into her pocket so she can cry without obstruction. People are often more emotional here than any place else in Egypt, more aware of the energy, even if they have no idea why or what's causing it. I have seen a literal field of Sekhmets. I have stood right at the statues, looked full into their faces, even touched them, and it is not the same. Sekhmet is tall, about seven feet including the sun disk over her head, made entirely from black basalt rock. She seems comforting, reassuring somehow, like she's already laid waste to your hard outer shell and is now licking the soft Tootsie Roll center.

We stand in a circle, each of us having brought things for Sekhmet to bless. It seemed old-fashioned in advance, smacking of a religious ceremony I was none too comfortable with, but in the moment it all makes sense. Energetically, it just feels right. The tour leader asks us to take hands, and says a blessing honoring Sekhmet. The energy hums in the small room, vibrating almost audibly. One by one, these pilgrims pick up the objects we have placed in front of Sekhmet, and slowly, ceremoniously, walk from her presence.

People are reluctant to leave. Some stay close until the last possible minute, until it is clear a few will outlast the rest to get a moment alone with her. When it is my turn, I stand in front of Sekhmet, feeling her presence on me like a hot desert wind in the middle of the cool, close space. I gaze up at her, uncertain, but my heart tells me this is the real thing. I love her! I actually love her. She is merely a statue, but this is an inexplicable moment and I allow the overwhelming feelings to pour in and out of me, giving up all pretense of whether I am doing it right, if it's okay to be sensing these things; for once, the part of my self that watches me do everything, ready to comment on the actions that might look foolish, is silenced. It is long past time to give up my place in front of Sekhmet and I leave reluctantly, pausing to pick up my hieroglyphic gold necklace from her feet. On my way out, I see Lyra's face, and realize she and Sekhmet share the same leonine features.

While I was waiting for my turn with Sekhmet, I saw something not even Shakky had noticed. The statue is placed about three or four inches from the wall, which is built from foot-tall stone blocks. Behind Sekhmet is a narrow parting in the stone, and because we were here in the early morning, the sun lit up that spot as we finished our ceremony. Since Sekhmet blocks the light and the space is so narrow, I stood at the side of the statue where I could see her back. I looked at her spine and observed the sunlight, through the fissure in the wall, hitting her at the perfect angle to travel up her whole back, a wink at the Kundalini energy which illuminates from the base to the top of the spine. There are no other chinks in the wall, not in the whole room—I know, I've looked—nor in the room on the far left where her counterpart stood. I am very proud of my little contribution to Egyptology, so now I point this out to everyone who sees her. The little light traveling up Sekhmet's spine is like a glimmer of hope inside the dark chapel.

WHERE WE SEE THE FLOWER OF LIFE

At least a half-hour before God is awake, we depart for Abydos. We have both breakfast boxes and lunch boxes, taking only a few minutes for coffee and a bite of pastry on the ship. Most of us have brought pillows from our rooms, and within about twenty minutes, we are all dozing again, leaning against the windows or each other like troops gathering strength on the long journey to the front.

We drive three hours across the desert, passing through small town after small town, each with a military checkpoint we have to clear. The buses used to be required to travel in a convoy of other buses and security trucks, but recently the government deemed it safe enough to discontinue the convoys. We are grateful to have the experience unfettered by other, more tourist-minded travelers—it's also much easier to have temples to ourselves this way. Along the way, we have the requisite potty breaks and I manage to snag a hot breakfast at a gas station we pull into—a major score.

By the time we arrive, it's already 9:30 in the morning. Thankfully, we are the only ones in the parking lot. Abydos is not particularly convenient, and it is often left off the schedule by the tour companies whose clients think, "You've seen one temple, you've seen 'em all." That's lucky for us, for whom

Abydos is practically the most sacred site in all of Egypt, even rivaling the King's Chamber in the Great Pyramid.

Abydos is the name of the city, not the temple. The "Temple of Seti I at Abydos," which was built by Seti I and finished by his son, Ramses II, is dedicated to Seti, along with a host of important gods: Osiris, Isis (and in alphabetical order, not to offend any of them) Amun, Horus, Nefertem, Ptah, Ptah-Sokar, and Re-Horakhty; I refer to it as Abydos because that's what we've always done—it's a lot shorter to say. The temple has several unique features and sacred spaces. One of its greatest anomalies is the remarkable "future wall"—a series of hieroglyphics high on a wall, clearly depicting a tank, a fighter jet, a submarine, and an airplane. Egyptologists have recently declared this an illusion caused by the plaster falling off a portion of overlapping hieroglyphics, but I've been right there, stood under them and looked hard. I've examined my own pictures and those of others, and ninety percent of the section is a single, smooth piece. People will see what they want no matter what, but one way or another it is a mysterious, exceptional feature.

When we went to Abydos, six months after the massacre at the Temple of Hatshepsut, we were the first visitors they had. I remember the shopkeepers flinging open the doors to their stalls, so happy that we were there with our cash, willing and able to buy their goods again. All the souvenirs had a half-inch of desert dust on them, but we ignored that and shopped anyway. I bought a colorful paper-mâché sarcophagus, about a foot long and six-inches high—inside was a bright, wrapped, paper-mâché mummy. I've never seen a piece like it since.

You cannot see the temple until you pass through the security checkpoint and into the main gates of the grounds. Like most of the complexes, a series of outer temples surrounding the main structure has fallen into ruin.

Schwaller de Lubicz's research show us that the temples are all built to echo man. As you go through the other temple compounds, the correspondence is roughly: outer courtyard=legs; main courtyard and hall of columns=ribs; main building=chest; sanctuary/Holy of Holies=head. Unlike any other site in Egypt, Abydos is built in an L-shape as opposed to a straight line. Directly behind it—attached to the temple—is a deep, older sanctuary. We enter the cool main building, streaked by shadows and thick shafts of sunbeams like follow-spots on the stones, and make our way through to the outside, until we finally gaze upon the Osirion.

Like the Great Pyramid, the Osirion is made of eighty-ton blocks of granite, imported from the Aswan region hundreds of miles away. These stones are so sharply and cleanly cut you could calibrate surveying equipment to them. Only two cranes in the world are capable of lifting these blocks into place today; we know of nothing in ancient times that could do the job. Also like the Great Pyramid—and nowhere else in Egypt—the entire structure is lacking in ornamentation. At all other sites, practically every square inch is covered in bas-relief or etchings. The columns are carved all the way up to the tops; hieroglyphics are all over the ceilings, on all the walls, even the cornice pieces. But here there are no markings except on one wall, stamped into it—actually, more tattooed into it, the way ink is tattooed onto skin—are depictions of a series of 144 interlocking circles known as the Flower of Life.

The Flower of Life is sacred geometry—in other words, geometry found in nature, like the Fibonacci Series in math, which is a sequence of indivisible numbers that, for example, describe the Nautilus shell's peculiar curve. It is also the symbol of one of the most powerful things that happened to us in Egypt.

The Osirion engenders two schools of thought: that it was dug into the earth by whomever built the temple for Seti I when he commissioned Abydos; or that the Osirion was already there, and that while digging Abydos' foundation, they found the significantly older Osirion and altered the path of the construction, which explains its singular L-shape. The silt layers in which the Osirion sits have been dated to 30,000 BCE. As in: *The world is way older than we knew. Now what?* Which does not sit well with the current administration in Egypt, let alone most of the world's theologians and more than a few of her politicians. Further, the idea that we don't have the technology now to do some of the things the Egyptians seem to have done all by themselves, including engineering and construction, is liable to piss off a few people and frighten many others.

A couple of years after seeing Abydos, Greg and I were in the northern part of Israel, visiting an active dig containing the newly uncovered Kingdom of Saul. It was late, around 6pm, and no one was at the site except a friendly black kitty. We wandered around for a few minutes, and found a marker for the city gates —or rather, the remains of them, stone structures obviously a few thousand years old, crumbling into the dirt. There, below the stones, jutting out underneath them like a skyscraper stuck under a house Fred Flintstone built, were huge granite blocks. They were perfectly carved, as if by a laser—as they are at Abydos, as are the stones of the Great Pyramid. If you compared them, you might wonder how they got Aswan granite all the way into North Israel. Visiting the temples today, we tell our groups what they are seeing, and what we believe; then we leave them to choose what is right for them inside their environment, and inside their own heads.

On our earliest visit, we went down to see the Flower of Life, standing on the wooden walkway about three feet away from the tattoos, which, though interesting, are too subtle to make much of an impression. Then we toured the main temple, including viewing the King List—the inscription of the cartouches of every Pharaoh in Egyptian history, except for Queen/Pharaoh Hatshepsut and Akhenaton, who by then were reviled. Afterwards, Lyra found the place she was supposed to conduct our personal initiation, a small annex called the Immaculate Conception Room.

Abydos' beautiful relief carvings are the quintessential example of Egyptian artistic production. The carvings are almost all raised relief, and the workmanship is exquisite; created from fine marble, it makes you feel as if you are standing next to these gods and goddesses, the priests and pharaohs. The Immaculate Conception Room depicts the moment where Isis, in the form of a kite, hovers over the reassembled body of Osiris, taking his essence up inside of herself so that she can become pregnant with Horus.

The carvings appear twice, on the left wall and on the right. In both, Osiris is lying on a couch that has lions' heads for legs, watched over by Horus the Elder. When Isis gives birth, it is to this god Horus the Elder, transmuted into Horus the Younger;

he represents the man's potential to become the living Horus, as each Pharaoh was.

Horus the Elder is standing next to—energetically supporting —Isis as she is impregnated by the golden phallus she has fashioned as a substitute for Sobek's snack. Look closely and you can see that Osiris is hovering several inches off the couch, levitating, his body fully rigid. The most erect is his phallus, which—thanks to later generations of people living in the temples—has been gouged out to a depth of an inch or more on all sides, leaving the indelible impression that Osiris was truly a god among gods.

In the Immaculate Conception Room we walk to where the light enters through a single skylight, which in ancient construction simply meant leaving out the requisite number of stones in the roof. The sun is streaming onto the floor, warming the pale gold reliefs until they glow. We begin our ceremony— chanting and toning our single note to awaken the throat chakra with which Abydos is associated. The last portion of the initiation is Lyra shaking her rattle around each of our heads, followed by our own silent meditation. When I finish, about five minutes later, I open my eyes to see that Greg has stepped forward, directly into the shaft of sun now lighting his face, his closed eyes.

Lyra approaches and we both watch Greg—we have a peripheral awareness that something powerful is playing out inside of him. He has this half-grin on his face, an appearance of being off somewhere; gently, he starts to laugh. His joy grows until the laughter dissolves into tears, but you can tell they are tears of happiness, because the sweet, goofy grin never leaves his face. Lyra puts her hands up, palms flat, near but not touching Greg, sending him energy through her hands, supporting him the way Horus the Elder supports Isis in the carvings, the way Set and Horus sustain Pharaoh in the Cairo Museum statue. I echo her, a little uncertain because I have never done this before, but knowing that it is somehow right. I push the energy out through my hands, probably forcing a little bit because of my enthusiasm and naiveté, but I can actually sense something there, as if I am holding it up, though my hands are floating in the air. Suddenly, Greg crosses his arms in front of his chest, and as he brings them in, he accidentally hits my hand. Immediately, his eyes open; he's still crying and laughing.

We don't know what to make of what has happened, but then Greg starts talking at us, rapid-fire: "The wall of the Osirion—that symbol—it's God, it's everything! It's the building block of all things. I saw God, and it was that symbol!" He had been transported, for lack of a better word, to stand in the presence of the Flower of Life, which was alive and on fire, and at the same time he "got" that it was the soul of cellular structure in nature —in essence: God. This was all so real and overwhelming that it's all we can do to get him out of the temple and onto the bus, because he just wants to stay and experience this place, and relive what has happened. I ask if someone or something told him this information; did he actually talk to God? Greg shakes his head, trying to explain. "It wasn't like that at all. It was just this 'knowing.'" I nod, trying to understand, to make sense of his unexpected epiphany.

As we leave the room we notice Akins, the head of our security detail, guarding the doorway. He has been there the whole time, quietly watching us and making sure no one tried to enter while we were meditating in what he observed as some sort of important experience. As we pass him, he asks, "Will you teach me how to pray?" This is the last thing I should probably be teaching anybody, having never prayed a day in my life (except for the usual *God, please let me get through this fill-in-the-blank*.) Of course, Greg, Lyra, and I all agree, and we make a date the next free day. Satisfied, Akins escorts us to the coach.

*   *   *   *   *

On current trips, when we take people out to the Osirion to the Flower of Life, we also tell the story of what happened to Greg. Then we bring them inside to the Hall of Osiris, off the main room of the temple. It is a large, long hall with many columns and a comparatively low ceiling, where the head of Osiris is supposedly buried. When we are all gathered, I sing for everyone.

At home, I sing in a choir; I'm fortunate to sing at Agape, the woo-woo center I belong to, in what is essentially a black gospel choir that performs New Age music. I have a good enough voice; fifteen years of singing leads in musical theatre and a lot of training ensured that. But there is something about singing sacred songs in these spiritual spaces (which have better acoustics than anywhere, including your bathroom shower) that is quite special; I feel so lucky to get to voice these pieces for our guests.

People have sometimes said, "You have the best voice I have ever heard." While this is almost certainly not the case, I understand that the energy of the temples magnifies, even glorifies, my vocal instrument and my words—it moves people. To me, this is the point. These spaces were created to shift people's energies, and by being there—without ever bothering to do any specific ceremony—by being in the room and committing yourself to connect to that energy, it changes so much in your life. Even today, these experiences are some of the best in my memory. I feel blessed to return over and over—to know the temples so well that I remember each room in Abydos with my eyes closed, the ins and outs of the sprawling Temple at Karnak, the experience of being in the King's Chamber by myself. Few people in the world get that privilege; I am humbled and grateful beyond words to be one of them.

After we left Egypt, when Greg experienced his unexpected enlightenment, he went through a depression that lasted more than seven years; Greg called it his "dark night of the soul." And it truly was. But after the gloom had lifted, when he accepted the call that he first received standing in the Immaculate Conception room in Abydos—which he had resisted for the entire seven years—he really blossomed as a person. Only Largo, who tried to climb the Colossi, had as difficult a time as Greg—reentry can be a bitch. But I know that we all make our own choices; we all learn the lessons that we are here to learn. For each of us, the experience of Egypt is truly so powerful, it is worth any price.

HALLE EAVELYN

HOUSE OF HORUS

Denderah is dedicated to the goddess Hathor, wife of Horus; the literal translation of her name is "house of Horus." Denderah is an architectural mirror of the Temple of Horus in Edfu, except that it fully walled and you have to walk up a flight of steps to get to the entrance, so it is years before I know the temples well enough to see the similarities and recognize the echoed locales.

Over time, the areas surrounding these sacred sites have changed considerably, Denderah being an extreme example. Where we once drove into a parking lot that was barely paved, we now have a low, sandstone visitors' center greeting us, and a state-of-the-art metal detector. Inside the building, we watch a short Nat Geo movie on the site, then move back out into the sun. We walk to the temple proper on a paved walkway, the large flat stones wide enough for at least ten of us to stroll abreast. To our left, vendors cry out; although they cannot reach us now, we will be funneled directly in front of their shops as we leave. This is fine by me because we always get an excellent price here for the heavy blankets we take up Mount Sinai.

One year, we visit Denderah on our anniversary, and even though I normally love birthdays and anniversaries, for some reason I feel awful all morning. We are returning from Abydos, and en route I make things worse for myself by re-reading my journal until I cry. I relive past failures and experiences, seeing the pattern of Spirit—what I have come to think of as God, the Universe, the little inner voice that knows what is best for me—trying to tell me over and over who I actually am, bypassing all the crap that I do to get in my own way.

My issues are always the same, and I find I can sum up my journal, all hundred pages, in about three sentences:

Stop resisting and let go.

Get out of your way.

Trust, and release the HOW.

Boy, am I concerned with the "how" of things. I can ask for help, but then I have to know the path to get there. Greg tells me, "You can tell me what to do, or how to do it, but not both." Of course, it's one thing to tell your husband how to do something, but my ego wants to tell God, too.

My private conversation usually follows these lines:

Thank you in advance, God, for unexpected income to build my abundance. Pause (I am thinking). *Hmmm… what could bring me income? A new tour. A location scout could come to our house, knock on the door and ask to use the house for a movie* (don't laugh, this very thing happened twice last year). *A refund for something. Ok, well, that's all I can think of.* Pause. *So some of those things, then.*

But in my well-meaning brain, I have just limited every option I haven't eliminated, which doesn't leave the Universe much latitude. It's discouraging, and I am only now learning to quiet these thoughts, and to choose others. It is an uphill battle, but often an uplifting one.

We arrive at Denderah, and I jump out ahead of the group to greet and feed Afwan, my favorite dog. She is so happy to see me I start to feel better, then we all go inside the main temple. Other buses are expected soon, but now, with the whole place to ourselves, we put off our tour until later and head to the birthing room at the right side of the temple.

The birthing room is an elevated space about twelve feet square, the ceiling covered by a large relief carving of the sky goddess, Nut (pronounced Noot). She is bent over at the waist, and her arms are out at an angle; she's folded into three parts in a variation of a yoga down dog. Nut is swallowing the sun, then giving birth to it again, so she's usually depicted with a sun, or rays, coming from her crotch; I'm glad the Egyptians see the vagina as a sunny place. This version, though, has a Hathor head inside a square frame below it, as if the sun is warming Hathor. Since this temple is dedicated to the goddess of love, joy, and childbirth, this seems apt.

We do our toning: Maaaaaa for the heart chakra, then three Ommmmms. I determine to throw myself into the ceremony, ignoring my negative feelings, my sadness. Greg asks us to form a circle, then pulls us into our hearts, reminding us that Hathor stands for the love and gratitude we find here. He invites us to "feel the thing we are grateful for right now,"

Immediately, my smallest dog, Butters, appears in my face, licking me in the insistent, wriggly half-puppy way he has, showing me that, in case I had forgotten from five minutes earlier, *HE LOVES ME!!!!* This movie clip in my head is quickly followed by the nape of Greg's neck—how his blonde hair curls down—my baby niece and nephew's faces, my other dogs, my family… tears start running down my face. I break into a smile. Greg is still talking, performing the ceremony, encouraging and guiding our group. He says, "Look how much Spirit loves us that it came into the world as each of us, unique, to see through our eyes. It loves us so much, it loves life so much—it loves life like a baby loves its toes! Remember when you were a baby, sucking on your toes—how happy that made you?"

The image, the exquisite image of a baby sucking on its happy toes, is so yummy that I begin to chuckle, then to laugh and laugh, the tears rolling down unchecked. Then the group starts to tone again: Maaaaaaa.

Since I can't stop laughing, my intonation keeps dissolving into chuckles and general hilarity, and soon it catches on—an infectious giggle wave—until we are all alternately laughing and toning and the room is filled with love. Afterwards, we take turns telling the thing that we are grateful for, and I thank Greg for reminding me that I am sucking on the toes of life. At the end of the ceremony, we all hug each other, and I leave the weight of the world in that room. Happy anniversary, indeed.

Now we start the tour, heading up the straight staircase to the roof, where we view the graffiti left by Napoleon's men, stationed there to see... what? Lawrence of Arabia thundering by? These men were so bored they fastidiously inscribed their names and the date as if they were printers engraving the rocks; each symbol is carved a half-inch deep in precise, even, professional-looking letters. It's as if someone had access to a Times New Roman font book as well as an excess of time.

Near the graffiti is a ceiling relief—this is one of the world's earliest zodiacs. Despite its size, about five feet in diameter, it is a replica. The original resides in the Louvre in Paris. Apparently prizing the rock off the ceiling was another occupation of these same soldiers. Next to the zodiac is a second etching of Nut, her nude body extended like a winged Balinese balsawood statue. Since the ceiling is low, some enterprising folks (I'm blaming the soldiers again) spent long hours digging out the genital area, and now Nut looks like she could be on the receiving end of Osiris' giant manhood back at Abydos.

Last, we visit what looks like a small rooftop temple, but turns out to be one of the oldest known sundials. The stone columns were topped with wood, long ago rotted or removed; depending on how the sun hit the beams, the angle revealed the time. This is a piece I wish had been restored, as I cannot see to my satisfaction how it worked. I watch the sun casting its shadows on the floor of this structure. No one knows who first created the sundial; it may have been invented here.

On our way out, at the bottom of Denderah, Shakky shows us another remarkable site. He directs us to the rear of the temple, where the eager Galabeya Boys stand waiting next to what looks like a storm shelter, the doors flung open as if a hurricane is imminent. Those of us who are not claustrophobic descend into the ground and find ourselves in a shaft barely big enough for two people to pass each other. Around the corner, in this crypt, are curious hieroglyphs of tall lizards walking on their hind legs, carrying what looks like kitchen knives. "It means they are teaching," Shakky explains.

Next to them are huge lotus flowers, each enclosed by an elongated bubble, snakes writhing from their centers. The lotus are supported by a huge djed with human arms. The whole image looks remarkably, uncannily, like an electrical transformer energizing a couple of giant follow-spots. This is the only place in Egypt these images appear, and they are bizarre. I believe they are a riddle, left here over the long centuries for someone to decipher. Can it be an accident that they look like modern spotlights and the electricity running them?

Riding back in our coach, Greg dozing beside me, it occurs to me that before the invention of the sundial, people only had a vague idea of what time it was by looking at the sun. Now, we carry our sundials on our wrists, and they tell us the time in digital format. So much creation had to happen between then and now. So much shifting and asking, "What if?"

I can choose to be like the inventor of the sundial, squinting up at the sky and asking, "What if we could tell time more accurately?" Instead of asking, *What if something bad happens?* I can as easily ask, *What if something good occurs? What if all my dreams come true? What if I am happy every minute of every day?* In choosing to turn each negative thought into a positive one, in choosing to "What If?" my way to a better place emotionally, I am shifting my own universe. Some day, if I start now, I may cover the distance between a sundial and a watch.

Babies are marvelous creatures in that they live in the moment. This is often the last time humans do this because we are paralyzed by the experiences of our pasts, and fears for our futures. As I take my first baby steps in this direction, I choose to suck on the toes of life instead, "What If'ing" my way to where I am meant to be.

WHERE WE PARTY LIKE IT'S 1999

I have only spent one New Year's Eve in Egypt. The price tag was kind of hefty—$110 a person for a single event including dinner, and if you were on the trip, you paid for that meal. This is Luxor, Egypt, not Luxor, Las Vegas, so I was a little surprised. We checked into the hotel that morning, and we weren't sure what to expect. But it was the Sonesta St. George, a five-star hotel with rooms and service to match, and we hoped for the best.

The evening doesn't even kick off until 8pm, giving us a chance to lie down after a long day visiting temples. Dress is semiformal to formal, and our festive group wears either suits and cocktail dresses or galabeyas they purchased in Luxor or Cairo. Though it is a Muslim country, a nod to the needs of the hotel guests gives us a champagne cocktail hour (well, half-hour, really) by the pool. After that, drinks are available to buy—as usual, the cheapest bottle of champagne costs somewhere north of $200, though beer and wine are somewhat more reasonable.

Hundreds of guests drift into a huge tent set up along the back of the pool. Normally, the space is an enormous deck overlooking the Nile, but tonight we can't see the river, a small price to pay when we spot the buffet. The sheer poetry of the food sculptures is impressive. Have you ever seen a giant standing fish made entirely of cream cheese, veggies garnishing fins and face? And a pelican, and a mermaid? Looking at the vast array of food, from the layered pâtés and savory pastries to the selection of fish, meat, side dishes, and desserts, I am struck by the ornate effort, by the beauty of the preparations and execution—at least fifty kitchen staff are on hand and I suspect many more are in the kitchens, making sure there is enough of everything for everybody.

I fill my little plate with giant shrimp, stuffed squid, and veal in a savory sauce, then return to try the variety of pâté en croûte. The dessert table, which is about twelve feet long, doesn't disappoint either: petits fours, baklava, chocolate mousse, cheesecake, pastries, and a new staple of Egyptian sweets—Spanish flan. Continuing the sculpture theme, one dessert features a piano made entirely from milk chocolate, with white chocolate for the ivories. The pièce de résistance is a four-foot long replica of the Luxor Temple, fashioned from gingerbread.

The buffet line dies down eventually and everyone gets onto the important business of eating. The music goes live; sadly, the initial set is a disappointment—two gorgeous girls in skimpy short dresses, wailing into the microphone on such chestnuts as "Volare" and "La Bamba." Worst of all—and I so want to enjoy them—the lead can't sing and her friend's harmonies are badly off-key. I wonder archly whose girlfriends or sisters have been hired. Who could have owed them a favor this big? The stack of giant speakers, much too close to our table, exacerbates the problem until we all want to run screaming from the tent, but luckily we "know people." Mohamed's tall, thin business partner, Ihab, has joined us for the evening. I pull him aside and point to the speakers. Ihab turns his usually sad-looking Spaniel eyes on me and smiles kindly, saying nothing since we cannot be heard over the noise.

Within ten minutes, the whole stack of speakers near us has been first turned to the wall, and then when that doesn't do the trick, mysteriously disconnected. Ihab winks at us and thanks the banquet manager, who shakes his head at the "unfortunate problem" and informs us that there is no engineer who could be spared to fix the electrics that night. Luckily, the girls' set only lasts another half-hour, and the sound is now far enough away from us to be manageable.

The Shrieking Siren Sisters are followed by Egyptian dancers, who wear traditional costumes that look vaguely Greek or Turkish, then a voluptuous belly dancer. A young man in our group, only about twenty-two, looks at her and exclaims candidly, "Boy, she's fat!" I gently explain that in many other countries, women are allowed to eat and are still thought beautiful. Judging from the response to her act, many of the men in the room are pleased by her cushiony figure; her rounded belly is considered a great asset in Egypt. Her performance segues into several other women of varying girths belly dancing, the group eventually flowing from the stage down into the audience, where they morph into a long Conga line that many in our group happily join.

By this time, we discover the party favors in gold bags by our chairs. In addition to butterfly masks in silver or red foil, we have various noisemakers and streamers. By far the most popular favor is a small baggie of colored papers formed into tight balls. Their purpose quickly becomes clear: to throw at your neighbors, of course! And to be made sport of in return. We get to know the people at the next table all too well as we lob the colorful pre-made spitballs back and forth at one another, and the grown men in their forties, fifties, and sixties quickly revert to six-year-olds.

A man in our group comes up as I am trying to decide if I have missed any of the desserts and do I have room in my full tummy for just a little more. Rick is supposedly traveling with his girlfriend, but my "gaydar" has picked out that she is his beard, not his sugar. He is smirking, dying to tell me that one of the waiters has tried to pick him up. He points out a young, curly-haired fellow who had delighted in participating in the paper-ball-throwing earlier. Rick went into the bathroom, and this guy followed him in, which was fine with Rick—only then our friendly waiter asked him for money. Rick, who is in his early forties, is a little put out by this turn of events. "Do I look like I need to pay for it?" he asks me, only half-joking.

At 11:30pm, I notice that the dance floor is empty, so I decide Julie the Cruise Director—as I call myself on these trips

—should make arrangements for the most festive of midnights. I amass our group, which despite some attrition as the magic hour has drawn closer, still stands at twenty-five or more. A few are reluctant—my darling Greg the most vocal among them—but peer pressure is a powerful thing. At 11:45pm, we all hit the dance floor, even Greg, dragged out there by several of the men in our group. Glad for the company, others flood onto the floor, and by 11:55pm, the joint is jumping, with the guy who's not into fat girls dancing on the stage, even performing back flips, much to the excitement of several slender young ladies.

So it comes to pass that, at midnight, the love of my life reaches across a crowded dance floor to plant the first kiss of the New Year on me. Since Greg doesn't dance in public, except an occasional slow number, and hates crowds, I take it at a sign that this will be a year of change. By 1am, Luxor has lived up to its promise of a great New Year's Eve party, and we drag ourselves upstairs to sleep. The price tag was well worth it.

The next morning, at 5am, Greg awakens, dresses quickly, and leaves to pick up whomever of the group is brave enough to catch the Winter Solstice phenomenon at the Temple of Karnak. For a few days in December, the dawning sun is perfectly aligned through the main temple entrance. This fact intrigues me greatly, just not enough to get me out of bed. Unfortunately, after Greg leaves, I can't fall asleep again. Then I remember: *It's New Year's Day. This is a chance to meditate by the Nile, to make my New Year's Resolutions where they really count!* I pop up, wrap a sleep-warmed blanket around my nude body, and head out onto the balcony.

The rooms at the St. George are grand enough, but the true beauties are the corner suites: a small separate living room, a side balcony, and a long hall leading to a large bedroom with a spacious balcony overlooking the Nile River. It gets cold in Egypt in January, yet I sit right down on the frigid marble deck, wrapped in my blanket. Dawn has already broken, and I can see the balloons starting their ascent, but today none drift from the pack to sail into forbidden territory across the Nile.

Sitting there, still toasty from the bed and half-asleep, I meditate for a few minutes and make my New Year's resolutions. I feel how fortunate I am to be on this balcony on this day. I declare the usual types of things—my intention to lose weight, my intention for further abundance—but this time it feels different. Egypt is primal for me somehow; it's the source, and saying these declarations aloud here makes them feel more real and stickier, like they will cling to me and help me to make these changes, even without my awareness, and despite any lingering resistance. I am shifting already, merely by being here.

I'M A SOUL SISTER

After you've been in Egypt even a week or two, you learn that a basic understanding of Arabic begins with the following conversation:

"Saba el khir?" (There are three ways to say Good Morning in Arabic, and this is the most common one. It means "Morning the Good.")

"Saba el ful!" (This is the second most common, and the most typical response. "Ful" is the way the scent of morning jasmine fills your nostrils, so roughly translated, this means "Morning the Nose Hit." The third way to say Good Morning is "Saba el noor," which is "Morning the Light." I know linguists would argue my etymology, but Arabic, in my humble opinion, is definitely a romance language.)

"Enta Quais?" (The next step is to ask how you are—colloquially, "You Good?")

"Hamdulullah. (One always responds, "Thanks be to God." Technically this is Hamdul'Allah, but it all gets run together.)

"W'enta?" (This means, "And you?")

"Hamdu'lah." (The even more foreshortened version. Apparently, He doesn't mind nicknames. In English, calling Allah 'Lah, might be translated into calling God "Big G.")

"Meya-meya." (This means literally, "a hundred/a hundred," or, "A hundred percent! Great!")

"Meya-meya." (Which you repeat to the person who just said it to you.) Congratulations, you can now speak Arabic.

This is all well and good when you are a visitor who has learned a little local. The above phonetic conversation will serve you well in almost any situation. When an Egyptian greets another Egyptian, however, the polite opening conversation takes on an elevated status. It's a Chip & Dale marathon where each person tries to outdo the other in a waterfall of welcoming speech. It's almost like a race to see who can get the greatest number of nice words out the fastest, a contest of kindness. Every conversation, whether in person or on the phone, includes this elaborate dance, each person saying the following to each other simultaneously:

Person 1: Hello, how are you?! I am well! Thanks be to God! I hope that everything is wonderful in your life and is as amazing as it is in my life! I am so glad to hear you are well! A hundred/a hundred!

Person 2: Hello, I am well! Are you all right? Thanks be to God! I hope that everything is wonderful in your life and is as amazing as it is in my life! I am so glad to hear you are well! A hundred/a hundred!

If the people are standing together at the time, they're likely shaking hands the whole while, nodding politely and smiling at each other. Mohamed and I were once walking the block between his home and his office when a man jumped out of his car at the intersection and ran over to shake Momo's hand. Even with his car stopped in the middle of traffic, the exchange sounded the same as if they had met in a formal setting.

On the phone it is simply a matter of both talking into their respective receivers simultaneously. In comparison, it makes the typical English greeting a mere shadow of adequacy. However, every Egyptian has done this tango a hundred million times by now, to every single person they have ever met. So there is a perfunctory quality about it that cannot fail to occur after many years, such as when an American says, "How are you?" to someone passing on the street and then keeps walking because the rote greeting wasn't actually an inquiry after that stranger's health. But in Egypt the speech must be made, in full, to nearly everyone. Even in a family, or a business where people talk to each other many times a day, the greeting is only a modicum less formal.

Our group aboard the *Sonesta Sun Goddess* is getting to know the waiters and the boat staff a little better, and we are also learning to converse with them. They all want to be your friend, I believe in a very genuine way. They want your address, to write to you after you arrive home. Of course the hospitality in our hotels and on the boat is always impeccable, which adds to the feeling of luxury as we sail down the Nile.

It's easy to spend afternoons learning Arabic. It's the hottest time of the day, so we also can rest, swim or read on deck. The sight of foreign women in bathing suits means that the crew finds excuses to watch, so the brass is always polished and all the deck furniture neat as a pin. Sometimes we dine on the upper deck, which means setting the tables to accommodate us and cooking part of the meal outside. Even in the heat, the nights are best outside, where water jets run through the deck's latticework roofs, the fine mist helping to cool us.

On the Long Cruise, I get to experience a real-life version of one of my favorite stories, the ancient tale, *Appointment in Samarra*. In case you don't recall this brief and exceptional allegory:

A servant is in the market and is jostled by Death. He runs to his master and asks for a horse. He tells him, " I will fly to Samarra and Death will not find me." Back in the market, the Master approaches death and chastises him for threatening his servant. "I was merely surprised to see him here in Bagdad," replies Death, "for I have an appointment with him tonight, in Samarra."

Given my fear of death you might expect the tale to bother me, but I find its inescapable logic and simplicity satisfying.

There is a group of elderly Australian veterans on our cruise ship. Greg calls them the "Dubya Dubya Two Vets." They served in Egypt during the Second World War, and none has returned since. Their Australian guide points out one of her guests in particular. He came to her and asked her to take him on the trip, explaining that he would be visiting Egypt to die. He had told this to several other travel agents, and they all turned him down. But this woman was willing to take the risk. About four days into the voyage, after a morning looking at sites, the gentleman does indeed keep his appointment. The ship docks and we spend several hours on the bank of the Nile waiting for an ambulance to come and take him off the boat to... I have no idea where. I hope that someone so sure of the time and place of his passing also remembered to prepare his funeral arrangements. Several on board are put out by the delay, but I am rather in awe of this man's brave choice, and quite impressed by his timing.

The shift to Osiris' and Isis' names and the monotony of their white wardrobe notwithstanding, Sun People are all really nice. It's bizarre. I watch them go into temples and "usher in souls" through a "star portal," which (to the uninitiated of us), looks a lot like people standing next to a sunbeam, trying to wave the dust particles closer to the floor. When we met them, I was indeed uninitiated and naïve and open to pretty much everything, but I still thought, *Okay, well, that's crap.* These days I know definitively that souls don't arrive by the boatload, riding on sunbeams, nor do they require the physical help of our arms waving about to do so. Yet the Sun People somehow also proved to be the real deal, and helped me in several vital, life-changing ways.

After a couple of days on board, we are hanging out with the Sun People more often and Greg is getting increasingly uncomfortable. He feels that they are "inauthentic." Possibly it is because he has to use the names of gods when addressing them, but I also sense he seems threatened, though I'm not sure why. They offer to do "psychic surgery" for whoever wishes. I have never heard of this—an operation that takes place only on the spiritual plane—but I am intrigued, and Lyra explains that it's quite a legit practice in some cultures. After what happened to me on the deck my first afternoon, I think, *What the hell?*

So one morning after breakfast, I find myself knocking on the door of Isis and Osiris' cabin, (which seems strange to write even now—"Had drinks with those swinging gods Hathor and Horus last night," etc.) Isis ushers me into the darkened room, and asks me to lie down, my head at the foot of their bed. Osiris is sitting in a chair next to the bed, hands on his knees, and Isis tells me he is already "in trance," which in woo-woo terms just means he's tapped in to something or someone on the non-physical plane that is now using him as a vehicle to communicate on this side. Though I had never experienced someone else in a trance before, I had already been guided to that state a couple of times myself, so I am okay with the idea of it.

I have to quiet my "fight or flight" mechanisms, which, as I lie down, include worrying that this nice couple will try to cop a feel, or throw a gunnysack over my head and sell me into white slavery in the Middle East (I have never heard of such a thing, but my overactive imagination certainly has no problems conjuring it up). After a moment, though, the silly thought passes, and I feel peaceful, ready for whatever challenge might present itself.

When I close my eyes I immediately notice that Osiris' energy is "different." Heavier than normal, more concentrated, somehow more compact. I sense another entity in the room, sitting where I know Osiris to be. He comes over and kneels down near me, breathing low and fast, grunting occasionally—these animal noises—but now I am no longer threatened, and I feel safe. Isis guides me. She asks me to visualize a green emerald, step into it, then surround it with a purple light. The whole time she talks, Osiris' hands are making swift, light little criss-crosses over my stomach. Once in a while, he emits a pig-like snort, and at one point, he stops, grunts as if dissatisfied, and then begins the process over again. It is like having a little troll working on me, and with my eyes closed, it might as well be. He performs his job well, and I sense that he has been doing this forever, his hands thickened by time but knowing the movements by heart.

Isis tells me Osiris is "bringing a different spirit in" and instantly, I feel the energy next to me shift. Now it is smaller, even more concentrated, and elderly—like a wizened old man.

Isis, who has been holding my hand the whole time, abruptly loosens her grip. She goes to my feet, at the head of the bed, and moves my ankles about a foot apart. Then she picks up my hand again. Now Osiris moves his hand swiftly, down the outside of my left leg, then down my right. Suddenly he shouts out, the first loud noise he has made during the whole session, and I can feel the motion through the air as he karate-chops down hard on the bed, right between my ankles. He mumbles and snorfles a few more times, and then Isis asks me to open my eyes, and escorts me towards the door.

As she puts her hand on the doorknob, she turns, her lilting English accent carrying the quiet words to my ear. "You had a great big chain weighing down your legs, my darling. It was holding you back and preventing you from flying. Now you can fly."

I hug her and say, "Yes, I will fly now."

Isis laughs. "Perhaps, my darling, you could start with little baby hops."

Outside the room, in the silent hall, I can hardly believe that a) this happened, and b) I don't think it is all complete bullshit. But something was in that room that wasn't Isis, or Osiris, or me, and I do feel different—lighter somehow and ready to accept the new version of whomever I am becoming on this trip. I have a strong intuition about who put the chains there, but though I recount the experience to Greg, I don't mention my hunch. I am also thrilled to tell Judith and Lyra what happened. Mother shakes her head, trying to make sense of it, but Lyra accepts it immediately as truth, not even seeming surprised. She's going to see the Sun People for her own psychic surgery later that day, so my story just whets her appetite.

The next morning, Greg and I have a big fight. I go a few minutes before him to breakfast, joining Lyra and Rose to say good morning to the Sun People. When Greg comes into the restaurant, he sees me talking with them; out of the corner of my eye, I catch him storming back out. I tentatively return to the cabin, where Greg is now in bed, pretending to nap.

"What's wrong?" I ask, sitting down on the bed, a little put out that we are going in for round twenty-three this early in the day.

"I'll tell you what's wrong!" he snaps, sitting up and throwing off all pretense of sleep, "Rose came up to the deck to find me last night after you went to sleep. She's afraid the Sun People are a bad influence on you. Lyra's grounded—she's been studying this Rosicrucian stuff for years, but you're a complete newbie, and you're letting them manipulate you psychically. They could be taking advantage of you and how the hell would you even know?"

I begin to protest. After all, I've still got all my faculties; I was aware, even discerning, the whole time. But Greg's building up a head of steam, and he continues to push: "Look, what if she's right? I have a bad feeling about them—I have had from the beginning! And you wouldn't know the difference! How could you? You don't have the experience!"

Well, I suppose he could be right. But I'm so enjoying myself, all this learning and new information and new ways of being. I am enthusiastic and stubborn, a volatile combo.

Greg starts to yell. "Why do I even bother caring! You won't listen to me—you never do! You are obsessed with the Sun People!"

I flash back: "I am not!"

"And you're being defensive!"

'No, I'm not, either!" Yes, of course, I am. But I've lost my patience, and I don't want to hear this, or be brought down from my effervescent high, so I jump up and head towards the door. "I'm sick of you trying protect me—I'm leaving!"

On the bed, Greg unexpectedly shoots bolt upright, yelling, "Fine, go! The chains are broken and you can go!"

I don't know why I had forgotten my intuitions from before, about Greg being threatened by Osiris, about him keeping me bound. All my anger falls away, and I run to him. "This is what it was about. I will never leave you! I want fifty more lifetimes with you now that we are healed in this one!"

Greg sobs, clutching me to him. "You've always been taken from me!" He is more upset than I have ever seen him, and for many minutes, I hold him, reassuring him that I will stay with him.

After he calms down, I tell him to put his hand on his heart and ask it what his greatest fear is. He answers quietly, "Losing you."

"Will I ever leave you?"

He shakes his head. "No," and begins to cry again.

"Can you trust me?"

"Yes." In all the times I have ever asked him this, in all the times he has ever questioned if he could trust me, I sense he is finally telling the truth. The chain feels like it's really broken, and indeed, this marks a turning point in our relationship, the first strong step on a lengthy road towards a deep peace between us.

TLE LONG CRUISE

The Long Cruise is now legend in the Egyptian travel and tourism industry. Originally planned as an annual event, the government gave its permission just once, and Greg and I were two of the lucky passengers to take that trip. Cruise ships are normally only permitted to sail between Luxor and Aswan because the middle of the country, from Luxor to Cairo, is considered less friendly to tourists; also, no temple sites here would be on someone's "must visit" list. You only see that part of the country if you take the overnight train to Luxor or Aswan, or fly over it on the short hop between the cities.

Besides all the ancient and marvelous sights, on the Long Cruise we also had full days of sailing where all we did was eat, relax, and recapitulate what had happened to us during the previous days. It's grand to sail the Nile, placid, easy—a decade ago, there were no cell phones, no Internet, no real access to the outside world. Eventually, I started to go a little stir crazy and got off the boat in Esna to call our office. It was around 9am in the States—evening in Egypt—and I was unhappy because no one answered the phone. Later I realized it was Sunday morning! By then, even picking up the phone seemed foreign—it was the only call I had made in ten days. At work, I was often on the phone over six hours a day, so it was strange to hold the receiver in my hand and have it feel unusual, to be aware of the act of dialing.

Some of the conversations I have had aboard the ships as we sail along will stay with me forever. We had a fellow on one of our tours, a gentle Southern accountant named Barry. He was a great guy, but he had gotten popped a few years earlier for cooking his client's books, exactly as the client had instructed. Yes, he knew what he did was wrong, but so did the client, and Barry was the one who went to prison. When he got out a couple of years later, he started over, rebuilding his business. But he no longer knew his purpose, and he was foundering as he tried to determine what act of fate brought him to this point, what the meaning of his life was supposed to be. In the middle of the trip, he announced to all of us that he finally figured it out. He had lived through that incident in his life so others wouldn't have to. His job, for the rest of his time on Earth, was going to be to help other people. A weight dropped from his shoulders; he forgave himself.

Another time, we were joined by part of a family of ex-Mormons: a recently widowed mom and her grown son and daughter. Peggy and her husband had chosen to leave their church rather than disown two of their five sons, both of whom were gay. It was a devastating *Sophie's Choice* for both parents, who were deeply embedded in the Mormon community. The parents and sons had participated in the process together, attending a meeting where they were excommunicated. In the Mormon faith, that's it—no Church equals no afterlife with your loved ones. You are literally cast into "outer darkness," cut adrift. For over ten years, Peggy and her family had suffered the effects of this cruel punishment. I suppose there is some bizarre Darwinian "survival of the fittest" justification: the parents created these gay boys, and the boys weren't able to exercise enough self-control to not be gay, or at least to keep it well-hidden, so we'd better get rid of them… the whole thing makes my blood boil.

The hardest part is that for a decade, as a result of this casting out, Peggy has had no spiritual home. When we spoke about it, she wept. The Mormon Church had convinced her that it was the one true faith, and she thought they were the only ones who preached this. I pointed out that most religions believe they are the truest and onliest path to God, whether it's Muslims,

Catholics, or Jews. She is not alone after all. I told her she has the opportunity to choose a new faith, a new spiritual home, and that Egypt is the chance for her rebirth. Many people think they come here for a vacation, when they really come to heal a hole in their hearts.

*　　　*　　　*　　　*　　　*

One afternoon on the Long Cruise, Lyra, Greg and I make good on our promise to teach Akins, head of our security detail, to meditate and pray. In our suite, we ask him to take off his weapons, and though he raises an eyebrow, he complies. All of a sudden we are participating in a scene from *Good Fellas*, as Akins removes guns, knives, handcuffs, a hand grenade—and begins to pile them all on the bed. We exchange shocked glances behind his back, not wanting to alarm him; this is more weaponry than any of us has ever seen in a single place. He takes a couple of steps forward, then turns around and bends over, sliding a forgotten knife from the hiding spot on his ankle. Adding it to the cache on the bed, he moves smoothly into the living room.

Nonplussed, we follow him and sit down on the big lemony sofas. Akins begins to open up to us, to describe the experiences he had as UN Peacekeeper in Bosnia. At one point, on a mission with thirty other men, his whole unit was killed; he was the only survivor, and he lost his two best friends that day. Another time, he worked desperately to airlift a special lung machine into a war-torn area, only to have the boy who needed it die as it touched ground. All these experiences have left Akins hollow and uncertain of his path, or why the human race goes on living. He wants to emigrate—to leave the police, go to the States and open a gas station. We show him how to meditate, then we do a long visualization, seeing him where he wants to be, peaceful and happy. Eventually, Akins does quit the police force and goes to work directly as security for Quest Travel, Momo's company. Then we find him again after several years, now an important official in the Giza Plateau security. He has made his peace, finally accepting his position and his choices.

Mornings, after breakfast but before it gets too hot, I go up to the top deck to journal, but I find myself drawn to the railing of the ship, where I stare off across the Nile to the verdant shores, the constant fields, the occasional fisherman. Other than an intermittent telephone pole or electric line, there is nothing to suggest this millennium, and my mind wanders off to a different time, a quiet life tending these squares of green and brown land. One time, a girl of around ten stands at the water's edge, and when she sees the ship, begins jumping up and down and waving, her arms up over her head, her whole body curving side to side. I imitate her body wave exactly, and she gets even more excited; even from a hundred yards away, I can tell she is thrilled to have engaged me. For as long as she remains in view, we stand there like that, locked in this reciprocal, soundless dance of joy.

Why do we remember one moment, but not another? What shapes certain incidents into memories while other languish or are forgotten altogether? Is this moment on the Nile more poignant than the next, the last? And if we are to create a life lived moment-by-moment, aren't they all equally weighted from a spiritual basis? The Ancient Egyptians believed that when you die your heart, with its baggage of all your good and bad deeds, is put on a scale and weighed against the feather of Maat, the Goddess of Truth and Order. If you are judged not to be righteous—if your heart is not literally "light as a feather"—you aren't let into the afterlife. Perhaps it's even simpler than that. Perhaps all your moments are piled together, and the question is just: Have you really lived?

Two days before we reach Cairo, Lyra suggests we purify ourselves before entering the Great Pyramid. It's more of the woo-woo, but it sounds intriguing and will keep us busy; otherwise, there is nothing to do but sail and eat. Everyone in our "bad kids" splinter group talks about it. Rusty doesn't want to because of his leg, and Carter is a Rosicrucian but as far as I can see, not much of a seeker. He drops out quickly, too. Rose doesn't think it's a necessary part of her process, and Judith, Eleanor, and Vivian all decide afternoon naps along the side of the Nile are enough purification for them. In the end, only Lyra, Greg and I visit the Turkish bath, which is a small steam sauna. We steam until we can't stand it, intone a note to open up the chakra we're working on, then go jump into the icy deck pool,

214

trying not to splash Judith, who is lying close to the water. We do seven rounds, one for each chakra.

The following day, we repeat the process in the Turkish bath earlier in the day, and no one is on deck with us. The last time we enter, for the crown chakra purification, Greg runs out after a few moments. When Lyra and I are finished steaming I find Greg on the sundeck right outside the bath, his eyes closed, lying prone as if wilted by the heat.

"Baby, are you okay?" He has thrown a towel over his head to block the sun from hitting his fair skin, and he pulls it up, squinting at me as the light hits his face.

"Uh…" he says slowly, "maybe not."

"Is there anything I can do? What happened?"

"No. I don't know. I felt something."

I sit next to him and he swings his legs over onto the ground so he can sit up, his head in his hands and the towel draped around his neck like a prizefighter. Unusually, I choose to say nothing, waiting quietly for the wheels to stop churning. After what happened in Abydos, I don't know what to expect.

"The bath was getting really hot and foggy. It was hard to breathe. Then I remembered—" he takes a deep breath—"being burned at the stake in another lifetime, suffocating from the smoke instead of being killed by the fire. It was awful."

"Sweetie, I'm really sorry." I touch his hair, still wet from the steam or the sweat of his fear.

After we are dressed, he goes to Shakky, still traumatized, and asks what the hell is wrong with him? The Magician is kind. He shrugs. "Don't worry, Dredj," he tells him. "It's okay. You are channeling your higher self. It will pass."

Later, back in Cairo, in the old city, we visit the Church of Saints Sergius and Bacchus (called Abu Serga) and go to the crypt where Mary and Joseph supposedly stayed for a long time when Jesus was a boy. It's several days later, but Greg is still experiencing the channeling, and he stands at the top of the crypt steps for several long minutes, silent, unmoving. The touristses come and go. When he returns I ask, intrigued, "Did you see or feel anything?"

Greg has a curious expression on his face, a faraway look, and when he speaks the words seem impossible: "Joseph had dysentery, and he was very sick. He went out to get bread for his family anyway, and had just brought some back. There were several families living in the room, and they were frightened. Later a Roman soldier found them, but he was sympathetic, and went away again without revealing their hiding place. Joseph went out every day looking for bread, no matter how sick he was."

I pull him to me and bury my face in his neck. Suddenly I am crying, overwhelmed. This is Joseph he is talking about, *the* Joseph, but now he is also a real man to me—a father trying to feed his family. I find this experience, this remembrance of Greg's, the hardest to believe, and yet I cannot question it. He wouldn't even think about making something like this up, and he is so somber and straightforward about telling these happenings, I know they are what he saw. Greg is living these moments.

On the way out of the narrow streets of Old Cairo, Greg stops and gestures into an alley. "Someone was killed—there." He points. "A knife between the first and second ribs." At the large banded iron door into the city, rusted with age, he pauses again and holds onto the door. Then he shakes his head. "The metal is vibrating differently. I am getting many vibrations, but no one thing stands out." It is the beginning of his talent for psychometry, the psychic ability to sense an object's past through touch, which he still practices occasionally. Like all these gifts, he accepts them reluctantly, as if he is afraid of their power.

Eventually, after we go home, the portal closes again, never to reopen quite so widely, although in the last five years, Greg has started to channel a group that comes through him, called the White Lodge. It's a lot like Abraham, the group that Esther and Jerry Hicks channel; they call themselves "non-incorporated entities." Where Esther and Jerry travel the world doing channeling sessions for individuals' self-improvement, Greg's work is focused on awakening the consciousness of the planet as a whole. Also, our roles are reversed with the Hicks'; Greg is the channel—Spirit calls him "the vehicle" and I am "the facilitator." We do what I call Spirit Sessions for friends, for clients, and for our groups as we sail down the Nile. In some ways, we've become the Sun People, an irony that is not lost on either of us.

THE MOON OVER
MOHAMED NAZMY

The Oberoi Sahl Hasheesh, on the coast in the Red Sea, is one of those spectacular, unforgettable hotels that make you wish you never had to go home. The hotel name initially threw me, because it has the word hashish in it; I was wondering if maybe that's why it's so popular. (As to the spelling, take your pick—remember, Arabic has no vowels.) But of course hashish is just the harvest; the Red Sea has nothing to do with smoking anything funny, at least nothing we ever saw. One year, we take our group to this paradise, to unwind at the end of the trip.

The Sahl Hasheesh has views from all over the grounds of the crystal, turquoise water. Like the houses in Santorini, Greece, each villa's whitewashed exterior stands out against the blue water and green land. The roofs are all gold domes, and inside, each spacious villa includes a deep marble soaking tub in the bathroom, a separate bedroom and a living room. They are all done up in Moroccan-style hangings and tall brass teapots on trays, with a cascade of bougainvillea outside your patio. A few of the resort's villas are even larger, and a couple (including Momo's) have private pools. Sure, you can visit the hotel's swimming pool, an infinity pool with the Red Sea behind the disappearing line and a bar you can breaststroke up to. But nothing beats being able to take a moonlight dip in your own backyard.

It is a beautiful, relaxing day, and several people go snorkeling or even diving, since the Red Sea features some of the best scuba and snorkeling waters in the world. This morning, Greg and I rent snorkeling equipment, and go down to jump into the sea from the dock that extends out over the water and ends in a large covered pavilion. We get to the pier, don our flippers and masks, and step from the ladder into the sea. Well, I do, anyway. Greg gamely goes down the three-rung ladder, but when the strong lapping waves begin their rhythmic rocking, he doesn't let go.

I'm already out eight feet from the pier. "Come on! It's awesome out here!"

"Uh, no, I'm going to stay at the ladder for a bit."

I swim back to him. "What's up? I thought you were excited to do this."

"Well, I'm not much of a swimmer. Remember, I almost drowned when I was six."

I rack my brain, recalling the sailboat where we both got incredibly seasick and had to sit staring at the horizon and comforting each other by singing "Sweet Baby James" over and over until we got to shore. I've been on a powerboat with Greg, too, on a lake in Alabama. Possibly, I have heard the drowning story before—his dad grabbed him by the nape of his neck and pulled him out—but I imagined we had been swimming together; after all, I was partly raised in Hawaii, and had spent all three years there in the water. Could I not have been swimming in so long? It dawns on me that this man, whom I consider my soul-mate and have spent most of my adult life with, has, in all my memory, never been closer to the water than sitting in those boats. How brave he was to try snorkeling in the Red Sea.

After much encouragement, plus a return trip to the snorkel outfitters for a life vest, Greg makes it into the water, and even swims a bit from the platform, his dog paddle transforming into something more elegant as he gets used to the waves. Our afternoon doesn't disappoint; just under the ocean surface, fish and plant life teem—a whole world living right under our noses. We see what looks like an angelfish with a four-foot wingspan (later I find out it's a batfish), entire reefs of coral, and a whole slew of tropical fish, including my favorite, a yellow tang, its tiny bottlenose leading it about as it swims merrily ahead of us.

Greg is captivated now, delighted to stay; for me, it brings back happy memories of lazy weekend afternoons in Oahu's Hanauma Bay, and I am pleased that Greg has taken to the sport. The water makes wavelets, and while we are swimming it seems somehow comforting, lapping at us as we snorkel; I even see a shine on the ocean floor and hold my breath and dive down to check it out, blowing the water out of the snorkel as I surface. We pet the floating jellyfish, which do not sting here as they do in Hawaii. But after two hours in the water, we are suddenly exhausted from the strain of fighting the current and ravenous from the exercise. Reluctantly, we swim to the platform and take off our duck flippers, turning them in before heading to the pool bar for a stylish-looking, yet sadly virgin, cocktail.

Tonight is a birthday celebration for Angie, a petite, older blonde; the spectacular Red Sea and the fabulous surroundings of the hotel are the perfect backdrop for an occasion. I am especially gratified because the catering manager came down earlier today and consulted on the menu, then allowed me to select the locale. I picked the porch outside the main dining room, overlooking both the pool and the sea. This evening we dine in wicker chairs at a long table set with yellow flowers and cobalt blue goblets that contrast prettily.

The food is Middle Eastern but not especially Egyptian: lamb stew, tiny pasta grains of steamed couscous, chicken in a tagine, the distinctive pot a cross between a stovepipe and a circus hat. In the middle of the meal, we are briefly joined by the head of Sonesta Cruise Lines, who is a good friend of Momo's. He charms us by telling stories of his travels through Europe with Mohamed, including a trick they played on a hotel clerk in Venice who was rude to them. They called an American friend of theirs to help get revenge on the clerk, and, after "Johnny from the American Embassy" called the front desk to make sure his VIPs were being well looked after, the clerk unexpectedly came knocking on the door to say they were being upgraded to suites.

Inside, the live music is an Ottmar Liebert-esque guitarist, and we open the doors to hear better. Greg smiles and offers me his hand in a romantic gesture, surprising me with his offer to dance.

We begin to sway a little next to our table, and as the main dining room has started to clear out, the guitarist moves outside to our party. We dance toward the side of the pool, the starry night clear overhead, the moon peeking out from behind a single cloud. I glance over his shoulder past the pool at the pavilion jutting out over the Red Sea and the moonlight reflecting on the water. I sigh happily into Greg's neck. At the end of the song, Greg kisses me, then we head to our table for birthday cake.

After dinner, a few of us are invited to Momo's. Greg and I go, as do Angie and Libby, an Amazonian brunette with crisp blue eyes—Libby has a bit of a crush on Shakky, as does her mother, who is also on the trip. Libby and Pamela have been estranged for a while, as Pamela is a woo-woo seeker, but also a raging alcoholic. Libby called her mom to ask her if she could babysit her grandchildren so Libby could go on this trip, but Pamela said she already had plans. When Libby arrived in Cairo, she was shocked to find that her mother's plans had unfolded as follows: Pamela had gotten off the phone, called us, and booked her own passage on the same trip without mentioning Libby. Families. You can't shoot them, you can't leave them. Not really.

They were oil and water at the beginning, but Egypt has that wacky influence, and one evening on the cruise, they both stayed behind to talk things out. They had their own private intervention and healing, and after that acted the way you would hope a mother and a grown daughter would. Now the only animosity between them is good-humored—which of them does Shakky like better? Since Libby looks like a taller, plumper version of Snow White, I'm guessing she would win, but Shakky is doing his best to keep them both at arm's length; the blessing and the curse of the tour guide is to balance the flirting so the guests all like you but you don't step over the line. Shakky likes to look at a lady, then grin evilly and tell Greg and me, "I would give her *no mercy!*" flinging his arm out for emphasis.

We always roll our eyes and agree, "Sure, Shakky," while trying hard not to imagine what that might look like. As Greg says, "Where is that stick so I can poke my mind's eye out?" But of course the ladies love it. Shakky once said it to Eleanor's face. Despite her cool façade, she laughed and shot back, "You might give me no mercy, Shakky, but it would kill you!" He looked astonished, but not the least bit unhappy at the thought.

We're all lounging on deck chairs near Momo's pool and talking as we look up at the galaxy above. The sky bursts with its own nightlights, and we are treated to the curve of the Milky Way. Greg relaxes near me, and Shakky and Mohamed, who are both staying in this villa, are deep in conversation with the women. Since it's a one-bedroom, I ask Shakky if he sleeps on the sofa. He wrinkles his nose at me sheepishly and points to my chaise longue. "I sleep here. It is better outside." He gestures up; though I agree it's lovely, I'm still wary. There's something about sleeping out in the open I can't reconcile with the enveloping coziness of my bed's duvet and soft pillows.

It is getting to be that time, but the company is so excellent we don't want to leave. The conversation drifts from topic to topic, everyone swapping favorite stories from the trip. Eventually, Mohamed breaks; he yawns, rises and makes his excuses. The floor-to-ceiling windows across the back of the villa reveal Momo as he passes through the living room, shuts off the light and enters his bedroom.

He flips on the bedroom light as we continue to chat. Through the glass, we see Momo head into the bathroom and close the door, then come out a few minutes later. He starts to undress, silhouetted against the opaque white shade, his disconnected ankles protruding beneath it. We are only half-aware, but the conversation slows, then stops, as the situation dawns on all of us simultaneously. Angie and I both turn as Momo walks towards the side of the room, where the shade is only pulled down to waist-height, and drops his pants. There is a moment's pause, then Greg takes a deep breath and announces: "There's a full moon tonight."

Screaming with laughter, all clutching each other, we watch helplessly—this is one car crash we cannot turn away from. A moment later, our beloved Mohamed turns around, revealing to us all what an Egyptian man looks like totally starkers. Angie and I are shouting, "Noooooooo" in the slow-motion way you see sometimes in a movie—I am trying to avert my head, and at the same time cover Angie's eyes, but it is too late. We are all laughing and falling on each other, chortling and wiping our eyes. Oblivious, Mohamed climbs into bed and snaps off the light.

It was five years before I worked up the nerve to tell Momo this story, and he took it in stride. He arched his eyebrow in my direction and asked, "So, what did you think?" And then he laughed his big, hearty, Momo laugh, and I knew all was forgiven

TUE LITTLE PRINCE

Louise, a friend from Australia, came on a Spirit Quest Tour one year. She brought her son, Tom, whose ninth birthday fell as we sailed up the Nile. Louise had five children, and Mum liked to take each child away alone on a special trip. Tom was mischievous from the start, a bright, energetic towhead with a wicked smile. I presumed it would be hard for him to integrate, as he was a good thirty years younger than anyone else in the group, but he had that uncanny ability to mix easily with adults, holding his own in a conversation and feigning interest on the rare occasions when he did not actively participate.

Over the course of the trip, Tom endeared himself to each of us. He constantly played practical jokes on Zach, another of our travelers, or Greg, and they both took to him immediately. Possibly Tom could see that in their hearts Greg and Zach were actually little kids, too. One day I watched the three of them chasing each other around the deck pool. Zach, a head taller than Greg, with a boyish haircut and a Dudley Do-Right chin, swept Tom up onto his shoulders and together they turned on Greg, who ran towards me in mock fear, his eyes lit by the chase.

After a few days, someone started calling him Prince Tom—probably Shakky—and his proud mum picked it up. Soon that was how everyone referred to him. After a few days, he got kind of a big head about it, and started strutting a little bit. And why not? He was very nearly nine, had the whole world ahead of him, and here he was singled out to take this most special of trips with his beloved mother—the fawned-upon only child in our whole group. I secretly wished someone would call me Princess Halle.

A few days before Prince Tom's birthday, we visited the Cairo Museum, and in the high-end shopping arcade across the street we saw a chess set that made Tom's jaw drop. Each of the pieces was an Egyptian god, goddess, or priest, wearing their finest clothes; their headdresses perched on their regal heads. They were laden with gold jewelry and the gold collars so often worn by the Egyptian royalty; modeled plastic has apparently come a long way. The pantheon stood on a board inlaid with gold and black alternating squares; to a child's eyes, it was a magical Technicolor incarnation of the plain sand-and-beige statues we had been visiting. Best of all for Tom, the bishops were renderings of Horus, the falcon-headed god at the Temple at Edfu, Tom's favorite.

Judith, who was with us on that trip, saw the light in Tom's eyes when he looked at the chess set, and motioned to Zach to distract the boy. Since Tom refused to leave the shop, Zach quickly became interested in another chess set, and asked Tom to look at it. Judith went up to the counter and slapped down her credit card, foregoing the almost obligatory bargaining process that can take place even in the high-end tourists shops. $150 later, the chess set surreptitiously stowed in Judith's backpack, we unglued Tom from the sets with the promise that we would try to return at the end of the trip, and maybe Louise would buy one for him.

As we cruised up the Nile, seeing and learning about the gods, we thought Tom had forgotten about the chess set until we saw a black basalt statue of a goddess. "Like the chess piece," he pointed out, "only not as dressed up." The unpainted black stone statue featured none of the finery of the modeled pieces.

The night of Tom's birthday, we had arranged a party for him on the cruise ship. Our group gathered in anticipation of the enjoyable evening, everyone dressed in their finest clothes—most in our fancy galabeyas. The chefs had prepared a special buffet, and afterwards the staff came out, singing, beating drums and a tambourine, and performing an Arabic dance. They pulled Tom out onto the buffet floor and let him go crazy as the chanting and the drumming built to a frenzied conclusion.

Afterwards, they served a beautiful birthday cake to the group, and we all sang "Happy Birthday" to Tom. As he blew out the candles, I asked Tom (as I always ask) what he had wished for. His look inquired if I was honestly that dumb, and he said in his strong Australian accent, "Of course I cahn't tell yew!"

Then it was time for the presents. Louise had bought Tom several souvenirs, including a Horus statue, so Tom was pleased. We all gave him a card that Judith had made (handy woman that she is) and passed around earlier for us all to sign. Everyone had chipped in money to pay for the chess set, and now the flat package was passed to Tom, who almost licked his chops, the way only a child with a huge present can. He tore into the wrapping, and when he saw his special gift, he hooted with glee. "Yes!" he cried, punching his small fist into the air. "Yes!"

At the end of the evening, as we were standing around saying goodbye, I felt a quick tug on my skirt. Tom motioned me down and put his hand around the nape of my neck, pulling my ear towards his face. The burr was soft, but still wicked. "You asked what I wished for? Well, I got it!" Then he released my neck and raced off, the chess set clutched under his arm. The rest of the trip, there was a chess game almost every night, and Tom turned out to be a good competitor. Louise told me that at home the chess set took up residence in their living room, in a special place of honor where Tom could see it every day and play as often as he liked.

*   *   *   *   *

You know on trips how you make friends sometimes, and then never talk to them when you get back? We've been lucky in that many of our guests have stayed in touch over the years. With Louise it was no different, and after she returned to Australia, she stayed in contact by e-mail, keeping us abreast of her family's goings-on almost every month. She even said she might join us for another trip.

A couple of years later, the night before we left for a scouting trip to Bali, we received an e-mail from Louise titled only, "Prince Tom." I opened it immediately, thinking Tom must have done something excellent at school to warrant the old nickname from the trip. It was addressed only to Greg, Mohamed and me:

Our Prince Tom was taken by God tragically yesterday to serve as an angel. We both loved and enjoyed our trip with you all and I will hold it in my heart forever.

Pray that Horus looks over him.

Love to you all.

I read it again, thinking it must be some kind of joke. Then I burst into tears, and started yelling for Greg, who raced into the room at the sound of my agonized voice. "Tom died. Tom… died." I could hardly believe it. My words were disembodied, useless things.

"Who? Who died?" I'm sure Greg thought some movie star had been carried off. This is the type of thing he imagines I would get hysterical over.

"Tom. Prince Tom." I tried to slow down. "Louise's Tom. Yesterday. She doesn't say how."

"Oh, my God." Greg's face collapsed, and he held me while we both cried.

Our whole trip to Bali was colored by this tragedy and I wept every day for the entire two weeks. It seemed so unfair, so wrong. Louise had five children, who ranged in age over a fifteen-year span, and Tom was exactly in the middle. After the funeral, after things had settled, Louise was a mess for more than a year. She couldn't go to the grocery store without feeling that life was hopeless, and I didn't blame her. She put her house, a gorgeous property in the tony district of Avalon, up for sale.

And then, finally, she made plans to bring her youngest children, Wyatt and Odette, to Egypt. She wanted Tom's ashes interred in a Horus statue she had commissioned in Australia, and she proposed we do a ceremony for him at the Temple of Horus.

Tom and Wyatt looked a lot alike, with the same blond haircut, green eyes and set jaw, and during the trip I began to notice uncanny resemblances in their characteristics. The kids had tried to put the tragedy behind them, but it was all still so raw, and Wyatt and Tom were only a year apart. They had done everything together, and now Wyatt had to make his way on his own, the little brother no more. Odette, two years younger, with a cheeky, joyous personality, seemed fairly comfortable. Wyatt was standoffish and quiet initially, but eventually they both warmed to us, enough that Greg and I felt is if we were taking on the role of family. More than once I wished I was mother to these beautiful spirits, strong and yet delicate, every breath still shaping their lives, but their future vastly uncertain now that Tom had abruptly gone.

Louise brought two things: a copy of the children's classic, *The Little Prince*, and enough laminated postcards for the whole group with Tom's face on the front and a quote from the book on the reverse. She lent me *The Little Prince*, and each night on the ship I read a little, marveling over it and wondering how I had missed this book as a child. Eventually, Judith reminded me that it had been one of my favorites. How strange it is that the things we often cherish as children are lost to us as adults. How could I forget these funny cartoon pictures of a prince standing on a planet so small that nothing but a few flowerpots fit on it? But it's these same forgettings that will serve Wyatt and Odette well, that will allow them to sleep through the night, and eventually the pain of losing their brother will subside until there is no more brother, just a few memories and old pictures. Louise will not be so lucky.

The morning of the memorial service I stumbled out of my cabin, hours before dawn. On my way to the stairs, I stopped stock-still, dazed to see Tom's face right in front of me. I blinked, yet it was still Tom, standing there in the flesh. I had little sleep the night before, and I was carrying the fuzz of waking up, so I blinked again. This time, when I opened my eyes, it was his brother Wyatt standing there, waiting for me to go first. But oh, how I was sure it had been Tom a moment earlier, come to join us on the morning of his memorial. I ruffled Wyatt's hair to cover my uncertainty, and then went to get Greg some coffee.

We went at dawn to the Temple of Horus, our first morning visit. We arrived in darkness and moved into the light, just as the people who built the temple did, moving from the dark god Set into the light of Horus, the falcon-headed son of Osiris. Outside the main walls, lit dimly, Greg spoke the familiar words of the myth of Isis and Osiris, Nepthys and Set. Then we entered the compound and while everyone else was looking at the architecture and listening to Shakky's lecture, I went in to prepare the space in the Holy of Holies.

The altar became Tom's altar—his picture went up in the center, and I lit a candle for him. When everyone else got there, we passed out the laminated postcards of Tom. Greg made a little speech, then Odette tried to read the quote from *The Little Prince*, but she began to cry too hard. The whole trip, she hadn't even shed a tear—I had even dared to hope she was past the grieving stage—but now she struggled to get a full sentence out. I picked up the card, put my arms around her, and with my own voice full of anguish, read the quote for Odette.

Then everyone who knew Tom talked about his or her memories. My favorite story was recounted by Debra, his mum's oldest friend. Apparently, Tom picked out a bright pink thong bikini for her as a present, and insisted on giving it to her over Louise's objections. Debra, not a small woman, put it on and did a cannonball into the pool, right over Tom's head. Everybody laughed and everybody cried, as it feels right to do at a memorial service, and Louise brought a little vial of Tom's ashes to sprinkle in the Temple of Horus.

Once, when we were in Munich and I was jetlagged, I stepped off the curb into the street, forgetting for a moment it was a one-way street and I had been looking in the wrong direction. Greg leaped forward, grabbed my arm, and yanked me out of the path of a car that was about to hit me. He probably saved my life, or at least prevented me from limping through the rest of it. Winston Churchill suffered a similar experience in New York City, 1934, and since Greg was not with him, Churchill was struck by a taxi. He ended up in hospital; a second later, a few inches, he would probably have been killed and perhaps the outcome of World War II would have been different.

Our lives are braided like DNA, and we so often fail to recognize that we are here, not by ourselves, not with our spouse, our children, our friends, but with everyone we touch, and everyone they touch and, by extension, the whole world. One boy's death changes that world, subtly or profoundly, depending on where you are in proximity to him. Tom's death now means we have created a scholarship in his name for Egyptian orphans, and our groups contribute when we go, as one of our ways of giving back to Egypt. Hopefully, in this small gesture, Tom's passing will help bring ease to the hardship in other children's lives. For Louise, Wyatt, Odette, and Tom's other siblings, I can only hope there are reasons though we cannot see them, and that time will bring more healing.

WHERE I FIND MUSIC IN THE WILDERNESS

Getting out to the Sinai is something of a chore. You have to wake up crazy early, check out of your hotel, board the coach and start the ride. It's six hours of straight driving, and if you're like most of the people I've traveled with, you'll need at least two (probably three) stops along the way, making the trip an all-day affair including lunch. I suppose not too harsh compared to the thousands of pilgrims who rode their mules, camels, or horses, or who walked hundreds of miles to get there. The fact that they made it at all is a real miracle.

We're delighted by the Egyptian landscape of empty calorie choices at the first rest stop, a modified gas station. Mini-croissants filled with dabs of chocolate (sort of a highbrow Little Debbie) share space with a huge assortment of roasted nuts and seeds. The potato chips—or crisps, as they say in Europe—come in a vast number of flavors, including lime and spice, tomato sauce, pizza, and my favorite: kebab, which tastes as if grilled lamb and a spud had a baby. Though the meat-flavored chip grosses out most of our troupe, I am intrigued. It reminds me of that scene in *Willie Wonka* where he walks Violet Beauregarde through her three-course chewing gum meal. Look what science has wrought; artificial flavoring has never before been used to such imagination. Tourist Eating is in full force as we stock up, but only Carter and I are brave enough to buy the kebab chips.

At the next stop, we go into the loo, where a young girl of twelve or thirteen is taking the toilet fees of one pound each. She sees my rings, and calls to me, very bossy, "Come here." Given my history of fun local interactions, I do. She audaciously takes off my little pinkie ring, a lovely orange polished stone set with a small diamond, that Greg bought for me at a fossil shop in Munich years ago. "Thank you," she says, putting the ring on her own finger. I smile, a little disconcerted, and ask for the ring. She starts to pull it off, but winces. "Owww—too hard!" Uncharitably, I think, "Enta f'kearny abeet?!" Vivian and Rose step out of the adjacent stalls simultaneously, looking concerned. I roll my eyes at them, step forward, and yank at the ring. "OWW!" she yells, perhaps in real discomfort this time.

I am shaking a little—I don't know why this encounter upsets me; she's barely more than a girl. But there is something about her swagger, her confidence, that makes me lose mine, and I feel suddenly close to tears. Instead, I hold my hand out and tell her clearly to take the ring off. She shrugs and hands it over without difficulty, then the three of us exit. Outside, I tell Shakky what happened, more shocked than upset. He makes a beeline into the Ladies' Room.

"Don't you EVER even joke with our clients!" Shakky yells at her, his finger wagging in her face. She shrinks before him, all the bravado going out of her in a whoosh, and I know it will be a long time before she tries to pull one over on a tourist again. Less than a month later, I lose the ring in an airport somewhere and wish that, as often happens when someone admires something of mine, I had given her the ring. Since I never lose my jewelry, perhaps this was a lesson for me. But by refusing to give into her, she learned that it was unacceptable to bully people. I am comforted by the true beauty of the situation, that both lessons were orchestrated simultaneously.

The big stop on the way to the Sinai is at the Red Sea, where we pull into a little beach town right around lunchtime. Many dining options are available in these streets, from street falafel to a half–chicken. We dine on seafood, of course, since it's been caught that morning: calamari, the slices thick and crisp; fried fish that would make the English weep; grilled fish served whole. Greg opens his to fillet it, and is surprised to discover the bones of the fish are blue. Some of the fish here eat so much phosphorus it turns the whole cartoon-length of the fishbone the color of the ocean.

The best thing is the fish soup—an assortment of tiny mussels and tender shrimp, sea snails, squid, and pieces of fish, simmered in a stock that tastes rich but not fishy. Observed by the surprised-looking taxidermied sea turtle perched on the counter, I eat two bowls of soup, and then have no room for the invariable French fries. Rusty helps himself to my leftovers.

After lunch, some of us smoke shisha on the grassy outdoor seating area of the restaurant next door, spending two dollars on enough shisha for six of us. We stretch out for half an hour, enjoying the sun on our faces and petting the local cats, who are obviously favored by the restaurant staff with leftover fish. Then we board the bus to get a closer look at the water, and a few minutes later are walking out into the sand of a local beach.

I am appalled at the garbage and litter everywhere. When will Egypt create a recycling program? More importantly, when will Egypt educate its citizens that the outdoors is not one big waste dump? But I know it's a cultural difference, and Egypt is certainly not the world's only offender. Recently I saw some jerk, in the middle of Las Vegas, open his car door and dump his ashtray into the road. This is the sort of thing that makes me roll down the car window and scream at them, my efforts at being woo-woo utterly shot in that moment. At least in the U.S. it's changing from the days of our parents, when people would routinely go camping or picnicking and simply leave all the trash wherever it fell.

Past the end of the line of garbage, this beach is better than most; the sand is soft and warm, the water laps gently, creating small whitecaps farther out. The sea is thick like opaque glass, varying from aquamarine to teal, and comes up no further than your chest for at least fifty yards. We have all been bad kids, as we have "borrowed" towels from our hotel in Cairo (we returned them when we got back two days later). Everyone has put their bathing suits under their clothes in anticipation of today, except Eleanor and Rose, who turn the rear of the coach into a quickie changing room. As gleeful as children, we run into the water to enjoy an hour in the salt of the Red Sea.

It quickly becomes clear that we are at a local (non-tourist) beach, because there are almost no other people here, and those who are enjoying this typical afternoon at the seaside are all Muslim. We are a significant source of fascination, for though the Egyptian men are in swim trunks (God knows what possesses men who are forty pounds overweight to don Speedos), the women wear long sleeves and long pants, wading in fully clothed. Some are even in burkas, their full veils trailing in the water. My American sunglasses don't recognize the scene at all, so the fascination is on both sides.

We swim further out and Greg comes across a reef that is effectively a low wall. We cross that reef, but the other side of the barrier is still surprisingly shallow and warm, the water only up to the tops of our heads. Here we meet a couple of young men in a paddle boat, who smile, calling, "America, Number One!" and circle us, trying to speak in what little English they have. They are so excited to meet us; I wonder how things would be if this were America, and someone ran into Arabs at their hometown beach. I turn away for a moment and say a quick prayer for peace in the world.

Too quickly, it is time to go and we wade to shore, turning the bus into a ladies' changing room again. Our suits hang on the overhead luggage racks to dry while we drive to the Sinai. I share my seat with Judith so that Greg and Lyra can talk quietly together about the temples. It's been a delightful afternoon, and Mother and I sleep until our next rest stop, a wadi—a desert oasis formed by a dry valley or riverbed that occasionally floods.

Wadi Feiran figured prominently in the Bible. Supposedly, it's the place where Moses struck his staff, causing water to gush from a rock, and where one of the most important battles of the time was fought—Israelites v. Amelecites. Exodus 17 is all about Wadi Feiran, today called the "Pearl of the Sinai" because it's a gorgeous oasis in the midst of stark Sinai desert cliffs, marked by a huge cluster of palm trees out in the middle of nowhere.

We pull into Wadi Feiran to visit a Bedouin farm. Even in the oasis everything seems mostly brown, including the high fence of dead grasses that acts as walls surrounding their compound. Inside, though, is a surprising half-acre of green—basil and mint alongside lettuces and what appears to be a live version of the fence grass. Around a small fire, on an eight-foot-long log serving as their bench, sit several Bedouin men. One detaches from the group and comes over to greet us, shaking hands with Shakky as he does, and gives us a tour of the place.

We are treated to a pen full of goats, several of them just days old, all bleating comfortably as the man tosses in armfuls of alfalfa grass. Stooping down over the chicken wire slung between the wooden gateposts, he scoops up a week-old kid and hands the speckled creature to me. Vivian, Rose, Eleanor and Judith exclaim over him and pet him as he is passed around, then he curls into my arms and goes to sleep, his head resting in my hand. Thank goodness my dogs are thousands of miles away and can't see their alpha mom falling in love with this foreign creature. I am glad there is no way I could bring the baby goat home, because I feel as if I could move heaven and earth right now to make him mine. As I reluctantly hand him over to his Bedouin owner, I focus on the older goats who have outgrown their cuteness and their playful high kicks in the yard. It's the only way I will get out of here without the kid.

When I rejoin the group they are drinking tea under a large open tent that has been constructed from thin tree trunks, using colorful Bedouin blankets as a roof. The log benches are here, too, lining the perimeter of the tent poles, covered in more blankets to further cushion our bottoms. I glance at Lyra, who smiles at me, then I drop down in an empty spot next to Greg. Grabbing the blackened kettle from the fire and pouring hot water into a small glass, a Bedouin adds a spoonful of crushed tea leaves, swirls it round and hands it over with a flourish. Encouraged by my ability to touch the glass without burning my fingers, I take a gulp of the tea, but nearly spit it right out. At least a tablespoon of sugar has been added to my four ounces of tea—I try to think of it as liquid candy, but I can't force it down, and take only another sip before abandoning the glass among the empties he is collecting. The rest of my group either has a more highly developed sweet tooth than mine or is much more polite.

Though we know there's a bathroom on the bus, it gets a little difficult trying to pee on a moving vehicle cutting hairpin turns through the Sinai. Several of the ladies therefore decide to brave the bathroom, basically an outhouse in a corner of the compound. At least it's fairly secluded, and when we get inside, we are thrilled to discover a real flush toilet in a concrete floor, and though it smells strange, it's no worse than the clean goat pen. Pleased, we take turns in the single stall and then climb aboard for the final hour of the trip.

Now awake, I notice the drama of the looming cliffs, the brown and white mottled layers, which have been standing since God was a boy. Outside the oasis is desert and wavy mountains, the occasional lone Sycamore tree and even rarer bush scrub. We are starting to see camels, some ridden by Bedouin, one tied to a tree (his master hopefully not too far off) and once… a whole herd of camels out on their own, foraging and enjoying the desert sun. Soon, too, appear two-story stucco structures—it is clear the Bedouin have brought schools and shops out into the wilderness, making it only a little less wild. It's strange to come around a corner and see a group of buildings nestled in the shadow of a mountain, but everyone has to reside somewhere, and a few have chosen to make their lives in these remote locales.

As dark settles in, we arrive at our destination passing through a wooden guard gate; the overhead crosspiece on the entrance makes it seem as if we're entering a desert dude ranch. An oversized wagon wheel reinforces this image, but Shakky quickly dispels this impression with the story of the Catherine Wheel and the saint after which it is named:

"In the fourth century was a lady called Catherine, who lived in Alex and refused to marry, even though she was very beautiful and many men want her. She went to the Roman Emperor Maximilian, who was persecuting the Christians. She begged him to stop, because Jesus was the way, you know? Normally trying to convince Max of something was punishable by death but he like her, and she was sooooo beautiful. He brought in fifty learn-ed men to show her she was wrong. Instead, she converted them all to Christianity! The Emperor is pissed! So he had all the philosophers burned at the stake, then he tried to bribe Catherine by offering her lands and marriage. But she refused! So he had her beaten and thrown into prison, then he goes off to war. By the time he return, she convert all his guard and also his queen.

Maximilian has everyone killed, even his queen, and sentences Catherine to die on a spiky wheel, like the one you just saw. But when they put her on the wheel, it break apart, and sends spikes out into the audience, where it kills some of the people who came to watch Catherine die. Now he has the poor lady behead. Her body is picked up by angels and carried to Mount Sinai."

Her ill-fated execution is how the modern Catherine Wheel, the spinning firework from which sparks fly off in all directions, got its name. Over a hundred years after Catherine's death, the Emperor Justinian built a monastery here, and now the whole area is known as St. Catherine's.

This story wakes everybody up a bit—almost none of us has heard of St. Catherine, not to be confused with St. Catherine of Siena, who was pretty feisty and outspoken in her own time, a thousand years later. We are still chatting about how much might be legend as we get off the bus and head to the dude ranch lodge for the requisite key ceremony.

They have cold towels and iced karkady waiting for us (in the winter, it's hot towels and warm karkady) and little tea cakes. We weary pilgrims are immensely grateful and, refreshed, segue into a little party under the high wooden rafters as we wait for our room keys to be handed over. They are on huge brass plates nearly four inches across—heavy to carry but hard to lose, though here it's too far to walk them to the front desk. Ready for dinner, we climb aboard and are driven to our rooms.

A few minutes later we are standing in the middle of a vast area of land with cozy stone cabins barely visible in the dark. The luggage is swiftly unloaded, we say farewell to each other, and the Bedouin staff whisks us off two at a time, humping all the bags they can carry; they will make as many trips as is needed. Tips are included, but we still hand our escort a few dollars as he leaves us. Even out here in the desert's desert, the dollar is still as accepted as the Egyptian pound.

We look around the large stone abode, one of four connecting cabins that make it seem we are in Sinai townhouses. We have a large living room, a tile floor, oversized benches and chairs, a back porch, and a separate bedroom. They have no double beds; Sen had advised me of this earlier. But we can move the heavy wooden nightstand out of the way and push the beds together if we want. The closet is larger than we have seen anywhere else on the trip, containing deep shelves on one side (though we aren't staying as long as in other hotels, the closet is so sensible I wish I could pack it and haul it back to Cairo). We have enough room it is not even necessary to fully unpack, as we can spread all the suitcases out. A large tumbleweed on the shelf over the heavy wooden door is the only decoration other than the red and white Bedouin seat cushions. The whole atmosphere is rustic; it reminds me of the desert in California or Sedona, only here everything is the color of sand.

Suddenly starving, we head to the restaurant, a friendly, lit building a hundred yards away at the top of a hill. Four or five flights of steps take us there, but I require several breaks. The high altitude is sneaky, and I'm fine one minute, winded the next, typical for those unused to mountain air. Inside is reminiscent of a ski lodge—a couple of huge rooms supporting a high wooden roof, a giant fireplace that sadly does not warm the space enough in the winter, and long trestle tables, sufficient seating for over two hundred people.

The food is laid out buffet-style in big chafing dishes, and it's the kind of food you want when you're climbing a mountain—lots of pasta, grilled chicken, a different fish dish each night, several choices of steamed vegetables and potatoes. The men carbo-load, and the women tentatively have their only bite of noodles in ages. We shrug, knowing we will work it off tomorrow. The food is good, not great, and it's hearty. No one lingers after dinner; the combination of the altitude and the long ride has us all exhausted and ready for sleep.

The next morning the Sinai mountains surround us on all sides as Greg and I leave our little stone cabin and climb the steps to breakfast. The hot buffet is unvarying: a chafing dish of little wieners, another of potatoes, one of grilled tomatoes, and one of boiled eggs. There are also many trays of pastry and fresh fruit, with large urns of coffee, tea, and hot milk alongside. Last, there is a tureen of porridge, seemingly made of short, broken pieces of pasta in a sweet milky soup. It's weird, but Greg likes it, and several others agree. Everyone sits with their own group, and there is little mingling between the various nationalities unless you run into someone at the buffet. I count cliques of Germans, French, Americans, and Israelis, all here to climb the mountain. Of course, Judith makes friends with several, speaking to the Germans and the French in their own tongues.

After breakfast, we sit outside the cabin enjoying the morning sunshine, the crispness of the air, the mild temperature. Our narrow porch has high rock walls on each side that allow privacy from the rooms flanking us, while affording a good view of the stark landscape. Greg is about to turn on some music—he carries iPod speakers on his travels like runners carry water—when there's a knock on the heavy wooden door. It's Shakky, at a loose end until it's time to leave. We invite him in, and the insistent rhythms of The Dave Matthews Band carry us out onto the porch.

The weather is perfect—cool in the shade, warm in the sun—and the clean, clear air of the mountains invites us to breathe deeply. Greg turns up the music and Carter ambles over, drawn to the sound. He's a daily cigar smoker (at least on vacation) and he lights one, sitting down on a corner of our porch where the smoke won't blow in our direction. Carter looks so happy to be here—it's exactly how I feel, too. I look with love at Greg, at Shakky, and I start to dance to Sonia Dada, the lush melodies and funky beat washing over me. With no one around to make him feel self-conscious, Greg joins me, grabbing me up in a kind of groovy waltz, and we dance to the whole song, laughing and simply enjoying this moment.

When the next song starts, Shakky asks how well we know Vivian, who is not certain if she will climb the mountain even now, because of the altitude and her personal fears. Because I am still drawn to the music I keep dancing on my own, uninhibited by the men I am with or my own concerns about any lack of grace. I'm more and more into it, and the guys are lost in their conversation, ignoring me completely. Suddenly, it's as if I can feel the inky black notes of the music being injected into my veins and I'm mainlining the tune. I look out into this vast desert and feel what jazz singers and sax players must feel, that deeper layer of understanding about the music that had always eluded me. I've had years of training, but this is different, like the music and I understand each other. I hear the harmony lines individually; I can pick out the instruments' unique sounds. Grateful for this new plane of existence, I stay connected to the music until it is time for our next adventure... climbing Gebel Musa—Mount Moses.

CLIMBING GEBEL MUSA

What did God say to Moses when he got sick?
Take two tablets and call me in the morning.
- Eric Sieverling, Egypt, 2009

Most of the people who ascend Mount Moses are instructed by their guides to summit at dawn. It might be a scheduling thing—many people spend only a single night here, whereas we prefer to spend two or three since it's such a long drive. They haul their cookies out of bed at 1am, staggering up the mountain in the dark, see dawn at the top, and then head down. By the time we are at breakfast, they are all back, triumphant, loopy from lack of sleep, and still planning a trip to St. Catherine's monastery in the next couple hours, after which they will return to Cairo.

We will start the climb after a hearty lunch and a last carbo-load. You're certainly more alert in midday and, if you stay at the top until the sun dips past the tippy-top of the mountain, you can still make it to base camp before darkness covers you. Then you can take your time winding down the path to the bottom in the dark, arriving at the hotel for a late dinner.

So we relax before lunch. We take a quick bus ride to the Bedouin craft collective. Most of the pieces you can buy in Egypt are dirt cheap because of the economy, the cost of materials, and the average low salary. Everyone takes advantage of the rock-bottom prices and shops a lot when they visit. Out in the Sinai desert, one woman is evolving past that.

Salema Gabely started off in a tent with four other women, creating beaded designs that are typical of the Bedouin people, the nomadic tribes who come from that area. Salema's work, and that of her small group, grew until now they have over 500 Bedouin women from multiple local tribes, all creating exquisite pillowcases, handbags, and jewelry. When you buy a scarf there, not only is it hand-beaded, but the same tribe wove the fine cotton or wool fabric themselves. The best part is it's all fair trade pricing, which is more expensive, but nothing more than you would pay at a shop like Pier One. This business method has allowed Salema to buy a house, a big one, and to create the store in what must have been the living room of the property.

There's also a large tiled porch where you can sit and drink mint tea, though the prices are fixed, so there's no bargaining to accompany your beverage. Knowing the money is going directly to the women who made the goods, it's easy to open your heart and your wallet wider, and this tiny pit stop has become a favorite of our groups, as people quickly remember friends at home who need extra gifts. Salema bustles around, accepting (as most merchants do) Egyptian pounds, U.S. dollars, and Euros, and no one minds standing in line for their flood of purchases to be counted and rung up.

Afterwards, the coach drops us off and Greg and I go to our cabin for a bathroom break, lacing on our hiking boots to face the mountain. Then we meet everyone at the bus, standing around as more brave pilgrims show up. Vivian has decided she's going to try, at least as far as base camp, 4,000 feet up.

There are two ways to get to the top of Mount Moses but both involve mucho walking. The first is to start at the bottom and walk all the way, then turn around and go down. It's many hours of using your feet, and the grade is somewhat steep despite a number of switchbacks. The second, more usual method, is to hire a camel and a Bedouin guide, and to travel by camelback up to base camp. This trip takes two-and-a-half hours, just to get there. Then you dismount, walk a little ways, and abruptly face the more strenuous outdoor workout known as the "700 steps," a steep set of stairs cut into the mountain itself.

At the top (6600 feet, according to the GPS of a man we met there) you turn around and go down the same path, though it is rare to see anyone return to the bottom on a camel.

A ten-minute ride brings us to the outskirts of St. Catherine's Monastery, which we will visit tomorrow, and we pull into a small parking lot filled with camels and Bedouin. We meet our main Bedouin guide—Shakky is careful to point him out, along with some of the shenanigans he has seen—such as it's double the price at the top if you want to get off the camel. Shakky knows his men, he hires them all the time; they are honest. Each Bedouin approaches one of us, takes us by the hand, and leads us off as if we were children, helping us onto our camels.

My hat is off to whoever figured out how to mount and dismount a camel so they could ride in the desert, thereby saving many lives and creating entire new trade routes across what had only been impassable land. The camel has to kneel on its front legs, then lie down on all fours as if it were a resting dog. The Bedouin accomplishes this by yanking on the metal bit in the camel's mouth, pulling the camel's head down until the body follows. Then you swing your leg over the camel's wide body and sit on his saddle. Get situated (which means the Bedouin guide thinks you aren't in immediate danger of falling off, not that you feel settled) then lean back and hold onto the saddle horn for dear life as the camel staggers to its feet like a drunk after an all-night binge. As we lurch into motion, the Bedouin leads the camel onto the mountain path. I'm sure my camel's thinking: "We have to be together for the next couple of hours. Get used to it. At least you get to go home after this."

After scooting around as best I can, trying for some semblance of comfort, I finally ball up my sweatshirt, which I brought in case the mountain air is chilly at the top. I stuff it at the base of my spine, right where the rear saddle horn is digging into my L-5 vertebrae. I try to post, like on a horse, but this is quickly exhausting. The camel's rhythm is more side-to-side, anyway, so I eventually give up and focus on hanging on.

We lumber along for a while, a dozen Bedouin spaced out alongside the camels, and I start enjoying the scenery from this new height. The Bedouin let the camels keep their own pace, and none of the animals seem bothered. It's like car traffic—we move in batches, wide clearings between us; Greg and several of the others are far enough ahead of me that we occasionally pass at different switchbacks and can wave before fanning out again into a straight line. Though we travel single file, camels have minds of their own, and my camel wants to lead. Once I am in the front position of our little section, my camel slows, content, and does not try to catch up with the group ahead of us.

I swivel around in my saddle, looking over my right shoulder at the valley below. Sen, who is riding near me, has pointed out St. Catherine's to us, nestled at the bottom of the V (for Valley?) making a picturesque scene. We stop for a moment to raise our cameras, then continue up the mountain. Occasionally we pass a trash bin, which though large, overflows with plastic water bottles and other debris. Since the garbage trucks can't make it up here (even if they had garbage trucks in the Sinai), the camels must pack refuse down the mountain every so often, but apparently not regularly enough for the mass of visitors.

The only other things that break up the pristine beauty of this mountain are the snack shacks. Little more than lean-tos, every so often there is a tiny tin roof shack, and a Bedouin or two swathed in cotton scarves serving tea, coffee, cold sodas, and an assortment of candy bars. I laugh when I realize that my backpack of provisions is not needed, and that contrary to my concerns, no one would starve on the side of this mountain, as there must be a week's worth of food and drinks at each place. It all seems to fall under the category of sugar and/or caffeine delivery devices—just the little lift you need when you're flagging. I suppose out in the middle of the desert you could still die of heatstroke, dehydration or starvation, but like most places in the world, gone are the days where the pilgrim's path was clearly delineated by the bones of previous travelers.

At the next bend, my camel continues to walk straight, ignoring the pronounced curve in the path and making me worry that we will plod right off the side of the mountain. I yell when the camel reaches the razor edge of the cliff and lurches back over to the right, now walking on the brink of the precipice as if showing off his camel tightrope act. My cries of concern bring Sen, Sen's camel, and the Bedouin leading them both. They pull up alongside me, and Sen asks if I am okay. I point down at my camel's circus performance. "Is this normal? Or does he just have the thrill gene?" Sen looks surprised for a moment, then laughs.

"Oh, my sister, this is nothing to worry about. The camel likes to walk like this. They never fall off—they have never lost a camel off the side of Gebel Musa." He speaks in Arabic to the Bedouin in front of him, who responds. "No," Sen confirms. "He says they have never lost a single camel." He pauses. "People, yes. But a camel, no way!" Startled, I look across at him, and he is grinning at me, expecting me to laugh. I give him a half-smile, half-grimace; after all, the camel is undoing six months of chiropractic care in a single afternoon. I lean hard to the right to compensate, talking with Sen for a few minutes until his camel falls back and we can no longer converse easily.

A little while later, another camel makes a break for the front of the line. But after he's ahead of me, I can see that it's the Bedouin, not the camel, who has caused this change of hierarchy. Most of our escorts are men, but this is a young boy, barely a teenager, and he is switching his camel with a thin stick. The camels are hobbled by their saddles, which have a short rope or piece of fabric slung down close at their thighs, hampering their movements, preventing them from running off or going too fast. Every three or four steps, the boy switches the camel, not lightly or lazily as I have seen drovers do to move their beasts along, but hard enough that I can hear the high swish as it whistles through the air. After a few times, I have had enough. I get the boy's attention and tell him, "La," Arabic for "No."

He smiles at me, and continues to switch the camel's hindquarters. "La!" I repeat, pointing at his stick. He looks at me quizzically, and then goes back to walking. I watch him—it seems to be a habit, a part of his rhythm: walk, walk, walk, switch. Walk, walk, walk, switch. "La, min fudluk"—I am trying to be polite by adding "please" (and hopefully impress him by my Arabic). He smiles. Walk, walk, walk, switch. I didn't realize my animal advocacy extended to camels, but apparently so. I give up and move to English, since I do not know the Arabic for, "Will you please stop beating that camel, you unfeeling jerk!" The closest adult Bedouin has come over, trying to help. I point at the boy, complaining that the camel is moving as fast as he can, that the boy is beating him for no reason. The older Bedouin speaks rapidly to the boy, gesturing at me, at the camel. The boy shrugs, points the stick towards the ground. We all keep moving, and for about five minutes, the camel has peace. Then, walk, walk, walk, switch.

I bite my lip. I watch the boy. Even it's nothing more than a bored gesture, I can tell it stings the camel, and I can see his or her haunches quivering in response to the blows. I try to tell myself there is a spiritual reason for this, a lesson. For the camel, for the boy, for me in relation to them both. Perhaps in their last lifetime together, the camel beat the boy.

Now we have a new rhythm: Walk, walk, walk, switch, "La!" These frequent reminders from me slow the rate of his wrist flicks enough that I am able to catch some of the scenery alongside the mountain. When we reach base camp, I pull Sen aside, point the boy out and tell him the whole story. Sen disappears to look for the Bedouin leader of the group, assuring me that the boy will not travel with us again. I try to explain that he is welcome, so long as he leaves the camel alone, but Sen cannot control the boy or the other Bedouin. If the boy chooses to beat the camel, it is his to beat. I have heard of camels sometimes raging against their masters—biting them, breaking away and running off, or even killing them. I can only hope that this camel chooses revolution over the plodding march of pain, with death his only other way out.

We reach base camp and dismount, the feeling returning to our legs as we hobble around a bit. Now I know why cowboys always look bowlegged in the movies, and they only ride horses. Ducking into the most elaborate snack shack we've seen—a second room off to the side and the dirt floor covered with carpets. I buy a Snickers for me and a Kit Kat bar for Greg, and watch curiously as the Bedouin stand off to the side doing their afternoon prayers. Even on the side of the mountain, they pray five times a day, or as close as their schedule will allow. Allah will forgive them if their prayers are a little bit late, since they must also earn a living.

There is a bathroom up here, which I have never been brave enough to enter, because from the outside it looks like a grass shed-hut-thingee that's about to collapse from age. Of course, all the men go. I mean, who cares about whether the toilet's clean if you're never going to get that close to the seat? It's really not fair. The women who need to use the loo do so, standing in a long line outside the grass shed. Judith comes back shaking her head, her face a little squinched from holding her breath. Luckily, in this regard, I am a camel myself, and it will be hours before I need to go again. Once everyone has pottied, and Vivian and the few others who have decided, "This is quite far enough" have headed down the mountain, the rest of us turn towards the upper path for the final piece of our pilgrimage.

It's kind of exciting—the narrow passage disappearing above us between two tall boulders reminds me of the scene from *The Lord of the Rings* where Aragorn goes into the foothills to find the ghosts of his mountain men ancestors. But after we travel beyond the boulders, the path widens again pleasantly, and we turn a corner to see the mountain range laid out below us. We continue up a fairly gentle slope, everyone spreading out so they advance at their own natural pace; then abruptly, we have reached the end of the road—the 700 steps.

"Steps" turns out to be a generous term for what I consider rough-hewn cuts into the side of sheer stone. When someone says stairs, I imagine uniform treads and shallow risers. These bad boys are steep, and they have been around for almost a thousand years; though surprisingly unworn by the feet of countless pilgrims who have crossed them, they are fairly uneven. I don't know how historians definitively determined the number of steps, as some of them could be counted as two, even three, depending on how you interpret the crumbling spots.

When we were in Greece, Greg and I went to Delphi, where the Oracle historically held court. Being the bad kids we are, we snuck behind the rope at the Elysian Springs, where, to our surprise, we found evidence of an ancient mystery school, including a set of stairs sculpted out of a cliff. In vain, we tried to scale them, but they were worn from thousands of years of use, to the point where they had become polished like pottery, too slippery to scale. Perhaps it was an initiation, climbing those steps. They were quite even, the rise only a few inches, and each time, after almost making it to the top, Greg would slide back down as if he were a cartoon character caught in a never-ending loop.

Many a pilgrim chose to ascend Mount Moses on his knees. Perhaps the Sinai steps were cut as a test for these pilgrims or maybe they were intended to ease their way, but imagine the agony, walking on your kneecaps all the way up the mountain, with its rocks and slope, only to get to this last part and be too winded to climb the steps. Maybe it's the altitude, or maybe I'm not in good enough shape, but I literally have to stop every two minutes to catch my breath. I think of my dogs. Tripod, who had a badly healed leg when we found him, is notorious for running through the canyon trails we take, throwing himself down in a shady spot, then taking off again a few seconds later when we've caught up to him. I try to adopt this method, but I find myself acting more like Tripod in the heat of summer— after he drops, he refuses to rise, and practically has to be dragged. In this case, I am both the dog and the leash.

Waving Greg on—I am too embarrassed to slow everyone down—I finally go at my own pace, climbing as long as I can, then resting an equal length of time until my heart stops yammering in my throat and I can continue. The sun has started to set, yet I am overheated from the exertion. When I reach the top, the rest of our group is already comfortable, conversing with a few other travelers, who I am quite surprised to see, as no one passed us on our way.

The top of Mount Moses is tiny, yet it is large enough for a miniscule stone chapel and another, even smaller, building—the interior no more than six feet square. A Bedouin goes about his business inside, ignoring us all as we settle in for sunset. Everyone hangs out on the stone steps of the chapel, or walks around the few paces that can be taken at the top of Gebel Musa, admiring the panoramic views. I observe the way the sunlight charges the surrounding mountaintops with an ethereal beauty contradicting the stone cliffs' massive weight.

Sunset is getting closer now and more people are arriving. Over twenty of us are on top of this tiny mountaintop, and it's beginning to resemble a UN summit, or at least a social club for world travelers: English, Scots, Americans, Australians, Canadians, French, Egyptians and Russians have all come to share this single point in time together. The seating is crowded, but because of the vast air space surrounding us, we don't feel cramped. After the spectacular sun takes her bow, several people stay to watch the light change, but Greg and I head down immediately, trying to beat the dark.

Since it took me over an hour to climb the steps, I am surprised at how quickly I race back; in only fifteen minutes, I am at the top of the trail again, where there is a spacious rest area—two rooms that overlook the cliff. The extensive outdoor seating tells me a lot more people come at dawn. I can't imagine where one would put them all at the top, but now am only concerned about getting down. We ignore the inviting tea and candy bars, and start quickly onto the path. Moving fast, the downward slope of the land working like a tailwind, we are able to get to base camp as twilight descends. Here we pause to pull out our flashlights and turn them on, grateful that Greg has bothered to bring his Mag light, which is whiter and brighter than the other lights and casts a wide glow.

Now the mountain is easy for me, and I walk at a fairly fast pace, my flashlight illuminating the ground in front of me, vigilant against the rocks that might otherwise trip me. Despite my best efforts, I stumble at least twenty times, and it constantly seems as if my ankle might twist or even break, but miraculously I have no pain or discomfort; I recover and walk on. Sen and I have fallen in together, as Greg and Lyra are embroiled in a deep discussion about Horus Temple. I take Sen's arm. He has a walking stick—this is not his first rodeo—so he leans on the stick and I lean on him. It's a good system, and I stumble a lot less. At one point, darkness now fully upon us, Sen takes a wrong turn, and we realize after a couple of minutes that we are on a meandering path off to the side. But as long as we head downward, it's the right direction, so we abandon the little side path, go straight through the rocks, and in no time have rejoined the main trail.

Sen points at the stars, which have come out enthusiastically. Without the ambient light so common in the cities and even villages, the stars seem to be millions of pinholes poked into a blackout curtain, and their beauty is a marvel. As I see the path above me, my breath catches in my throat—the flashlights of all the pilgrims heading down the mountain have created a chain, as if the mountain is hung with white running lights from a Christmas tree. I stop for a moment and the voices of some of them carry down to me—two girls, singing Donna Summers' '70s hit, "I Will Survive." I suppose this is what passes for pilgrimage in the modern world, but I turn away, walking a bit more quickly until I can only hear Sen's quiet voice, until I can hear my own thoughts again.

WHAT IF MOSES HAD A CELL PHONE

St. Catherine's monastery is nestled at the base of Mount Moses, and when you're way up on the side of the mountain it's lovely, but this is nothing compared to what it looks like when you visit it. A cross between a Tudor village and a Mediterranean villa, St. Catherine's was for many centuries literally the only show in town. These days, souvenir shops and a couple of little cafes have sprung up around it, as well as the St. Catherine's hotel down the street where we are staying.

When I enter St. Catherine's, I am struck by the overwhelming number of touristses. Because many people aren't fit enough to climb Mount Moses, or aren't even interested in trying, this monastery is the biggest draw in the area, and people journey from all over the world to visit St. Catherine's and its most important attractions: the Greek Orthodox church, and the burning bush—yes, that burning bush—on the monastery grounds. It looks like a big bougainvillea, but without all the colored leaves. The burning bush is vigorous and grows so fast that they constantly have to give it a haircut so it doesn't cascade onto the path below and block visitors' ability to walk by it.

As I understand the story, someone at St. Catherine's has tested the sap and figured out that if you go back in time over thousands of years, this is the actual plant that Moses stood in front of when God set the bush ablaze and spoke to him. You would think that a bush on fire would burn up and no longer exist, but since it was God, not an actual fire, it has been determined that this is the shrub in question. I sure hope so, because they built the entire monastery around it, and the singular massive display of greenery is now approximately fifteen feet tall and is gawked at by around ten thousand people a day. I suppress the thought that someone planted this bush for marketing purposes, once the Moses story had gained widespread popularity. It is, after all, a very nice bush, though it was not on fire during any of my trips there.

Visiting hours at St. Catherine's are limited to 9am—noon, six days a week and no public hours on Sundays, affording the priests at least one day entirely in peace to celebrate their mass. We arrive a half-hour before the monastery opens to visitors, and stand in front of the entrance, a low, medieval castle gate of leather bound in wide belts of thin metal. As we wait, we stand near a woman whose face and neck are covered in a fine pale down, so thick she looks as though there is a halo beard around her when the sun lights her profile. *Gee, she could use a good shave.*

My mind begins to wander... after many years and much traveling I have seen it all. The lovely woman whose nose hairs were so long they curled down onto her upper lip, traveling with family who could have suggested a trim sometime in the two-week trip. Isis, the leader of the Sun People, whose buckteeth belonged to Roger Rabbit as opposed to a middle-aged Englishwoman. An older woman whose hairdresser apparently cropped her bob to show off the deep wrinkles on the back of her neck. The lady who wore the wrong color consistently, as if someone had mentioned that mustard or green brings out the yellow undertones of her skin, and she took it as a compliment.

This is the hard candy when it comes to considering myself a spiritual person. Although I have this deep desire inside myself that says I want to be a better person, or want to love everyone no matter who they are or what they look like, I also have this judgmental streak, and it's usually a lot bigger. I know people who will start sentences with, "I'm a spiritual person, but that's some messed-up shit," and then bitch for at least ten minutes. I know others who say, "I try to be good, but..." and it is this "but" that can get us in all kinds of trouble. I struggle over this judgment of mine, this thing that makes me human. You don't see monkeys in the wild saying, "Well, you have this boil on your face, so I'm not going to groom you." If anything, it makes them more interesting to each other.

I often ask myself, should I mention the nose hair or the tendency to choose colors that make one wonder if you're going to pass out? One time I had dinner with friends of my father's, a lovely couple. The wife ordered spinach and when it arrived, she got some caught in the front teeth of her wide, frequent smile. I almost said something to her, but I didn't know her that well. Instead, I waited for her husband to mention it. But he didn't. She sat through three more courses, a dark green spot in the middle of her lovely white teeth. After a while, I thought, *I should probably say something*. But then I mused, *if I now mention she has spinach in her teeth, and she's eating tiramisu, she will immediately be aware that I have kept quiet about this for nearly two hours. If the situation were reversed, I would withdraw any trust I had in that person at that very moment*. Instead I said nothing, willing her husband to cave. Which he never did. I can only imagine her, in the car on the way home, checking her lipstick and then wondering what the heck that piece of spinach was doing there?

Does this make me a bad spiritual person, for being judgmental? Or does it make me a better human? Do I get extra brownie points for thinking about it, for letting it bother me? Is anyone even keeping score (doubtful) and if not, does it help me to become more enlightened by ignoring these all-too-human tendencies? These are the questions I still have, standing in line, waiting amongst the unwashed masses.

Perhaps I am having these thoughts because St. Catherine's is terribly crowded; it's almost impossible to feel the holiness of the place because the touristses are everywhere. At 9:01am, Shakky begins banging on the door and shouting in Arabic at whoever is inside. When Shakky has gotten good and riled up, they finally meander over and push back the bolt.

Following our marching orders, our group rushes in and makes a break for the left side of the monastery, where the burning bush is waiting for the crush. Everyone else has gone to the church, which is the biggest draw inside the grounds. By choosing the second-most popular stop, we have bought a few minutes to ourselves for a silent prayer, before the hordes exit the church. Eventually, people start coming up, and as they step into our little circle, Shakky catches their eye and quietly requests silence, his finger to his lips, then arcing out into an expansive hand gesture that seems to say, "that is the way it must be."

As more people join us, an energetic reverence is established. It is remarkable; all of these people around the burning bush are respectful, quiet, even if most of them don't even know why. As we leave, filing out in a straight, silent line to the church, I can hear the sound of the voices spilling into the vacuum our band of pilgrims created.

This experience was even more powerful than a private visit, because Shakky was able to achieve the same effect with the crowds around us as if we had been by ourselves. People appreciated the space, the silence, which they otherwise would have ignored in favor of taking pictures and a quick glance at yet another religious icon. This is one of The Magician's special gifts.

The church is terribly crowded. You are not allowed to talk inside, and they ask you to turn off your phone. You enter through a long, narrow antechamber where they have beeswax candles available, four for a dollar. Like all Orthodox churches, you can light a slender candle for someone you care for and stick the bottom into a large basin of sand where, in twenty minutes, it will drip down into nothing but a strand of ash left by the disappearing wick, and be replaced by the next person's candles and fervent wishes for their own loved ones. You follow the crowd into the main part of the church, which has individual, small, carved wooden pews on either side of the chapel floor, creating two hallways behind them. On the right side, the only tourists allowed are Greek Orthodox; on the left is the corridor you walk down to exit.

Though the main chapel area is large, only the front half is available to visitors; a velvet rope blocks the rear. We make a sort of square as we walk along the pews on the right, across the main chapel at the rope, peering towards the marble floor, bibles and religious art you cannot get close enough to see, admiring the stained glass windows across the back of the church. After a minute, the crowd pushes you along by the left side of the pew and then scoots out the corridor behind it. Here you view paintings of saints and priests and monks' relics on your way to being funneled out of the side of the church, where you are deposited onto the monastery's main path. The whole time, I feel jostled and hurried. *God is in this church, so God must feel jostled and uncomfortable, too.*

I duck into one of the individual high-backed carved wooden chairs, which pulls me out of the crowd's way though everyone is right in front of me, brushing my knees constantly as they pass. Perhaps it's the tall wooden sides of the chair over me, the top of it cutting in a bit as if it were a nascent roof over my head—but I feel safe all of a sudden, protected from the throng, and I start to enjoy the church. I am exploring what God might think of this view when a ringing cell phone startles me into the present. I narrow beady eyes at the young Egyptian who answers it, staring at him from below my brow. He takes the call in the church, not even bothering to keep his voice down, and when he gets off the phone, I glower at him again. He shrugs at me. "What's wrong? I'm a guide!"

"Then you should know better," I tell him, turning away disdainfully.

"But I need to use my phone!" He tries to engage me again.

It is my turn to shrug. "Then you should use your phone outside." As Shakky would say, I give the guide no mercy because I am so annoyed at his rudeness in this holy place.

The ceiling of the church is covered with hanging chandeliers. I notice the roped-off portion has all the gold chandeliers hanging behind it, whereas the brass and silver ones are hung high over the heads of the visitors. It's a practical solution to potential theft, though it is also possible that without the roped-off section, there would be no place for the priests to stand. As it is, a gray-bearded, scowling, black-robed priest hovers behind the division, observing us all under heavy eyes. As I pass by, I make eye contact and smile—sending my energy across the space to make a connection, and he nods in return, his lips turning up in what is surely a smile. Later, I hear Greg and Shakky (both practically allergic to authority figures) complaining.

"Dredj, did you see that priest?" Shakky asks.

Greg responds, "The mean one, with the hanging forehead?"

Shakky nods. "He is always here. He never smiles."

"He smiled at me!" I can't wait to point out the results of my international olive branch.

"That man?" Shakky asks, astonished. "Because you are a pretty girl, perhaps."

"Uh, no. Because I smiled at him. The two of you might consider making the initial gesture next time." They don't get it, looking at each other and shaking their heads.

"Lookit, what if the priest is mean-looking because no one is ever nice to him?"

Greg squints at me a little. "I suppose."

Shakky's voice is melodious, warming. "You could be right. I will try to smile next time." Good. Another set of converts to my plan for world domination through kindness.

*   *   *   *   *

A private visit to St. Catherine's is so rare as to almost be unheard of. Just once, we were lucky to bring a group of librarians who specialized in religious texts, and our Surgeon Mohamed pulled giant strings to get us a private visit; like at the temples, it was an entirely different experience to have the place to ourselves. We went on a Sunday morning, when the priests at their Mass were the only ones there, and had a magnificent visit, experiencing St. Catherine's as it was meant to be. We were given a full tour, including a visit to one of the dormitory buildings. The highlight was the St. Catherine's Library, normally wholly off-limits to visitors of any kind. A guest wrote to us months later to say she had been at a party with a woman who did Catholic tours to the Sinai and had been visiting St. Catherine's for twenty years. It had taken our librarian two hours to convince the tour leader she indeed had been in the St. Catherine's Library, because the woman refused to believe her.

Outside of the Vatican, St. Catherine's Library houses the largest collection of sacred books on the planet, making this is a remarkable locale. To the untrained eye, the primary impression is of age, not individual history. Books these days are colorful, with beautiful jackets, well-designed titles, and florid fonts. Walk into any library and you will see all that, plus labels identifying the books in the Dewey Decimal system.

These books, being infinitely older, are plain, either bound by thread or leather, and indistinguishable, with few or no markings on the bindings. It's not as if someone wrote the name of the author and the title of the book on the leather spine in calligraphy—they are simply blank—and many of the books are in manuscript form, their only binding the thick thread holding the pages together. I suppose all that info is inside on the flyleaf but, to my modern eye, it's enigmatic, as if the books, despite all our efforts to get a glimpse of them, refuse to reveal their secrets. Only a few of the cases are glass, so you often can't see into the shelving, either.

In one glass case a book is open to an ornate black and white map, next to an illuminated text, the colors hidden inside like covert operatives in a Technicolor spy game. On a shelf below it sits a tiny book of prayers in the finest hand I have ever seen— so small it looks as if it were written by fairies who crept into the library at night when the priests were asleep, and worked this imaginative art of letters. Of course, these texts are written in languages I do not read; they are all Greek, Latin, or Arabic to me.

The library, too, is surprisingly small; the room is approximately 20 by 40 feet. The upper story is off-limits even to us so perhaps there are other rooms we were not shown. I have never visited the Vatican Library, but in the *DaVinci Code*, it was big enough to hold valuable cars next to the stacks—you couldn't fit half a Mini Cooper in this place. I expected the library to be much bigger—a building unto itself, but perhaps there aren't that many sacred texts left in the world. Greg has quite a collection, which he has been amassing for over twenty years, and we have only filled twelve shelves.

Father Justin gives us a lecture on the library, which I do not hear much of because the room is crowded and I defer to our guests. I spend the time on the balcony walkway with the kind manager of St. Catherine's who has coordinated this adventure for us, and we talk easily about tourism in Egypt and the Sinai as I enjoy the unobstructed view of the monastery rooftops and the burning bush below.

At the end I sidle in, mostly to observe Father Justin, who was an American professor from San Francisco when he petitioned to join the order in the '70s. He is the only non-Greek priest, though at this point his beard is long and gray, his cassock black as the others—we are hard-pressed to differentiate him as American. To my mind, he is as indistinguishable from the other priests as the books in the library, except that he can speak English, which he does in a quiet, gentle voice. I didn't ask him if he considers it a blessing or a burden to be the resident guide to all English-speaking visitors, but he is kind and generous with his time. For these librarians and teachers, this is the pinnacle of their trip, their Great Pyramid, where they can see and even touch the history of writing, of religious works.

We are taken to the roof, where we can view St. Catherine's and the mountains that surround us, a scattering of Bedouin men far below sunning themselves on the flat rocks across from the monastery, the majestic views of Mount Moses and, across the way, the St. Catherine's hotel. I feel blessed to be here and experience such deep peace.

*   *   *   *   *

Once you have seen the church and the burning bush, you can visit two souvenir shops. The one inside the main entrance is tiny and crowded. The other, around the back of the monastery, is much larger and doesn't get as much traffic, so it's a lot more pleasant to browse. Amongst the wooden, crystal or pearl rosaries, CDs of Gregorian chants, and racks of postcards, are pictures of the relic of St. Catherine's—her shriveled and dried hand covered in jewels. Since Catherine herself refused the gifts and marriage that would have afforded those riches, to focus on God, I don't know what she would think of her hand draped in gold and encrusted with rings. Possibly she is even more understanding in the afterlife than she was on Earth.

My first time here, I walk through the charming environment to see a line around the rear of a stone building. Shakky tells our group to go stand in the line, which is for the ossuary, where the bones of all the monks are stored after they die. Given our cultural predilection for respecting the dead, the monks' practical approach to their remains quite surprises me. Rather than take up space with human-sized resting places, a dead monk is buried, and then after decomposing, dug up to be put into this room where all the bones of all the monks are grouped together—the femurs on one shelf, the tibias on another. Of course, the skulls are kept together, too, piled on top of each other like grinning children performing a Halloween pyramid trick. The bones reside in a cell with iron bars and a gate to prevent anyone from disturbing the monks, creating a dungeon of bones—this serves to give the monastery its own "Chamber of Horrors," hence the line.

My first ossuary was Meteora in Greece, a group of skinny pillar-like cliffs. Monasteries were built on their plateaus, enabling the monks to avoid invading Turks. The monasteries are only a couple city blocks square; space is at a premium, so I understand the need for a bone dungeon. But ossuaries seem standard practice everywhere, especially in centuries past. I admire the juxtaposition of the practical issues—the space, and the desire to keep and maintain the bones of the dead. At St. Catherine's, where the ossuary is large, there's a glass case where one lucky priest has been dressed in full robes, his skeleton intact in his chair, keeping watch over the rest of his fellows. I wonder if these monks died easily, having long before made their peace with God.

People's fascination with death is constant; "how" we might die is the subject of horror films, even snuff films, and "when" is the eternal question. I am always collecting people's thoughts on death, in case I might happen upon a nugget I can use to ease passage through my own terror. I remember digging in our new backyard in Hawaii when I was thirteen, and finding a small skull. I flattened myself against the fence in horror, my breathing coming so fast it shocked me as much as the object itself. Finally, curiosity overcame fear and I knelt next to it to examine the skull further, to discover that a cat had died years earlier and the owners had buried it in a shallow grave. I was too terrified to touch it—it was a dead thing, perhaps the first one I had ever seen. Now I stare at the empty round eye sockets of the monks' skulls, the grinning upper jaws. They don't seem like people, really. Just empty shells. This is exactly what I fear most. Where did they go—Sebastian, Benedict, Franciscus, Thelonius? Are they in heaven? Are they off in the ether? Do they know? Can they remember walking these stone paths, eating their meager meals, loving their God? Will I know? How can I still be me after I die? How can I retain the one central thing that keeps me in orbit, my sense of self? My inner child is still begging the darkness, *Please, please—I'll do anything—please don't make me "not me" any more!*

In full panic now, I push past the line of people waiting to get into the cramped room. Greg grabs my hand on my way out. "Are you okay?" I can only shake my head and keep going and he turns and follows me into the sun. "Sweetie?" I'm trembling, breathing raggedy breaths. "Did it happen again?" I nod and he pulls me to him. "Shhhh. Shhhhh. It'll be okay." I let him hold me, listen to his soothing words, but I'm not certain it will be okay AT ALL. How can he possibly know?

Judith joins us. "Haddie, are you all right?"

When Greg's daughter was a toddler, she couldn't pronounce my name properly and called me Haddie instead. Around the same time, she cut my lip open by flinging her little head against it in a fit of laughter. Terrified by the blood, she pointed at my mouth. "Haddie wip?" she asked. "Halle's lip is fine," she was told. The next day, Greg and I left on a business trip, and the whole time we were away, her poor mother had to listen to plaintive concerns for "Haddie wip?" It got to where her mom would respond, "What about Haddie wip?" And his daughter would get a great big smile on her face and announce, "Haddie wip fine!" It's still a cherished nickname of mine, so Mother smiles when I tell her, "Haddie wip fine," even though I am still a little shaky. She puts her arm around me and Greg holds my other hand as we walk to the bus.

*   *   *   *   *

On our last night, we are picked up in a number of Jeeps, and drive off toward the desert to have dinner with the Bedouin. On the way, at a typical stop by the Sinai guard patrol, they refuse to let us pass (no explanation is ever proffered). We are kept by the guards for over thirty minutes. I become certain we will not be allowed to proceed, so it is quite a relief when they finally wave us on; we are almost like teenagers being released from school early on a Friday afternoon—that sense of exhilaration and relief that comes after freedom.

It is quickly clear why we need the four-wheel-drive Jeeps, as we leave the paved road after twenty minutes and head toward the mountain range. Eventually, we pass a Bedouin standing in front of a palm tree, holding his camel's tether. I wish I could draw like David Roberts and capture this scene from my imagination, since the Jeep is far too jouncy and fast moving to attempt a photograph. We see two more camels, then nothing for a long time.

Abruptly, the vehicles slow, and the Bedouin drivers pull off in the middle of nowhere, which I suppose is the point. We clamber out of the Jeeps, while the Bedouin arrange a couple of fallen logs and spread blankets on them and over the sand. It immediately lends this space a sense of belonging and a floor. They put a couple of teapots into the quickly built fire, and some of the group relaxes on the carpets while Judith, Eleanor, Vivian, Lyra, Greg and I climb to the top of the hill to look for Mount Moses. Eventually, we see a small building at the top of a mountain, and using this familiar landmark as our guide, we discern that there is a whole mountain between Gebel Musa and us; we cannot see it, though the landscape is analogous. We sit at the top of the hill, watching the Bedouin below us preparing dinner, and enjoy this special treat of sunset in the Sinai. As the sun dips below the mountaintop, we are called for our meal, and we scramble and slide down the hill in anticipation.

The Bedouin have brought drums and tambourines, and they sing and play, sharing their homemade instruments so we can also partake in the music-making. They pull the pots from the fire and pour tea all around, serving us from a beat-up silver tray in the standard small glasses. Though it is already evening and I will probably be up half the night because of it, I have cup after cup of the steaming tea, this time lightly sweet, the way I like it. We enjoy the camaraderie as night truly falls and bright pinpoints of light begin to dot the blackness. There are so many winking stars it's as if I'm seeing double, and the Milky Way winds in a ribbon across the sky, showing us the curve of the universe.

They have roasted a goat for us over the open fire. This makes me sad as I think of the little kid I held in my arms on the farm two days ago, but it's a natural part of life—there is no question that we are eating a creature who was raised for a purpose, fed with love, and killed humanely for this desert feast. In many ways, I am happy to feel this close bond to my dinner.

The Bedouin drivers, who are also our cooks, pull out a flat cast-iron griddle and make the puffs of Egyptian bread we have eaten often on our journey. There is something about the fire, the lightly browned bread pockets opening as we pull them apart to reveal their steamy middles, that makes this the best bread we have had on the whole trip. The rest of the meal is soup made from goat—so light and tasty that everyone remarks on it— salad, potatoes (boiled in the soup, and equally delicious) and rice, each served in giant metal salad bowls, alongside sodas passed in two-liter plastic bottles. I smile after a few bites of goat meat; sadly for my taste buds, it is a little tough and stringy, but this tells me it is an older creature, lean and well-lived, and my kid made it through another day.

As the darkness deepens, we lie easily on the blankets enjoying each other's company, finishing off the last of the painstakingly prepared food. We know that our morning drive to Cairo will come too soon, and we savor the last few minutes of our Sinai trip before heading to the hotel to pack. In the morning, the coach returns us to the big city for the final leg of our pilgrimage. But first, a tale of giving thanks...

AN AMERICAN
THANKSGIVING IN
CAIRO

The year Greg turned fifty, his birthday also fell on Thanksgiving. We were staying in the new apartment building Momo had just gutted and remodeled for his "American friends." Ostensibly, this means the tour leaders who come and go, and it's good business since it mean he no longer has to put us up in hotels. However, it is actually for much more altruistic reasons— he wants us to stay as long as we can, each and every time. Not only an America-phile, but also possessed of the most generous spirit I have ever seen in another human, Momo wants to keep us around for weeks, even months, after our tours are completed.

We are staying an extra week, as we do each time now when a tour is over. We have discovered that it is better to work in Cairo after the tour ends, and then to deal with a couple days' recovery from jet lag, rather than to rush home exhausted. So Greg and I sit, our view of the Pyramids and the rooftop garden neglected, typing away at our keyboards—in the same room, but separated by our thoughts, our words, our projects.

However, no computers for me for the next two days. Mohamed has told me a white bird came to him in a dream and said I should cook Thanksgiving dinner for everyone. Of course, this is complete bullshit. Upon my arrival I had offered

263

to make this same dinner, and was turned down flat by my gracious host. Now he has changed his mind, and a white bird is his charming way of telling me. For Greg's birthday, we will have American Thanksgiving, and it will allow Momo to relive a memory he has harbored since his twenties at University in New York, when he sat in a kitchen and watched a girlfriend cook, her family joining them for this most American of holidays. He tells me, "I love this day better than Christmas!" I'd better get to work.

To start, there is the shopping. In trying to recreate Thanksgiving as it is traditionally celebrated, I forgo any of my usual twists—the oyster cornbread stuffing, the brined turkey, the ginger streusel on the pumpkin pie. We will have a Plain Jane Thanksgiving meal, as traditional as I can make it. First stop: Carrefour.

Carrefour is in the big shopping mall, less than 30 minutes from Giza. It was certainly not here when we started coming to Egypt, and now it is bridging the gap between Giza and New Cairo, just as Shakky said—new cities in the sand. Carrefour contains an assortment of Euro-trash shoppes and the almost de riguer Coffee Bean, an ultramodern McDonalds and a sign that says, "Coming Soon: Marks & Spencers." Ignoring the vast choices, we head straight to the WalMart-like grocery store, where electronics sit cheek-by-jowl with baby clothes, meat, toiletries, and the largest fish counter I've seen outside of London's Harrods.

The Surgeon has offered to take me so he can participate in choosing the turkey and the china (the serviceable breakfast dishes in the flat are not the sort of thing you can put a big meal on, nor are there enough for the fourteen guests we are expecting). Accompanied by Momo's daughter, Nancy, who serves as our driver, we visit two days before Thanksgiving, because my father has threatened me long-distance: "If that turkey isn't defrosted starting today, you'll never have Thanksgiving dinner on time!" Plus I need to buy my bread now, so it can get nice and stale for the stuffing. As I make my way through Carrefour, it is clear this will be a Thanksgiving of flexibility, of adjustments, of less-than-traditional offerings.

For starters, there is no sage. Zero. Not in the extensive spice section, nor at the spice deli, which is its own counter staffed by workers who scoop saffron, cumin, or turmeric from huge piles like colored sand, echoing the stalls found at the open markets. I search everywhere for sage, convinced that without it, Momo will taste that it's not traditional turkey. Eventually, I settle for bunches of fresh rosemary, oregano, and parsley.

I am planning to bake both apple and pumpkin pies, and the apples look good—a Golden Delicious-type that will peel and slice nicely. I see a sign for pumpkin and head towards the display, bemused to discover that what the Egyptians call pumpkin looks like a mottled green butternut squash on steroids. The smallest I can find weighs something like five pounds and is two feet long, the bulbous part measuring at least ten inches across. Despite my trepidation I knock on the base, listening for the hollow sound that tells me it's ripe, and place it in my cart.

Unfortunately, both the onions and the carrots look like they've seen better days—the onions in particular must have been stored for months, as they are shriveling in their skins. The celery is as much bitter leaf as it is stalk, and I have to buy three to make up a single head of American celery. Mohamed and Greg laugh when they see me, my arms so full of leaves I look like I am holding a pageant bouquet.

Now for the potatoes. Only there aren't any. As I wander aimlessly, looking for something that resembles a spud, I hear an American conversation lamenting the same problem. I turn around, surprised, to see two male teachers who live in Cairo shopping for their family's respective Thanksgivings. As we strike up a conversation, I feel a certain relief, a connection to these friendly strangers that makes me feel less out of place—someone else in Cairo is also going to be cooking Thanksgiving dinner. I am not alone in my nutty search for exotic things like cranberries. Though I can find none fresh, I do locate a can of Ocean Spray.

The Americans are planning on stuffing chickens, since they can't find turkey. "Come with me!" I tell them, triumphantly leading them to the meat department. Turkeys—four beautiful birds—sit trussed and wrapped next to whole turkey breast, and to my great pleasure, everything is fresh, not frozen. The teachers are ecstatic—one man calls home to make sure his wife will approve, and she is more than happy give the nod to a turkey breast. I pick the largest turkey—over eight kilos (about seventeen-and-a-half pounds)—and we drop the birds into our carts in the vegetable department. During our absence, The Surgeon has been working his magic. Mohamed is thanking the clerk who has brought four packages of organic potatoes from the back, about six potatoes per cellophaned and styrofoamed container. I ask the teachers how many they want.

"All of them!" the older one tells me. "You take them, since you need them."

I laugh. "I don't think that's necessary." I look over at Mohamed, who instructs the clerk in Arabic. The chap runs off and a minute later returns carrying another six packages of potatoes. We gleefully divvy them up and wish each other a Happy Thanksgiving. I am grateful knowing that we made theirs a little better, but more so for the chance to commune with people who fully understand our strange little traditions. I only truly feel American when I am abroad.

In the housewares section, we select china from an open stock of dishes, choosing gold-rimmed plates edged in blue that will make an attractive base for the dinner. After much searching, I find a deep-dish glass pie plate and a nine-inch standard one. It is now obvious that the Egyptians don't bake many of the same things we do—to find my treasures I had to wade through shelves of pizza pans and flan sets galore. Worse, when I go on the hunt for measuring cups I can find only a 16 oz. liquid measuring cup, no dry measures. No little plastic graduated bowls nestled in a one-cup. No glass bowls of the right size, and even if there were, none of them have the size stamped on the bowl—I would be guessing. I finally settle for scoops—the kind you use for flour or buying dry goods in bulk —all on a single loop so they sort of seem like the absent measuring cups; three of them, labeled 1/4 cup, 1/2 cup, and 1 cup. If you need 1/3 of a cup of something, well, you just wouldn't, apparently. They will be difficult to work with, since to get a full measure you have to scrape your knife along the wide slope of the scoop, but it is my only option.

Eventually, a grocery cart-full and hundreds of dollars later, we make our way to the car. Momo has paid for everything, and at the end has pronounced it a great evening—he has gotten so much pleasure from this, he says; the money doesn't matter. It is a good reminder, as I had sticker shock and a little guilt when I saw the total rung up on the cash register. I am determined not to let down my end of the bargain.

At the flat, everything barely fits in the refrigerator, which is undersized in an otherwise large and well-appointed kitchen. Mohamed's love of America and attention to detail has led him to create a kitchen you can truly cook in—black marble countertops spanning three walls, room for a breakfast table that seats four comfortably, a six-burner gas stove and an oversized oven.

Though I had never made more than toast in the kitchen before this trip, we had the great good fortune of meeting the celebrated writer, John Anthony West, author of *The Traveler's Key to Egypt* and a dear friend of Momo's for nearly thirty years. He and Greg hit it off so well John stayed until midnight after we all went to dinner, then came back for breakfast the next morning and stayed all day. We also hosted an Australian tour leader who came up from the ground floor, Rhonnda—I had whipped up omelets for them this morning and was now feeling confident that I could work in this space. I wash and roast the pumpkin, cutting it into four slices and sprinkling them with salt.

My concern is the piecrusts. My go-to recipe, the one that made me feel like I could bake, is a no-fail piecrust from *Cooks Magazine*. The problem is its secret ingredient: vodka. This is haram—forbidden—to Muslims, and my reasonings to Momo ("no taste, no odor, the alcohol burns off") all were sweetly ignored. He pleaded for me to use something else. Thank God for the Internet, where I discover a recipe that calls for 7UP. Vaguely recalling a *Cook's* experiment that also used soda, I choose this recipe and cross my fingers. Next: I haven't baked without my Cuisinart or stand mixer in... never. A long time ago, I had learned the basic principals, and my first piecrust (an abject failure) used the timeworn method of cutting the butter into the flour: two knives. Since the recipe makes four crusts, I am going to be here a while. No mixing bowl, but I find a large plastic lettuce spinner that will do the trick, and spend the next fifteen minutes dicing cold butter into tiny pieces. Time for the flour, which I scoop from a kilo bag using my new one-cup scoop. I am dismayed to discover that after 4 scoops I have used about three-quarters of my kilo bag, which my swift iPad calculations advise is the total amount of flour I need. Glancing over the flour in the bowl, my eye agrees. I stomp to the cupboard and pull out my new liquid measure, transferring a cup of water to the scoop. Great. My dry scoop is measuring for liquid, not volume, and therefore is off by about a third. I blame the conversion from metric, but I suspect it's more likely to be a product designer who doesn't bake and has no clue that these two one-cups should not be equal. At least I caught the problem before I moved on—the pastry is the hardest thing for me, and I promise myself that if I can get it right, the rest of my American Thanksgiving in Cairo will be a snap.

Estimating the flour as best as I can, I attack the bowl with my criss-crossing knives. After a few minutes, it becomes clear that I will be getting my full upper body workout from this task, since my biceps, triceps and torso are all engaged. Perhaps I should cook like this from now on—it would save me time at the gym. I have to take it in stages, as it requires over thirty minutes of crosscutting before I have the right size crumbles in the bowl. The crust is all butter because I did not find any shortening at Carrefour. I'm sure there is an Arabic word for lard, but I was reluctant to ask—I don't trust that my apple pie wouldn't wind up tasting beefy.

I add the 7UP and the dough ball forms; though it's a little soft looking, we have a winner. I divide the dough and refrigerate it for the morning, giving myself a little pat on the back. Turning my attention to the now-roasted pumpkin, I am chagrined to discover that the pumpkin's meat, though well-cooked, resembles spaghetti squash, its fleshy strands long and stringy. It occurs to me that this isn't a variation on pumpkin at all—the word "squash" has simply been mistranslated as "pumpkin" from the Arabic. After trying every tool at my disposal to cut the strands, including my by-now-expert crisscrossing knives, I reluctantly give up and move on to getting the flavor right. I bought a few pinches of fresh nutmeg at the store, which I sprinkle sparingly over the mashed squash (no sense even calling it pumpkin). To this I add cinnamon and the crushed heads of about 20 whole cloves—which equals only a quarter teaspoon. Milk, eggs, brown sugar, then the whole thing is ready to be put into pie shells. It's enough for two pies, and since I also have an extra crust...

I take a quick trip downstairs to see Rhonnda, the tour guide. She is a sweet-faced, round woman with short red hair that wisps everywhere and a tendency towards dressing in the same fall colors as I do. She opens the door for me then goes into the kitchen, calling over her shoulder, "I have a surprise for you," in her melodic Australian accent. I follow her, but she is already heading back to me, a twinkle in her eye and a whole bottle of dried sage in her hand. "Look what I found!" I consider this a gift from the Gods, Anubis thanking me for feeding all the dogs I see, or the Goddess Bastet for the cats. Rhonnda and I raid her kitchen cabinets, retrieving two large mixing bowls, a pie dish, and a lovely plate I can use as a relish tray, the painted Muslim design serving as the perfect backdrop for the assortment of olives and pickled lemons that Greg picked out from Carrefour's olive deli.

Armed with my assortment of kitchen supplies, I head upstairs to finish baking. Though the apple pie has only a sprinkling of cinnamon and clove in the filling, tomorrow I will be pleased to discover the spicy peppery flavor, as if I had precooked the apples overnight in some complex combination of fabulous ingredients. All the pies turn out perfect, the pumpkin especially well-flavored, but the texture so off as to confuse you terribly if you closed your eyes while eating.

Leaving the pies out overnight to cool and meld their flavors, I am in bed by 9pm. Tomorrow, I will be up early to prepare the feast.

*   *   *   *   *

It's 4pm on Thanksgiving and I am a little concerned. The early part of the morning went well—I brought Greg coffee in bed, "birthday coffee"—and he opened his presents: a small silk rug exquisitely woven with an image of the God Thoth, and a set of antique camel bone beads highly polished by diligent fingers praying over them for many years. Then Shakky picked Greg up and whisked him off to play in the back streets of Cairo for the day. I stayed home to cook, to be joined by Rhonnda, Doaa (an excellent new female guide who we had just met) and Mohamed, who I expected at 1pm. Greg smiled when I told him to be home by then, but I knew Shakky. He would have Greg out until the last possible minute. Now here it is after four o'clock and I am still alone. Momo had told me earlier he would be there when his work was finished; I laughed and said, "See you in a couple years," but I hadn't meant that he should stay away all day.

The cooking went better than I could have hoped. In an unfamiliar kitchen, using an oven that had never been turned on before—not until the pies a day earlier—with a single oven rack, a dial only marked every ten degrees (in Celsius), and no meat thermometer, clearly Anubis and Bastet were still smiling on me. Having come out of its wrapping looking fresher and more beautifully trussed than any American grocery store bird, the turkey had only an hour left to cook. The herbed butter I rubbed under its skin had basted the bird all day, enhanced by occasional spoonfuls of pan juices I spooned up and poured over the turkey whenever I had swapped the side dishes out. Apparently, a turkey baster is an optional kitchen tool, though I would have sworn by it until now. Under the bird, the mirepoix of carrots, celery, garlic and onions has practically melted into the dripping fats, assuring at least a moist—and hopefully flavorful—finished dish.

On the stove, zucchini casseroles and a pan of mushroom, fennel and sage stuffing sit side by side with the mashed potatoes. These are yummy but sadly lumpy, as I have neither potato masher nor sieve. Everything is staying warm until it can go in the oven for a final reheat once the turkey comes out.

The only real hitch in the whole process took place in the morning, when I was cleaning the turkey. I removed the package of glossy giblets, reassured that this bird ate more healthfully than I do. Then I felt inside the cavity for the neck. It seemed—well, a bit long. But I kept pulling, it came all the way out and I found myself face to face with the bald head, his eyes now narrow slits that stared at me balefully as if to say, "You did this to me. I was just scratching at some seed in my yard, minding my own business, and *now* look at me."

Of course I did what every savvy American cook would do when unexpectedly coming into contact with the head of her food—I screamed. Greg was still home at this point, so I recreated the whole experience on video for him, sans hollering. The plucked head had been half-decapitated and sort of bobbed up and down as if nodding—I could develop a whole comedy routine were I better at ventriloquism. And the beak had been chopped off—luckily, from the looks of it, post-mortem, because I can't imagine how the turkey could have eaten otherwise. Or breathed. It reminded me of the head of the desert cat in Denderah, and of how far away we have gotten from our mortality and even being aware that the animals we call food were once living beings, who functioned on their own and didn't know they had been born simply to sustain us for another day.

The doorbell rings. Finally, a guest! But when I open it, Greg is standing there, his galabeya muddy, smelling of greasy Cairo, wearing an ear-to-ear grin. Shakky took him to the antique booksellers, where he bought the "Hymns of Akhenaton" and an Arabic book of translations dating to the 1930s. He can tell because it's called "The Dragoman in your Pocket" and Egyptians haven't been called that since then—it was actually a name for Turks.

"Where is everybody?" he wants to know. I shrug. It's Egypt. Besides, two people from Mohamed's staff came by an hour ago and blew up over two dozen balloons, which they have left strewn across the apartment floor, so I know we are not forgotten. I show Greg the multicolored balloons. Most of them are plain, but a few say things like, "Happy 18th Birthday!" and "Happy 50th Birthday!" On closer scrutiny, I also find, "Happy 90th Birthday!" and "Happy 4th Birthday!" It's clear they are covering their bases.

The doorbell rings again—it's Rhonnda, joined by Mohamed, who stops theatrically inside the door, enjoying the Thanksgiving smells. While Greg goes off to shower, I tour Momo around the kitchen, showing him my three pies, the beautiful turkey, the pans of side dishes. "I'm also doing sautéed green beans and steamed julienne carrots, and there's fresh bread and butter," I tell him proudly, certain of having achieved my foodie goals. Mohamed nods, smiling, and then gets on the phone, which is standard operating procedure, as he gets a call every five minutes all day long. I check the turkey one last time and turn to my friend and mentor as he hangs up.

"I called Felfela Restaurant," he says. Felfela is so close we go out the front door of our building and through their kitchen to eat there, an almost daily affair. "They are sending up extra forks for dessert. Do you need anything else?" I tell him I am fine. "Good," he responds. "I also ordered some macaroni."

Excuse me??

"Momo," I inform him, "I cooked all day. There's a ton of food. What do you mean, you ordered macaroni?" He gestures dismissively.

"This is not a lot of food for Egyptians. One person will eat half your turkey. Have you ever seen the amount of food for Ramadan?" I have. It's a lot. But still.

"Mohamed," I say, trying to keep the frustration out of my voice, "I have cooked Thanksgiving dinner many times. I made plenty of food, people can even have seconds. NO macaroni! It's insulting!"

"I understand! I get it!" he responds, his voice rising in excitement to match mine until we are both yelling, "but you have to trust me—I know Egyptians! They only want to taste the turkey—they won't eat anything!" *Well, which is it?? They'll eat too much or they won't touch the food?*

I'm searching for a solution. "Okay, well, can we leave it here in the kitchen and I'll only bring it out if we run out of food?"

"Sure! Let's do that." He is eager to compromise. It's five o'clock. I pull the turkey, wearing its tin foil cloak, out of the oven and slide my big pans in to heat. I take a quick peek at the roasted turkey, which is a glorious deep golden brown, and pour the pan juices off into a tall saucepan so I can take the final step, the one most likely to trip up the educated cook: the gravy. The doorbell rings again.

"I've got it," sings Rhonnda, happy to be of use and away from Mohamed's and my clashing energies. I turn to see two waiters from Felfela, each laden with a tray full of small metal pans covered in broiled cheese. Mohamed has ordered that classic Egyptian dish, a huge favorite here: macaroni in béchamel —penne pasta mixed with ground beef and slathered in a thick white cream sauce, then smothered in cheese and baked. From the looks of it, there is one for each of us, a full meal to itself.

I turn the pan juices down and clang my spoon onto the marble countertop. "I have to go in the other room now." I stomp off into the bedroom, pissed. Greg waits a polite minute, then follows me in.

"It's a little like having a kid's party with grown-up food, and then someone brings cheeseburgers," he sympathizes.

I groan. "I know! It's bad enough I have to explain all the food to people and try to get them to eat it! But," I take a deep breath, trying to calm myself as fast as possible, "I refuse to ruin your birthday over it." Still releasing my feelings as quickly as they come up, I return to the kitchen to finish the gravy.

Rhonnda is already there, on bean duty as she snaps the ends off the perfect green legumes. Her eyes flicker over me as I enter the room, but I smile easily, determined to regain some of my lost grace. "Mmm, macaroni looks good," I say to her, my grin only semi-sarcastic. She laughs, brings the finished beans over, and offers to help with the next task.

The doorbell is going every five minutes now, and almost everyone is here: Ihab, Momo's partner at Quest; Sen, whose wife had a baby girl just days earlier, Shakky, who had rushed home to take a shower after dropping Greg off; Doaa and her husband Hashem, a member of the Giza tourist police; Momo's plump, sweet wife, Hannan; his daughter, Nancy, her big eyes taking in everything even as she spends almost every minute texting; his son, Marawan, who towers over everyone but is too shy to say a word; several of Momo's loyal staff. They traipse in and out of the kitchen, looking for food, uncertain of what is supposed to happen. "Dinner in ten," I announce, straining the gravy through a sieve so that it is perfectly smooth (would that I could have done the same with the mashed potatoes) and putting the veggies on to sauté.

Rhonnda helps me arrange the serving dishes, Greg gets the last of the napkins and silverware on the buffet, and I ask everyone to join me in the kitchen. They crowd around the room, spilling into the dining room. The flat is huge, but no table seats more than six and despite Greg's vehement protestations, Momo was unwilling to yield to our collective pleas that we push tables together. The idea of a single place, where everyone holds hands and then eats together, is apparently wholly American and sacred only to us. We will eat scattered about the den, living room and dining room, making this preface is doubly important. I'm not sure where to begin.

"Uh, this is the turkey." I point to it on its table, waiting to be carved. "And this is stuffing and mashed potatoes—all of them get gravy, which is on the stove" (more pointing). "This is a zucchini casserole, and then, well, you can see the veggies and the bread and butter. And this is cranberry sauce; take a little. It goes well with turkey." I sound completely lame, but it's the only time I've ever had to explain a meal to my guests. Everyone looks at the macaroni, which is sitting out on the side counter. *Can't I pretend it doesn't exist, or order people not to eat it? "You can't have your macaroni until you eat a plate of turkey and trimmings."* All this runs through my head in a flash, but what comes out is, "Oh, and Momo ordered béchamel in case anyone wants some."

I head to the turkey and begin to carve while everyone sniffs around, taking a plate and small tastes of everything. Even Momo, who knows the food, doesn't help himself to much, and I'm starting to worry. Over at my carving station, the bird seems dry and overcooked, cutting in thick strands instead of smoothly. After serving a few people and encouraging them to douse it in gravy, I finally sneak a bite. To my surprise, it tastes nothing like the meat looks—it's moist, tender, fully flavored. A slight gaminess reminds me this is not farm-raised bird, and I smile to myself and carve more confidently. After I have served half the turkey in slices, I help myself to my favorite parts, a wing and the tail, then head into the kitchen to finish filling my plate. It's clear there is plenty of food left, though everyone is served now, but a glance over at the counter where the few remaining macaroni dishes sit tell me it's the most popular item.

I take my plate past Greg, Momo, and Shakky, sitting with some of the other men at the dining table, and go into the den, joining the group of women seated in there. Hashem, Doaa's young husband, is the only man who sits next to his wife, which puts him in the women's corner.   I listen to the Arabic conversation, flowing over my head like fast-running water, and turn to Rhonnda.   "How's the food?" I ask her, feeling surprisingly out of place.

"Grand," she responds, smiling warmly at me. I am suddenly grateful for her presence, for her simple understanding of what might need to be done in my kitchen as I finish preparing and serving the meal. These other women cook, but obviously not the same way.   They want to know how I prepared the vegetables, which are quite undercooked by Egyptian standards. Momo's wife, Hannan, asks me if I cook at home. When I tell her yes, almost every night, she looks surprised, even though I hasten to assure her it's nothing as extensive as Thanksgiving dinner.

Abandoning my plate for a moment, I greet some late-arriving guests of Mohamed's and press food on them. I go into the kitchen to drop a dirty dish in the sink and see the normally elegant Ihab slathering a large piece of bread with cranberry sauce. I am tempted (controlling thing that I am) to tell him that's not how you're supposed to do it, but instead I keep my mouth shut, and am astonished to see him add another piece of bread on top of the first, take a pat of butter from the plate, and smear it thickly on the bread, using his fingers.   I should probably remember to put out a butter knife next time, but he seems perfectly content, standing in his expensive suit jacket, his fingers covered in butter. I giggle to myself as I watch him take a large bite, savoring the mix of flavors and textures. Momo explains later that jam sandwiches are popular among Egyptians.

I wander through the guests, looking at plates where food has been tasted or left untouched, but a few that have been cleaned completely. My eye catches on Marawan, who has balanced a pillow on his lap and a bowl of béchamel on top of that; he is devouring it with a large spoon. The unwanted leftovers will be fed the next day to the family of six dogs I have discovered living in a vacant lot only a block away; they eat from my hands and sit patiently, waiting for me to feed them and pet them. By now I am okay about the dogs, for the most part—accepting that their short lives are the truth of their existence. Live hard, play hard, die young. Wasn't that originally my own motto? The dogs will not go hungry tomorrow.

When I sense everyone is almost finished eating, I invite them all into the dining room. I had planned to ask everyone to hold hands, but now, seeing them together, it feels futile and inappropriate. I console myself that this gesture of gathering is enough.

"Happy birthday to Greg," I say, smiling at him. Everyone applauds loudly; Greg is truly beloved by Egyptians, and each trip he is always ready to stay longer, even when I cannot wait to be home. "Thank you to your host, Mohamed." Everyone applauds again, louder this time, and Momo accepts the acknowledgment graciously. "We have a tradition in the States— each person says what we are grateful for, and I ask all of you to join us in this giving thanks. Greg, would you like to start?"

He smiles, sitting up straighter in his chair. "I am so grateful to all of you for being here, for enjoying this experience and my birthday. What a magnificent day!" More applause. Each person says something as we go around the room. The Egyptians always say, not: "I am grateful for" or "I am thankful for," but: "Thanks to God for" whatever they are feeling. More than once it's simply, "I am giving thanks to God." When it's Momo's turn, he says how happy he is that he built this apartment building for his American friends, so they can come here and experience being in our big Egyptian family. It truly gives him the greatest pleasure to see us enjoying ourselves. Shakky gives thanks for our continued health. He mostly means his and Momo's—with four heart incidents between them, their health is a lot to be thankful for. Then I give thanks for the Long Cruise, which brought us all together.

"Yes!" Shakky and Momo agree, joined by Sen. We reminisce for a moment; Nancy was there, at eight, and Marawan at four—Sen carried him in his arms. Shakky starts to tell a longer anecdote, but I interrupt him, anxious not to lose everyone's patient attention.

"Shakky, can you sing 'Happy Birthday' for Greg?" He starts, and everyone joins in, singing the most traditional of birthday songs in English as Greg smiles and conducts.

Then I cut the pies. While serving, I discover that no Egyptians actually like pumpkin pie. I have to keep sliding a little onto everyone's plates, though the apple is rapidly disappearing. I watch as two women move into the kitchen and spoon the leftover cranberry sauce all over their apple pie. Again, I stop myself from interfering. It's not my tradition, but what the hell? Perhaps we will start new ones this evening, and in honor of our Egyptian family we will have cranberry-sauced apple pie and no pumpkin ever again, or I will insist on retaining and roasting the turkey head.

Mohamed comes up and puts his arm around me. "Was it what you remembered?" I ask him. "Did it taste right?"

"Perfect," he says, rubbing his round belly.

"The macaroni was the right thing for people," I acknowledge grudgingly, looking at the only two untouched metal dishes.

"Look." He motions with his head and I follow his eyes into the kitchen. "It's Thanksgiving."

I see what he sees, the counters full of food and dirty dishes, a well-used oven, a stove covered in half-full pots and pans. He squeezes my shoulder.

"This is my favorite part." We stand there for a moment, together, the Arab and the Jew, the Egyptian and the American. I wish they would let us settle the peace talks. Then we'd all have something to be thankful for.

THE KING'S CHAMBER

On the very last morning, the coach pulls into the deserted parking lot and we all climb out in front of the Great Pyramid. My group dresses for climbing, hiking, and crawling, wearing their sturdiest shoes and thickest pants. I usually wear a galabeya. By the time we leave, in another two hours, the lot will be jammed full of buses, slammed with vendors, tour guides, and touristses. There is a lottery each day that allots only 150 tickets to get inside the Pyramid. For many others, it's enough to see the place, and most folks don't bother to disembark as busload after busload push through this route each day. For us, and for our guests, our private visit is the biggest highlight of our trip. We leave the bus behind and walk to the entrance. It is silent, reverent, as if the sands themselves are holding their breath, waiting for us.

I have been here many times by now, but since The Great Pyramid is considered perhaps the greatest riddle on earth, it is as fascinating for me as on my original trip. Built ages ago, much longer than is currently accepted, it has many anomalies and bizarre features; so much weirdness, in fact, that in one of his talks on the subject, Greg has two full screens called "WTF?" devoted to the laundry list of outlandish facts and data. Some of my favorites are that no plane can fly over the Great Pyramid because its instruments go wonky, that it's such an advanced structure we cannot replicate it even today, and that there was no known entrance until a Caliph named Al Mamun forced his way in during the ninth century, discovering several perfectly usable and laser-precise passages that led right to the entirely concealed entrance.

The Great Pyramid is known as Khufu's Pyramid, since supposedly he built the structure around 2500 BCE as his burial chamber. Of course, facts totally screw this theory up, since there was no way in until Al Mamun dynamited, and he reported finding nothing inside but a lidless coffer in the King's Chamber. This coffer is too small for a modern man of medium build to lie in without bending his knees—hardly appropriate when you compare it with, say, Ramses' granite sarcophagus in the Valley of the Kings, at least three times larger. The Pyramid was also devoid of both the treasure always found in an unspoiled tomb and any debris left behind by tomb robbers—these guys must have been pretty anal-retentive, to have taken the time to sweep the place out after they were done looting it.

The reason the Great Pyramid is attributed to Khufu is that his name appears inscribed in red paint in one of the hidden "relieving" chambers, so-called because they were thought to alleviate the pressure of the building's angles. In 1837, by dynamiting his way into the South entrance, an Englishman named Howard Vyse discovered Khufu's hieroglyph under mysterious circumstances: by then the Pyramid had been scoured for any markings and none had been found for the last thousand years; also, Khufu's name is misspelled, the same misspelling which appeared in a contemporary book that Vyse was known to own. The best analogy I have heard is that it's like discovering the Empire State Building thousands of years from now, seeing graffiti that says "Kilroy wuz here," and thus inferring it is the tomb of Kilroy, as well as attributing the building's architecture to him for good measure.

That the Pyramid has not a single carving anywhere is most unusual. The only other place this occurs is at the Osirion in Abydos—also the only other place the eighty-ton granite blocks are used for building. Most people think kings and queens are buried here because of the names of the chambers, but the King's Chamber gets its name because it has a flat roof, typical of the type used by Muslims in their burial of men. The Queen's

Chamber has a peaked roof, so named because the Muslims choose to bury their women under pointed roofs.

Inside, the Great Pyramid is a little intimidating. At Disneyland, if you've ever been through the caves on Tom Sawyer's Island or the walking part of the Indiana Jones ride, they are the closest I have come to the experience. Al Mamun opened up the entrance by super-heating the exterior blocks and then pouring cold vinegar on them until they cracked, then his men tunneled into the Pyramid, now the main "forced shaft." About a hundred feet in, they met up with the original tunnel to the Grand Gallery, which is completely smooth and perfectly made. We had a stonemason on our first trip who was especially interested in the massive cut rocks used in the building of the Pyramid, and he was shocked when he got inside. He told Greg and me that you can't slide a piece of paper between the stones, that they are so exact they seem to be laser-cut.

No one has a clue how it was done, but when he was initially inside, Greg suddenly "remembered" that the stones were moved using sound. The molecules of the stones rearranged themselves in response to toning, and became light enough to lift the stones easily. Then the stones were "sung to" again after they were in place, and became heavy once more. Many years later, we visited a twentieth century corollary which still exists in Homestead, Florida, where a single Latvian immigrant (a small man, at that) built the Coral Castle as an homage to his lost love, using only homemade tools and something he called a "perpetual motion generator." The coral stones, cut from the bedrock underneath him, weighed many tons each, and were so precisely carved that no light could get between them. Though it took the gentleman twenty-eight years to build his castle and he refused to allow anyone to see him working, two teenagers snuck in and reported that he was moving the rocks around as if they were helium balloons.

Where Al Mamun's forced shaft meets the original entrance shaft is The Pit. I've been down twice, ten years apart. The shaft is extremely long and straight, and as I descend slowly into the earth, I hold tight onto the handrails on both sides. The narrow floor is covered with wood planks, with helpful crosspiece cleats every few feet. I say a silent prayer of thanks to the men who did all this work, enabling me to climb down to the pit or up to the King's Chamber in a matter of minutes instead of hours. There is enough room for one person to go down the shaft, bent over so far that it is easier to walk backwards, feeling for the next foothold as you go.

At the bottom, my original impression is that The Pit was dynamited out—it is the most unfinished part of the whole space, rough-hewn blond rock crumbling under an oppressively low roof. The most intriguing part of the space is blocked off— a pit in The Pit that goes deeper into the ground. But it's scary down here, mostly because I know that people have died in The Pit over the years, and those who have lived to tell the tale had terrifying experiences. There are stories that both Alexander the Great and Napoleon Bonaparte spent the night in the Great Pyramid and neither would ever speak of it.

On the way out of The Pit I have no problems, but Greg reports feeling a great emotional weight hit him about a third of the way from the top, a tremendous fear and feeling of worthlessness. He pushes on through and by the time he reaches the top of the shaft it is gone. Others report similar feelings— shame, fear, or sorrow—in this very spot.

To get to the other rooms in the Pyramid, we go up the long ascending shaft. Here we have to creep single file, bent at a 90° angle, and it is too much for some of the older, less-fit people in our group, who turn back. After what seems an eternity, but is probably no more than three or four minutes, we emerge into the Grand Gallery.

No matter how tall you are, you can stand up here since the walls are nearly thirty feet high. Inside the Grand Gallery, I notice that it's somewhat cooler. In fact, it's a constant 68° degrees inside, exactly the temperature of the earth's interior. What makes it seem hotter is all the other people, as well as the strenuous workout we get clambering around inside.

Next we visit the Queen's Chamber, duck-walking to get there. A guest who had problems with her knees brought kneepads and tried to crawl, but she moved extremely slowly and was uncomfortable. Crouching low is the trick if your legs can manage it. Inside the Queen's Chamber, the room is empty, the walls smooth, and it's fairly uninteresting except for the peaked roof and a passageway that is both gated and locked. Again, people are reported to have died there, but we enjoy toning and meditating here, and some people feel a great sense of peace in the Queen's Chamber.

To get to the our final initiation in the King's Chamber, we climb a short metal ladder, then traverse the wooden walkways on either side of the Grand Gallery. We reach the low chamber entrance tunnel, perfectly squared off. I duck-walk three or four paces, only to find a surprisingly high space inside, then another low tunnel as before. I cannot imagine what the purpose might be of the two low tunnels with the high one in between—another of the Great Pyramid's mysteries. I emerge into the King's Chamber, which is a 34 by 18 foot black granite room, around 10 feet high. I am immediately peeved, as I see that a fan has been forcibly inserted into the granite wall by randomly gouging out a huge spot. I can only imagine the long-term implications of this choice, but it is clear that we humans have left our stamp on this place. In the corner sits a dehumidifier, since 150 people a day plus the private visits take their toll.

Other than the granite sarcophagus, the room seems quite empty. Later, our pictures will reveal tons of what we call energy blobs, large circles of energy or light that appear only in pictures but cannot be seen with the naked eye. Though they are often passed off as dust motes on the photos, some of the ones we have captured in the King's Chamber are several feet across. I also have a picture of Greg and a friend doing energy work in here, and over their heads appears an inexplicable huge gray mist in a mysterious swathe around them.

Once everyone is here, at the agreed-upon time, Shakky turns off the lights and darkness swallows us—we are lit only by our own flashlights. We begin our ceremony by toning. The coffer, when struck, emits a perfect A; off this note we take our opening sound. I recall my first visit here—Rusty kicking the coffer with his prosthetic leg to achieve the tone—and smile.

We come forward individually and Greg leads the initiation, asking if each person is ready to leave his or her old self behind. He asks for a password, and each one speaks his or her own, a single word that marks the passage to their future.

When it is my turn, though I plan to say something else, I hear the word, "truth" resonating loudly in my head, so I give that as my response. Climbing over the left, broken corner of the coffer (the easiest way to get in) I lie down in the rectangular red granite box, the sides rising over me into a rough edge. Around me, my fellow initiates wait quietly, while Greg asks me the question I have heard so often over the years: "Are you ready to leave your old self behind?"

Of course I am. I look around, sensing all of my past fellow travelers with me. My mother, Eleanor, Vivian, Rose, Rusty and Carter, our dear Lyra—all joining me for this transcendent moment. I nod solemnly to Greg and cross my arms, mummy-like. I close my eyes and drift to the Long Cruise, reliving the most important moment of my life:

Isis, my favorite of the Sun People, stops by my lounge chair as I am journaling the events of my "psychic surgery." She asks if Greg and I will join their table at dinner that evening, so they can explain to us what had happened to me. I eagerly accept, and when I tell Greg about it, he shrugs and says he is curious about what they have to say.

But in the ship's restaurant as we greet the other members of our group, Greg reneges, now unwilling to join me at the Sun People's table—he is still tender about the psychic surgery I underwent, agreeing with Rose's concerns that I am too naïve to know what's best for me. I go by myself anyway, which is unusual, but I feel very strongly; we made the commitment and something tells me I need to be there.

I am at a long table of about twenty people and, although I have met several of them, other than Isis the only one really I know is Lyra. I sit in the middle, directly across from Isis, comfortable and ready for a nice meal. The Sun People start discussing the psychic surgeries each of us received. Isis beams at me. "My dear, you were the healing of the day!"

"But nothing's wrong with me!" The words are out before I have a chance to realize how defensive they sound. Isis looks at me carefully across her oversized, owl glasses.

"You really think so, my darling? Nothing?" I go through it: What problems do I have? Everything okay in my family? *Good relationships with my parents, a sister I could kill sometimes, but love a lot... Check.* Personal life? *Screwy, but madly in love, lots of friends... Check.* Money issues? *I work too much, but who doesn't, and we always get by.* I mean I feel perfectly normal, possessing all the normal idiosyncrasies that make us human, except... *ah, yes. My old fear of death.*

Well, that. I mention it aloud easily, shrugging it off as if it's a little tremor, not 9.8 on my personal Richter scale.

Isis extends her arms towards me across the dinner table, her floaty sleeves falling away to reveal surprisingly slender wrists and delicate white English skin. "Take my hands, child," she says in her throaty accent, turning my palms up towards the ceiling. "Close your eyes."

Yeah, okay. This motherly lady is doing something strange to me, again, but hey, I don't really know any of these people; if I lose it I won't ever have to see them, so I am going with it. I shut my eyes. Isis begins to walk me through a meditation.

"Put your hand on your heart, imagine a flower in your heart and see how many petals the flower has." In my mind's eye, I look, and I can just sense a flower, hovering over my heart. I hear in my head, rather than count, that it has twelve petals, and I tell her this.

"Open the flower's petals and see inside of the petals a pearl, then see inside of that pearl a flame." I can feel my hand, how warm it is, the heat spreading out from my heart.

"Now look around, see what you are wearing." I look down in my mind, and I am clothed in a heavy, violet-silk cape, with square gold buckles fastening it to my shoulders.

"Where are you?" I haven't paid attention to the locale, but now, in my mind's eye I suddenly see myself in a temple. "You are standing in a circle, and you are healing Body, Mind, or Spirit —which one?"

I'm still at the dinner table, I feel in no way hypnotized and I've been doing this meditation for possibly sixty seconds at this point. Despite all this, as I look around inside my head, I "hear" that I am in the third circle, that of Spirit, and I see I'm standing on a platform of stone in the temple. Isis tells me, "I am approaching you. What am I giving you?"

I see a woman dressed in purple robes, who does not look like Isis, but who I somehow know *is* Isis. In the little movie unfolding in my brain I look down at my cupped hands, palms toward the sky, as she places an ankh in my left hand and a little jeweled bird in my right. The bird is covered in lapis, carnelian and jade (upon returning to the States I found an almost identical bird and it has sat on my altar for over ten years now). I laugh out loud, sitting there in the dining room. It's all so vivid: the bright sun, the pretty day, and the feeling of these things in my hands. Isis says, "And what did I promise you?" I can feel the answer immediately in my heart, and I am instantly and utterly flooded by these four words:

YOU WILL NEVER DIE.

It's almost impossible to describe the feeling I have at this moment... as if I am completely filled up, in every particle of my being, with knowledge and truth with a capital T. I get it in my pores, in my bones; I feel it in my soul and indeed it is the first moment of my life that I know that I have a soul. Isis asks me again, but I can't answer her because I am crying a hot torrent of tears as the joyous awareness fills me that I will never die; that I without any doubt have a soul.

The massive burden of fear is lifted—I am Atlas, and Earth itself has been taken from my shoulders. More importantly, an entire new world opens at that moment, a world where my eyes no longer tell the whole story, where there is a significance, a sacred meaning behind every mundane thing. It is like being granted admission into the world's most exclusive club, being told the most important secret ever, and thereafter seeing everything through different eyes.

That was the last time I ever worried about death. I have never had another recurrence of my panic attacks, even when I deliberately tried to bring one on years later. It simply was a piece of information from Spirit, the universe, God—that was imparted to me in that moment. I am forever grateful to this woman for being the conduit, because it eliminated the only deep terror that I've ever had, and it gave me a knowing that I am cognizant most of us never receive. I wish I could bring to others the peace I have, especially to those who are in the process of making the transition to the other side of existence, and tell them there is nothing to be afraid of. But somehow, everyone must figure this out when they are ready, and sometimes their lesson is contained in that fear, that "not knowing."

At the table it takes me some ten minutes—or a lifetime—to get the words out, and still sobbing, I finally am able to stammer, "I—Will—Never—Die!"

Isis simply says, "Yes." Then she brings me back quickly, out of whatever semiconscious state I was in. I have to excuse myself immediately because I am by now a puffy-faced, deranged person with a head full of snot, but it is also the most joyous moment that I have ever known; so powerful that when I go upstairs a few minutes later to tell Greg what happened, I slip inside my sandals because the energetic rush has caused sweat to pour from my hands and feet.

I'm still so grateful for it, every time I think about it. I can still recall each detail of that event, of that exquisite knowing, and of the release that came after the unburdening.

In the coffer, as my attention returns the King's Chamber, I remember the initial time we were inside; when Greg went into the sarcophagus, he was unexpectedly struck by the realization that this was an ancient mystery school initiation, that our souls were separated from our bodies in the coffer, and flew out along the shaft at the top of the Pyramid, then back into the shaft on the other side. These shafts exist, of course, closed only at the surface of the Pyramid, an illogical engineering choice. I remember this each time I enter this granite coffer, and I am reminded that in the ancient mystery schools, perhaps the greatest lesson was learning that your body and soul are two separate things. This knowledge was on the deepest level, but I had forgotten it until I came to Egypt.

Over the years, I have watched as people from all walks of life get into that sarcophagus and come out changed. It is an exceptional opportunity to be here, and the blessing of recurring annual visits to share this experience with so many seekers on the same path, has been the most amazing gift of all. I hear Greg toning, his voice deepening to a basso profundo coming from his core. He is joined by the rest of the group, then he invites me to

"Rise, Horus—reborn," and I step out of the coffer to take my place alongside the others.

In the dark, after everyone is initiated, Greg gives me a nod, and I sing one of the sacred songs I have learned. Despite singing as gently as I can, my voice echoes and bounces off the walls; the acoustics in this chamber are simply the best in the world. Everyone is still, my tone clear and bell-like. I can feel them being showered by my musical offering for the last time.

When the lights come on, we make our way to the front of the Pyramid, and I sing some more, enjoying hearing my voice float down through the Grand Gallery. I traverse the last of the passage, unexpectedly encountering a Galabeya Boy, a clear-eyed older man. He asks me in halting English if I was singing. "Aiwa," I reply. He grabs me to him in a bear hug, and when he releases me, he has tears in his eyes. "Shokran," I tell him, grinning.

Then reborn, as I am each time I come to this wonderful country, I step out into the fullness of the morning sun.

ACKNOWLEDGMENTS

Because of my experiences, I became a Rosicrucian by the end of my first Egypt trip; it was my original spiritual home, for which I will be forever grateful.

Dad, I just couldn't have done it without you. Thank you for being my most constant reader. Mother, I would travel with you anywhere on Earth. Thank you both for making me possible.

To Momo and Shakky, thanks for pointing the way.

My little circle of Beta readers, I truly appreciate all your feedback and kind corrections and continued reading. Thank you.

Thanks very kindly to the editors and consultants who both took an interest in my writing and helped give me the keys to unlock the doors of rooms I could not peer into on my own.

Greg, thank you for being my True Companion. After the ride is over, I'll meet you at the turnstile. Let's go again.

ABOUT THE AUTHOR

Halle Eavelyn is "Julie the Cruise Director" for Spirit Quest
Tours and a spiritual seeker of truth. She is delightedly attached
to her partner, Greg, and counts amazing people all over the
world as her friends. When she is not traveling, Halle writes
screenplays and edits. This is her first travel book.

If you enjoyed this book, we welcome you to join the Spirit
Quest Tours' mailing list, invite you to subscribe to Halle's blog,
Confessions of a Cruise Director
www.spiritquesttours.com/blog
or even come with us to experience Egypt for yourself.
www.spiritquesttours.com

Made in the USA
Charleston, SC
02 May 2012